Protestant Liberty

MCGILL-QUEEN'S STUDIES IN THE HISTORY OF RELIGION
Volumes in this series have been supported by the Jackman Foundation of Toronto.

SERIES ONE: G.A. RAWLYK, EDITOR

1 Small Differences
Irish Catholics and Irish Protestants, 1815–1922
An International Perspective
Donald Harman Akenson

2 Two Worlds
The Protestant Culture of Nineteenth-Century Ontario
William Westfall

3 An Evangelical Mind
Nathanael Burwash and the Methodist Tradition in Canada, 1839–1918
Marguerite Van Die

4 The Dévotes
Women and Church in Seventeenth-Century France
Elizabeth Rapley

5 The Evangelical Century
College and Creed in English Canada from the Great Revival to the Great Depression
Michael Gauvreau

6 The German Peasants' War and Anabaptist Community of Goods
James M. Stayer

7 A World Mission
Canadian Protestantism and the Quest for a New International Order, 1918–1939
Robert Wright

8 Serving the Present Age
Revivalism, Progressivism, and the Methodist Tradition in Canada
Phyllis D. Airhart

9 A Sensitive Independence
Canadian Methodist Women Missionaries in Canada and the Orient, 1881–1925
Rosemary R. Gagan

10 God's Peoples
Covenant and Land in South Africa, Israel, and Ulster
Donald Harman Akenson

11 Creed and Culture
The Place of English-Speaking Catholics in Canadian Society, 1750–1930
Edited by Terrence Murphy and Gerald Stortz

12 Piety and Nationalism
Lay Voluntary Associations and the Creation of an Irish-Catholic Community in Toronto, 1850–1895
Brian P. Clarke

13 Amazing Grace
Studies in Evangelicalism in Australia, Britain, Canada, and the United States
Edited by George Rawlyk and Mark A. Noll

14 Children of Peace
W. John McIntyre

15 A Solitary Pillar
Montreal's Anglican Church and the Quiet Revolution
Joan Marshall

16 Padres in No Man's Land
Canadian Chaplains and the Great War
Duff Crerar

17 Christian Ethics and Political Economy in North America
A Critical Analysis
P. Travis Kroeker

18 Pilgrims in Lotus Land
Conservative Protestantism in British Columbia, 1917–1981
Robert K. Burkinshaw

19 Through Sunshine and Shadow
The Woman's Christian Temperance Union, Evangelicalism, and Reform in Ontario, 1874–1930
Sharon Cook

20 Church, College, and Clergy
A History of Theological Education at Knox College, Toronto, 1844–1994
Brian J. Fraser

21 The Lord's Dominion
The History of Canadian Methodism
Neil Semple

22 A Full-Orbed Christianity
The Protestant Churches and Social Welfare in Canada, 1900–1940
Nancy Christie and Michael Gauvreau

23 Evangelism and Apostasy
The Evolution and Impact of Evangelicals in Modern Mexico
Kurt Bowen

24 The Chignecto Covenanters
A Regional History of Reformed Presbyterianism in New Brunswick and Nova Scotia, 1827– 1905
Eldon Hay

25 Methodists and Women's Education in Ontario, 1836–1925
Johanne Selles

26 Puritanism and Historical Controversy
William Lamont

SERIES TWO IN MEMORY OF GEORGE RAWLYK
DONALD HARMAN AKENSON, EDITOR

1 Marguerite Bourgeoys and Montreal, 1640–1665
Patricia Simpson

2 Aspects of the Canadian Evangelical Experience
Edited by G.A. Rawlyk

3 Infinity, Faith, and Time
Christian Humanism and Renaissance Literature
John Spencer Hill

4 The Contribution of Presbyterianism to the Maritime Provinces of Canada
Edited by Charles H.H. Scobie and G.A. Rawlyk

5 Labour, Love, and Prayer
Female Piety in Ulster Religious Literature, 1850–1914
Andrea Ebel Brozyna

6 The Waning of the Green
Catholics, the Irish, and Identity in Toronto, 1887–1922
Mark G. McGowan

7 Religion and Nationality in Western Ukraine
The Greek Catholic Church and the Ruthenian National Movement in Galicia, 1867–1900
John-Paul Himka

8 Good Citizens
British Missionaries and Imperial States, 1870–1918
James G. Greenlee and Charles M. Johnston

9 The Theology of the Oral Torah
Revealing the Justice of God
Jacob Neusner

10 Gentle Eminence
A Life of Cardinal Flahiff
P. Wallace Platt

11 Culture, Religion, and Demographic Behaviour
Catholics and Lutherans in Alsace, 1750–1870
Kevin McQuillan

12 Between Damnation and Starvation
Priests and Merchants in Newfoundland Politics, 1745–1855
John P. Greene

13 Martin Luther, German Saviour
German Evangelical Theological Factions and the Interpretation of Luther, 1917–1933
James M. Stayer

14 Modernity and the Dilemma of North American Anglican Identities, 1880–1950
William H. Katerberg

15 The Methodist Church on the Prairies, 1896–1914
George Emery

16 Christian Attitudes towards the State of Israel
Paul Charles Merkley

17 A Social History of the Cloister
Daily Life in the Teaching Monasteries of the Old Regime
Elizabeth Rapley

18 Households of Faith
Family, Gender, and Community in Canada, 1760–1969
Edited by Nancy Christie

19 Blood Ground
Colonialism, Missions, and the Contest for Christianity in the Cape Colony and Britain, 1799–1853
Elizabeth Elbourne

20 A History of Canadian Catholics
Gallicanism, Romanism, and Canadianism
Terence J. Fay

21 The View from Rome
Archbishop Stagni's 1915 Reports on the Ontario Bilingual Schools Question
Edited and translated by John Zucchi

22 The Founding Moment
Church, Society, and the Construction of Trinity College
William Westfall

23 The Holocaust, Israel, and Canadian Protestant Churches
Haim Genizi

24 Governing Charities
Church and State in Toronto's Catholic Archdiocese, 1850–1950
Paula Maurutto

25 Anglicans and the Atlantic World
High Churchmen, Evangelicals, and the Quebec Connection
Richard W. Vaudry

26 Evangelicals and the Continental Divide
The Conservative Protestant Subculture in Canada and the United States
Sam Reimer

27 Christians in a Secular World
The Canadian Experience
Kurt Bowen

28 Anatomy of a Seance
A History of Spirit Communication in Central Canada
Stan McMullin

29 With Skilful Hand
The Story of King David
David T. Barnard

30 Faithful Intellect
Samuel S. Nelles and Victoria University
Neil Semple

31 W. Stanford Reid
An Evangelical Calvinist in the Academy
A. Donald MacLeod

32 A Long Eclipse
The Liberal Protestant Establishment and the Canadian University, 1920–1970
Catherine Gidney

33 Forkhill Protestants and Forkhill Catholics, 1787–1858
Kyla Madden

34 For Canada's Sake
Public Religion, Centennial Celebrations, and the Re-making of Canada in the 1960s
Gary R. Miedema

35 Revival in the City
The Impact of American Evangelists in Canada, 1884–1914
Eric R. Crouse

36 The Lord for the Body
Religion, Medicine, and Protestant Faith Healing in Canada, 1880–1930
James Opp

37 Six Hundred Years of Reform
Bishops and the French Church, 1190–1789
J. Michael Hayden and Malcolm R. Greenshields

38 The Missionary Oblate Sisters
Vision and Mission
Rosa Bruno-Jofré

39 Religion, Family, and Community in Victorian Canada
The Colbys of Carrollcroft
Marguerite Van Die

40 Michael Power
The Struggle to Build the Catholic Church on the Canadian Frontier
Mark G. McGowan

41 The Catholic Origins of Quebec's Quiet Revolution, 1931–1970
Michael Gauvreau

42 Marguerite Bourgeoys and the Congregation of Notre Dame, 1665–1700
Patricia Simpson

43 To Heal a Fractured World
The Ethics of Responsibility
Jonathan Sacks

44 Revivalists
Marketing the Gospel in English Canada, 1884–1957
Kevin Kee

45 The Churches and Social Order in Nineteenth- and Twentieth-Century Canada
Edited by Michael Gauvreau and Ollivier Hubert

46 Political Ecumenism
Catholics, Jews, and Protestants in De Gaulle's Free France, 1940–1945
Geoffrey Adams

47 From Quaker to Upper Canadian
Faith and Community among Yonge Street Friends, 1801–1850
Robynne Rogers Healey

48 The Congrégation de Notre-Dame, Superiors, and the Paradox of Power, 1693–1796
Colleen Gray

49 Canadian Pentecostalism
Transition and Transformation
Edited by Michael Wilkinson

50 A War with a Silver Lining
Canadian Protestant Churches and the South African War, 1899–1902
Gordon L. Heath

51 In the Aftermath of Catastrophe
Founding Judaism, 70 to 640
Jacob Neusner

52 Imagining Holiness
Classic Hasidic Tales in Modern Times
Justin Jaron Lewis

53 Shouting, Embracing, and Dancing with Ecstasy
The Growth of Methodism in Newfoundland, 1774–1874
Calvin Hollett

54 Into Deep Waters
Evangelical Spirituality and Maritime Calvinist Baptist Ministers, 1790–1855
Daniel C. Goodwin

55 Vanguard of the New Age
The Toronto Theosophical Society, 1891–1945
Gillian McCann

56 A Commerce of Taste
Church Architecture in Canada, 1867–1914
Barry Magrill

57 The Big Picture
The Antigonish Movement of Eastern Nova Scotia
Santo Dodaro and Leonard Pluta

58 My Heart's Best Wishes for You
A Biography of Archbishop John Walsh
John P. Comiskey

59 The Covenanters in Canada
Reformed Presbyterianism from 1820 to 2012
Eldon Hay

60 The Guardianship of Best Interests
Institutional Care for the Children of the Poor in Halifax, 1850–1960
Renée N. Lafferty

61 In Defence of the Faith
Joaquim Marques de Araújo, a Comissário in the Age of Inquisitional Decline
James E. Wadsworth

62 Contesting the Moral High Ground
Popular Moralists in Mid-Twentieth-Century Britain
Paul T. Phillips

63 The Catholicisms of Coutances
Varieties of Religion in Early Modern France, 1350–1789
J. Michael Hayden

64 After Evangelicalism
The Sixties and the United Church of Canada
Kevin N. Flatt

65 The Return of Ancestral Gods
Modern Ukrainian Paganism as an Alternative Vision for a Nation
Mariya Lesiv

66 Transatlantic Methodists
British Wesleyanism and the Formation of an Evangelical Culture in Nineteenth-Century Ontario and Quebec
Todd Webb

67 A Church with the Soul of a Nation
Making and Remaking the United Church of Canada
Phyllis D. Airhart

68 Fighting over God
A Legal and Political History of Religious Freedom in Canada
Janet Epp Buckingham

69 From India to Israel
Identity, Immigration, and the Struggle for Religious Equality
Joseph Hodes

70 Becoming Holy in Early Canada
Timothy Pearson

71 The Cistercian Arts
From the 12th to the 21st Century
Edited by Terryl N. Kinder and Roberto Cassanelli

72 The Canny Scot
Archbishop James Morrison of Antigonish
Peter Ludlow

73 Religion and Greater Ireland
Christianity and Irish Global Networks, 1750–1950
Edited by Colin Barr and Hilary M. Carey

74 The Invisible Irish
Finding Protestants in the Nineteenth-Century Migrations to America
Rankin Sherling

75 Beating against the Wind
Popular Opposition to Bishop Feild and Tractarianism in Newfoundland and Labrador, 1844–1876
Calvin Hollett

76 The Body or the Soul?
Religion and Culture in a Quebec Parish, 1736–1901
Frank A. Abbott

77 Saving Germany
North American Protestants and Christian Mission to West Germany, 1945–1974
James C. Enns

78 The Imperial Irish
Canada's Irish Catholics Fight the Great War, 1914–1918
Mark G. McGowan

79 Into Silence and Servitude
How American Girls Became Nuns, 1945–1965
Brian Titley

80 Boundless Dominion
Providence, Politics, and the Early Canadian Presbyterian Worldview
Denis McKim

81 Faithful Encounters
Authorities and American Missionaries in the Ottoman Empire
Emrah Şahin

82 Beyond the Noise of Solemn Assemblies
The Protestant Ethic and the Quest for Social Justice in Canada
Richard Allen

83 Not Quite Us
Anti-Catholic Thought in English Canada since 1900
Kevin P. Anderson

84 Scandal in the Parish
Priests and Parishioners Behaving Badly in Eighteenth-Century France
Karen E. Carter

85 Ordinary Saints
Women, Work, and Faith in Newfoundland
Bonnie Morgan

86 Patriot and Priest
Jean-Baptiste Volfius and the Constitutional Church in the Côte-d'Or
Annette Chapman-Adisho

87 A.B. Simpson and the Making of Modern Evangelicalism
Daryn Henry

88 The Uncomfortable Pew
Christianity and the New Left in Toronto
Bruce Douville

89 Berruyer's Bible
Public Opinion and the Politics of Enlightenment Catholicism in France
Daniel J. Watkins

90 Communities of the Soul
A Short History of Religion in Puerto Rico
José E. Igartua

91 Callings and Consequences
The Making of Catholic Vocational Culture in Early Modern France
Christopher J. Lane

92 Religion, Ethnonationalism, and Antisemitism in the Era of the Two World Wars
Edited by Kevin P. Spicer and Rebecca Carter-Chand

93 Water from Dragon's Well
The History of a Korean-Canadian Church Relationship
David Kim-Cragg

94 Protestant Liberty
Religion and the Making of Canadian Liberalism, 1828–1878
James M. Forbes

Protestant Liberty

Religion and the Making of Canadian Liberalism, 1828–1878

JAMES M. FORBES

McGill-Queen's University Press
Montreal & Kingston • London • Chicago

ISBN 978-0-2280-1070-8 (cloth)
ISBN 978-0-2280-1071-5 (paper)
ISBN 978-0-2280-1277-1 (ePDF)
ISBN 978-0-2280-1278-8 (ePUB)

Legal deposit third quarter 2022
Bibliothèque nationale du Québec

Printed in Canada on acid-free paper that is 100% ancient forest free (100% post-consumer recycled), processed chlorine free

This book has been published with the help of a grant from the Federation for the Humanities and Social Sciences, through the Awards to Scholarly Publications Program, using funds provided by the Social Sciences and Humanities Research Council of Canada.

Funded by the Government of Canada | Financé par le gouvernement du Canada | Canada

Canada Council for the Arts | Conseil des arts du Canada

We acknowledge the support of the Canada Council for the Arts.

Nous remercions le Conseil des arts du Canada de son soutien.

Library and Archives Canada Cataloguing in Publication

Title: Protestant liberty : religion and the making of Canadian liberalism, 1828–1878 / James M. Forbes.

Names: Forbes, James M., author.

Series: McGill-Queen's studies in the history of religion. Series two ; 94.

Description: Series statement: McGill-Queen's studies in the history of religion. Series two ; 94 | Includes bibliographical references and index.

Identifiers: Canadiana (print) 20220175535 | Canadiana (ebook) 20220175594 | ISBN 9780228010708 (cloth) | ISBN 9780228010715 (paper) | ISBN 9780228012771 (ePDF) | ISBN 9780228012788 (ePUB)

Subjects: LCSH: Liberalism (Religion) – Canada – History – 19th century. | LCSH: Liberalism (Religion) – Protestant churches – History – 19th century. | LCSH: Protestantism – Canada – History – 19th century. | LCSH: Religion and politics – Canada – History – 19th century. | LCSH: Protestant churches – Relations – Catholic Church. | LCSH: Catholic Church – Relations – Protestant churches. | LCSH: Canada – Church history – 19th century.

Classification: LCC BR570 .F67 2022 | DDC 280/.4097109034 – dc23

This book was designed and typeset by Peggy & Co. Design in 11.5/14 Adobe Garamond Pro.

For Hannah

Contents

Acknowledgments

This book represents the better part of five years of research, writing, and rethinking much of what I thought about Canadian history. A project that had started for me as a fascination with the evangelical worldview turned ultimately into a deeper exploration of the ideological underpinnings of Canada and the nature of political power in our liberal democracy. As with any project of this kind, its realization would not have been possible without many people working behind the scenes to offer their generous support, whether intellectual, material, or personal.

For intellectual support, I am especially grateful to my doctoral supervisor, David Marshall, and my secondary field supervisor, Jewel Spangler, for their insightful feedback, patience, and encouragement throughout my PhD program at the University of Calgary. My entire panel of dissertation examiners, including Lyndsay Campbell, George Colpitts, Elsbeth Heaman, and David Stewart, offered many insightful questions and comments that helped to shape my subsequent revisions. Thank you to Kyla Madden of McGill-Queen's University Press for believing in this project and guiding it through the transformation from dissertation to monograph. The three anonymous peer reviewers provided excellent critical feedback, which ultimately strengthened the arguments and presentation of this book. Thanks also to editor John Parry, who made significant improvements in textual brevity, consistency, and flow. Of course, the opinions expressed below and any faults thereof are mine alone.

The staff at several archives in Ontario provided assistance with my research, including the Archives of Ontario, the Dundas Museum and Archives (special thanks to archivist Sandra Kiemele), Lambton

County Archives (special thanks to archivist Dana Thorne), Library and Archives Canada, and the United Church of Canada Archives.

Next, I must express my abundant gratitude for the financial support I have received along the way. Thank you to the Social Sciences and Humanities Research Council for awarding me three years of support through the Joseph-Armand Bombardier Canada Graduate Scholarship. A generous travel grant from the Canadian Corporation for the Study of Religion enabled me to conduct extensive research in Toronto-area archives, the fruits of which are evident throughout this volume. The Department of History and the Faculty of Graduate Studies at the University of Calgary made available many resources and opportunities that made this project possible.

For early inspiration, I would like to thank my high-school history teacher Mr Westaway, who challenged his students to think about why history is important, and encouraged me to ask questions unapologetically. I am grateful also to the wonderful faculty and students of the University of Lethbridge, Queen's University, and the University of Calgary for the many discussions over the years that helped to nurture my passion for history.

For personal support, I want to thank every friend and family member who has ever offered a word of encouragement. I am immensely grateful to my parents for telling me stories of my ancestors, some of whom played as children in the halls of Scottish castles, and others of whom pioneered new lands during the "horse-and-buggy days." Their legacies live on in my children, Briar and Jubilee, who will inspire many new chapters of our family story. Finally, this book is dedicated to my wife, Hannah, with whom I am proud to have shared every step of this journey.

Protestant Liberty

Introduction

These Ancient Feuds

Before leaving his post as Canada's governor general in October 1878, the Earl of Dufferin felt "irresistibly compelled to convey a last and parting entreaty." Speaking before an audience of Irish Protestants in Toronto, he warned his listeners not to allow religious animosities to spiral into a perpetual state of inter-religious violence: "Your very existence," he insisted, "depends upon the disappearance of these ancient feuds."[1] For many in the audience that day, Dufferin's own experiences as a youth in Belfast would have been a familiar story. He spoke of visiting a hospital lined with gunshot victims, some lying dead on the floor, others writhing in their beds, each one, he said, casualty of a war between two religions. He pleaded with his audience, and by extension all Canadians, not to import such old-world quarrels into the "stainless paradise" of Canada, where all were welcomed "upon equal terms" and where no branch of Christianity was dominant over another.

Despite his glowing review of the country's supposed purity, however, Dufferin's six years stationed in the young dominion had impressed upon him the strong potential for sustained religious conflict. Although he remained vague about the "recent course of events" that inspired his speech, the outgoing viceroy had no doubt noticed the heated role that religious differences played in the nation's party politics and the tendency for public expressions of sectarianism to lead to clashes on the streets. Only the previous March, a two-day riot had broken out between Protestants and Catholics in reaction to the Fenian O'Donovan Rossa delivering a lecture in Toronto.[2] It is possible that this event, or something like it, was the reason Lord Dufferin felt the pressing need to issue his final entreaty.

The idea that Canada could be immune to old-world religious strife was the dream of statesmen, especially those champions of an emergent liberal order: if only Canada had impartial institutions and every religious group was "freely admitted upon equal terms," Dufferin proposed, there should be no justification to import "the brutal quarrels of the Old World."[3] The sentiment speaks to a version of liberal thought that, according to political scientist Janet Ajzenstat, underlay the very founding of Canada itself. Ajzenstat has suggested that the "Fathers of Confederation" crafted neutral laws and institutions within which various ideologies, ethnicities, cultures, and religions could co-exist on an equal footing.[4] She called the founders' approach "the great alternative," wherein the new nation's cohesion would be based not on a particular social identity, but "on the fact that our national institutions are inclusive."[5] In his own way, the earl sought to advance this kind of vision to the Protestants of Toronto: whether Protestant or Catholic, all Canadians were equally subject to law, so such differences should not result in conflict.

The great hitch in Dufferin's entreaty was that it was not so easy for Canadians to check their ancient feuds at the door. The logic of this liberal statesman – that fair rules and institutions would ensure peaceful religious coexistence – was not necessarily the perspective of the average Canadian. The typical nineteenth-century man or woman in Canada saw the world not in conciliatory votes and handshakes, but often in terms that reinforced their own particular worldview through sermons, scriptures, editorials, and public celebrations. Whether they were Protestant or Catholic, many of the conceptual tools through which they interpreted the day's events had been passed down to them in some form or another over centuries.[6] Stories about past religious wars, persecution, and discrimination from one side or the other were bound to reinforce mutual suspicion and, in some cases, outright hostility.[7] In this context, it was not always clear that equality of religions was in itself a desirable goal, especially when politicians used the concept in ways that seemed to justify ceding ground to religious rivals. For some liberal politicians in the 1870s, allowing Catholic religious processions through predominantly Protestant neighbourhoods was simply a matter of religious freedom, but for many concerned Protestants, it was an example of misguided cultural relativism giving sanction to idolatry.[8] Beyond the liberal statesman's immediate purview of political diplomacy and neutral institutions, there lay a rich world of the religious imagination where "these ancient feuds" refused to simply vanish to suit the demands of political civility.

This book examines the role of religion in the development of nineteenth-century Canadian liberalism. Focusing on Upper Canada (later called Canada West and Ontario), where politics frequently revolved around questions of church establishment and the management of Protestant–Catholic relations, this study proposes that the liberal-reform movement and its articulations of liberty, tyranny, and self-rule emerged out of the concepts and meanings of Protestantism. For many devout Protestant liberals in the mid-nineteenth century, the best way to safeguard "liberty" was to ensure that Protestantism remained the dominant cultural force, especially that Catholicism did not expand its influence in the colony. In the words of an editorial in the Toronto *Globe* in 1852, "Catholicism is utterly opposed to the free institutions which we [Protestants] have chosen and those which we will alone endure … They [the Catholic hierarchy] cannot suit themselves to the freedom of thought, the result of democratic institutions. As liberty advances they must decline."[9] This Protestant-conscious understanding of liberty was part of a much longer English tradition of resistance to Catholicism in the early modern era, wherein the English contrasted their own parliamentary institutions with the absolutist Catholic monarchies of Spain and France. Even John Locke's foundational treatises on religious liberty in 1689 reflected this Protestant-conscious understanding of liberty, wherein the philosopher raised suspicions about Catholics on the basis that they were more likely to be loyal to foreign governments.[10] Throughout the seventeenth century, the English were extremely wary of "popish" encroachments in their government and ultimately deposed their own Catholic king, James II, in favour of the Protestant William and Mary in 1688. Nearly two centuries later, the Glorious Revolution's achievement for "liberty" remained a defining moment for nineteenth-century Protestants in Canada.[11]

While this Protestant-conscious idea of liberty appears to have been prevalent among Upper Canadians in the early years – the 1830s – of the liberal-reform movement, it soon came into conflict with a competing conception of liberty, which sought to neutralize religion within the political sphere. This book summarizes these two versions of liberalism as "Protestant liberty" and "neutral liberty." The proponents of "Protestant liberty," such as William Lyon Mackenzie, James Lesslie, and George Brown, carried on the spirit of 1688 by insisting that Upper Canada would be free only as long as it remained Protestant. By contrast, the proponents of "neutral liberty," such as Robert Baldwin and Francis Hincks, rose to prominence after the Union of the Canadas in 1841 by building alliances between English Protestants and French Catholics and attempting to minimize the place of religion and culture within political discourse. They often accused their Protestant-liberty counterparts of "bigotry" and articulated instead a version of liberalism focusing on economic opportunities and property values.[12] For about five decades, from the origins of the liberal-reform movement in the 1820s to the early national period of the 1870s, these two conceptions competed for dominance within Upper Canada. Although Protestant liberty had helped create the Liberal party, by the last quarter of the nineteenth century that party had begun to purge the loudest voices of Protestant liberty from its ranks in an effort to reach out to Catholic voters.[13] Despite its eventual marginalization, however, Protestant liberty played an indispensable role in the making of early Canadian liberalism throughout this tumultuous half-century.

The main purpose of this book is to restore an understanding of Lockean thought as resting in large part on the foundation of Protestant culture, particularly that of Protestant Dissent, and consequently to appreciate the paradigmatic transformation that took place when that cultural foundation was uprooted in favour of secular materialism. Several recent studies of Canadian liberalism have captured well the neutral-liberty side of this story – describing a liberal order based on impartial institutions and market economics – but have largely overlooked the ideology's early religious and cultural imperatives.[14] Of course, other historians have long noted the religious dimension of Upper Canadian politics, but most have downplayed its significance, focused on a particular denomination or politician, or chosen to leave the detailed examination of this topic to someone else.[15] This study is the first to offer a narrative analysis of Upper Canada's liberal-reform movement in a manner that accounts for this sea change in liberal thought.[16] While this study does not claim to be a comprehensive analysis of all mid-nineteenth-century liberal thought in Canada, since it concentrates on select members of the liberal-reform movement in one region, it nevertheless seeks to contribute to a broader conversation about the nature of Canadian liberalism. By examining these early liberals' views over the span of fifty years, and by showing how they applied these ideas at both the provincial level and the new federal level, this study explains how these developments in Upper Canada ultimately became relevant to Canada on a national scale.[17]

Definitions and Parameters: Liberalism, Dissent, and Evangelicalism

Since this study wrestles with the contested nature of liberal thought in Canada, it would be counterproductive to begin with a rigid definition of liberalism. Instead, I start with the loose premise offered by historian Ian McKay, that liberalism is based on the primacy of the "individual" above all other categories such as community, society, and state. From that philosophical assumption there have emerged a host of political and economic practices, and a collection of principles (i.e., the idea of the individual's rights to life, liberty, property, equality) that various liberal thinkers have prioritized differently.[18] As historian Jeffrey McNairn has emphasized, scholarly characterizations of nineteenth-century liberalism can differ considerably depending on what they choose to include in the list of its defining principles.[19] Rather than imposing a single definition, then, this analysis follows McNairn's suggestion to examine the arguments among liberals and present a more "pluralized" view of liberalism.[20] From that vantage point, it is possible to see how early Canadians competed with one another to claim the mantle of "liberty" and, consequently, to see how the defining principles of liberalism changed over time.

The main proponents of liberalism in Upper Canada typically belonged to one of several non-Anglican denominations often called the Dissenters. Anglicans also contributed to the liberal-reform movement and the discourse of Protestant liberty, but they had a complicated relationship both with Canadian liberalism and with other Protestant denominations throughout the nineteenth century. Although a small handful of Upper Canadian Anglicans (e.g., Robert Baldwin, Benjamin Cronyn, and Edward Blake) would become prominent liberals, the Church of England's strong positions on church establishments, social structure, and imperial ties meant the Anglican church in Upper Canada started out, in the words of Curtis Fahey, "immersed in the conservative ideology of the age."[21] Voting records available from this period indicate that Anglicans usually supported conservative candidates, whereas Dissenters such as the Baptists and Congregationalists made up the voting base of the liberal reformers.[22] In some cases, Anglicans who openly espoused liberal views faced significant opposition from within their church, as in the case when the liberal Anglican Benjamin Cronyn was lambasted by a superior in 1851 as "better fitted for a political agitator than a Bishop."[23] One of the reasons for this political alignment: the colony initially gave exclusive privileges to the Church of England, such as a major land grant known as the clergy reserves. This contentious issue, among others explored below, helped to place Dissenters and Anglicans on opposing political sides for much of the first half-century of the colony's history after its founding in 1791.[24] It was only after the elimination of the clergy reserves in 1854 that Dissenting liberals began to speak more openly about reaching out to Anglicans as a group for political purposes.[25]

Anglicans' relations with other Protestants were also complicated by the public prominence of the "high church" tradition within Anglicanism. Its emphasis on bishops' apostolic succession from Christ and on church sacraments, notably embodied in England's mid-century Oxford Movement, made many Dissenters see Anglicans as theologically akin to Catholics and "only barely Protestant," often unfairly mischaracterizing low-church Anglicans.[26] Thus, although the contributions of Anglicans will be noted, this volume explores principally how Dissenters shaped Canadian liberalism. That said, future studies can build on my brief discussions of Anglican liberals to analyse their contribution to the concept of Protestant liberty.

The term "Dissenters" refers to those Protestants, initially those in England, who worshipped outside of the established Church of England (the established Church of Scotland was of course Presbyterian). Such groups have existed since the time of the English Reformation in the sixteenth century and have also been called at various times "Separatists" and "Nonconformists."[27] The category includes a variety of Protestant denominations, each with its own distinct doctrines and practices: in Upper Canada the most prominent were Baptists, Congregationalists, Methodists, Presbyterians, Quakers, and Unitarians. It appears odd that such diverse groups would find themselves in the same category. For example, what did the Quakers' quiet cultivation of "inner light" have to do with the Methodists' raucous camp-meeting revivalism?[28] As well, denominations such as Methodists and Presbyterians had internal divisions between those who supported and those who opposed the church establishment, which at times complicates their Dissenting status.[29] However, as the historian John Seed has explained, eighteenth-century adherents to these often-dissimilar denominations in England constructed a common Dissenting identity based on a shared history of persecutions at the hands of the established Church of England.[30] The basis of this alignment evolved during the rise of transatlantic revivalism in the mid-eighteenth century, after which evangelicalism (discussed further below) provided new points of unity for what historians David Bebbington and David Ceri Jones called "New Dissent."[31] Despite the Dissenting denominations remaining distinct from each other, throughout the nineteenth century they regularly worked together for common causes wherever they found themselves in the far reaches of the British Empire.[32]

The Dissenters' loose alliance was politically important in Upper Canada, where they made up a significant portion of the population. Whereas the Dissenters were always a minority in Britain,[33] in Upper Canada their combined numbers more than doubled that of their Anglican counterparts for much of the nineteenth century.[34] Several historians of the colony have noted a consistent correlation between religious and political affiliation, in which the Anglicans and Catholics typically voted conservative and the ones that this study classifies as Dissenters (Baptists, Congregationalists, Methodists, Presbyterians, and Quakers) typically voted for liberal reformers.[35] Noticing this pattern, George Emery wrote that "ethno-religious differences were the chief influence on voters' party preferences."[36] These denominations regularly joined political forces in the mid-nineteenth century, especially to challenge their perceived common enemy: the church establishment, and anything resembling it.[37] Several previous studies have explored specific aspects of Canadian church–state relations, notably the clergy reserves and religion in public education, many of which are referenced throughout this volume.[38] Although the Dissenters also famously took up a number of other political causes like temperance and abolition of slavery, explored in detail elsewhere,[39] this book concentrates on the intercultural conflicts between Protestants and Catholics and on the various applications of liberal thought that attempted to manage such conflicts.

By the eighteenth and nineteenth centuries, most of the Dissenters (except Unitarians) had embraced the transatlantic evangelical movement.[40] Since evangelical beliefs and practices feature in this study, it is necessary to introduce them here. To define evangelicalism, historian David W. Bebbington articulated a four-point checklist of the movement's characteristics: 1) *conversionism*, belief in the necessity of a personal conversion experience, 2) *biblicism*, adherence to the doctrinal authority of the Bible above any other authority, 3) *crucicentrism*, a gospel message focused on the atoning power of Jesus Christ's blood shed on the cross, and 4) *activism*, the imperative to express one's faith through some form of public engagement, such as evangelism.[41]

Together, the Dissenters' religious concerns became the rallying cries around which the early liberal-reform movement took shape in Upper Canada.[42] Over the five decades from the time the reformers first formed a majority in Upper Canada's elected assembly (1828) to the time that devout Dissenter Alexander Mackenzie left office as the first Liberal prime minister of Canada (1878), the Protestant Dissenters were an indispensable part of the reform party. This book cannot hope to give equal and extensive attention to each of the five Dissenting denominations mentioned above; for greater detail on each group, it refers readers to previous works about a single denomination. However, in focusing on Dissenting culture, this study traces the thematic links between each denomination, as they all invoked claims to a shared Dissenting heritage to advance common political goals.

Though set almost completely within Upper Canada, this volume acknowledges that its subjects often situated themselves within the broader events of the British Atlantic world. The Canadian movement against a state church, the liberal-reform movement more broadly, and the evangelical movement each perceived itself as part of a transatlantic whole. Despite operating within a very different church–state context than Britain's, for example, Canadian Dissenters still saw themselves as fighting alongside their like-minded compatriots in Britain. This international orientation was one of the reasons why disestablishmentarianism continued in Canada into the late nineteenth century, despite its facing no formal church establishment. Even after the Canadian colonies eliminated elements of church–state privilege such as the clergy reserves and the Anglicans' exclusive rights to perform marriage ceremonies, in 1863 Canadian newspapers could still publish news about the church establishment in Britain and sympathize, saying, "The spirit of persecution still lives amongst us and struggles to assert itself."[43]

With a large influx of British settlement in the 1830s and '40s, and increasing connection with the British world through regular transatlantic mail and (by the 1860s) telegraphs, the era's English Canadians were also, in many ways, Britons. British concerns were also theirs. J.M.S. Careless emphasized this connection in his analysis of nineteenth-century Canadian liberalism, arguing that the English-Canadian community "kept looking to the centre of the British world for the source of its thought."[44] In many cases this orientation determined how churches operated in Canada. For example, historian Todd Webb has examined the transatlantic mentality of Canadian Methodists who, despite starting out with exclusively North American leadership, began in 1833 to share resources, preachers, and objectives with their compatriots in Britain.[45] Rather than supporting the longstanding notion that Canadian churches were forerunners of an emerging Canadian national consciousness, then, Webb found that throughout the nineteenth century Canada's Methodists were "increasingly integrated into a British world."[46] Similarly, Denis McKim wrote about "loyalism's religious component," emphasizing the ways in which Dissenters such as Egerton Ryerson leveraged their religious connections to claim stronger ties to the British metropole.[47] These Canadian studies correspond with a similar international emphasis in scholarship outside the country. For example, David Hempton suggested that Methodism should be understood as an inherently international community rather than the product of any particular national context.[48] This book also highlights the transnational context for liberal reform, particularly as it fed into Upper Canadians' sense of participation in a wider British Atlantic world.[49]

Understanding the Religious Foundations of Canadian Liberalism

An earlier generation of historians often recognized the religious context of Canadian ideological development, but we must integrate these insights into the new scholarship on the liberal order. Writing in the mid-twentieth century, historians such as Arthur Lower and William Kilbourn took for granted that the prevalence of evangelical Dissenters in Upper Canada nurtured the liberal ethos during its infancy in the colony.[50] In 1989, William Westfall even wrote that "the study of reform has become the study of religion."[51] The last two decades have produced a windfall of new scholarship on the history of Canadian liberalism, inaugurated by Ian McKay's proposal to integrate various strands of scholarship into what he called the "liberal order framework." Following McKay's premise that liberalism became the hegemonic ideology of Canada beginning in about 1840, many scholars have set to work explaining and debating the various contours and consequences of this liberal order. However, this reconnaissance has tended to neglect these religious influences, overlooking or downplaying their role.[52]

This marginalization of religion may reflect a blind spot in our own secular society, wherein religious concerns arguably have less direct public influence. Historian Mark Noll explained that Canada has undergone a "rupture with the past" due to secularization since the 1960s. Along those lines, he argued that Canada's public sphere was gradually de-Christianized and that the public values that had been rooted in religion were relegated to the private sphere.[53] Now immersed in a Canada that excludes Christianity from political discourse, people today may not immediately appreciate the highly public nature of religion for their nineteenth-century predecessors. Therefore it requires a concerted effort to recover that religious context anew, to reconsider what it meant for the ideological development of their day, and to ask questions relevant to the next generation of scholarship.

Some scholars have made similar efforts to examine the religious foundations of liberal thought. For example, Kevin Anderson explained the Protestant context of twentieth-century liberal thought in Canada, arguing that the supposedly "universal" values of "liberty, freedom, and parliamentary democracy, were distinctively Protestant values … for which Catholics were [regarded as] unsuitable."[54] Tracing the Protestant roots of liberalism also necessitates an understanding of the sixteenth-century Protestant Reformation and its long-term consequences. Brad S. Gregory, for example, argued that Western liberalism emerged as an unintended consequence of Protestantism in part as a means to address "the serious problem of religio-political disruption in early modern Europe" initiated by the Protestant Reformation.[55] Philosopher Larry

Siedentop suggested even earlier Christian origins for many of the concepts that would later inform and ground Western liberalism. For him, the concepts of the individual, natural rights, moral equality, and representative government all emerged in the Middle Ages through the deliberations of Catholic philosophers and canon lawyers.[56] Although these proto-liberal ideas have pre-Protestant origins, Siedentop further explained that the Reformation facilitated the forging of liberalism as a coherent doctrine and made it possible to reimagine religion as a matter of individual conscience relegated to the private sphere.[57] Similarly, James T. Kloppenberg examined the "religious origins" of North Atlantic democracy, including the Protestant inspiration for foundational English liberal thinkers such as Algernon Sidney and John Locke.[58] Following the examples of these and other studies, I propose to re-examine nineteenth-century Canadian politics and the foundations of Canada's liberal order itself.

To that end, this book offers three conclusions about Canada's early liberal order, which I analyse in detail below. 1) *Liberalism emerged from a culturally specific origin*: Upper Canadian Dissenters' early advocacy of liberalism reveals a cultural basis for its ideas. Although liberal leaders went on to pitch their ideas as culturally neutral and therefore universally transferable, liberalism emerged from a specifically Protestant cultural context. 2) *Liberalism changed in order to appeal to non-Dissenting political allies*: The Dissenters' disillusionment with liberal leaders by the 1870s reveals just how much the bases of Canadian liberalism changed in five decades. As McKay suggested, in order to integrate groups on the periphery of the liberal order, liberal leaders were willing to alter aspects of liberal policy to accommodate their needs. Religion, particularly Catholic communitarianism, played a leading role in these compromises. 3) *Liberalism's accommodations failed to supersede collective religious interests with its individual-based paradigm*: The persistence of interreligious animosity throughout the nineteenth century, despite regular pleas from liberal statesmen for such conflicts to end, reveals the liberal order's failure to supersede collective identities and interests.

First, early liberalism emerged from a culturally specific origin. When the liberal reformer and would-be rebel William Lyon Mackenzie wrote in 1827 that he agreed with "Locke's opinion" on religious tolerance, he invoked an explicitly Protestant Dissenting heritage. Mackenzie believed that the clergy of the established Church of England could not be trusted to uphold the principles of religious freedom and would if given the chance promote "tyranny" and engage in "bitter persecution" of Dissenters: "Such was Locke's opinion, and such is ours."[59] Thus, Mackenzie articulated a culturally conscious version of Lockean liberalism that differs markedly from the idea that Locke epitomized neutrality and non-discrimination.[60] This interpretation was not unique to Mackenzie. Scholars such as the aforementioned James Kloppenberg have explained that John Locke's ideas of tolerance were circumscribed by his generation's "anxiety concerning the even greater threat represented by 'papists' and atheists."[61] Locke's writings on religious tolerance in the 1680s must be understood in large part as a response to King Louis XIV's Edict of Fontainebleau (1685), which revoked the Edict of Nantes (1598) extending tolerance to the Protestant Huguenots and ordered Roman Catholic uniformity in France and the crushing of the Huguenots.[62] In this context, Locke wanted England to offer tolerance for a range of religious beliefs, but also to withhold full political participation from religions deemed incompatible with a free English society.[63] Mackenzie and many other Upper Canadian liberals drew inspiration from this aspect of Locke's writings.

The notion that Lockean liberalism originated with a particular culture or had particular appeal to a specific culture is not widely embraced by scholars of Canadian liberalism today. Janet Ajzenstat, for example, has argued against the idea "that political institutions reflect prior commitments and prior loyalties" and has instead emphasized the cultural neutrality of liberal ideas even in the nineteenth century. Whatever its origins, she said, Lockean liberalism "could serve people who did not share the memories, the culture, and the historical experiences of British North America's English-speaking settlers."[64] However, in Upper Canada, early proponents of liberalism generally believed that British Protestants were uniquely suited to defend the "light and liberty of the nineteenth century," in contrast to those faiths described as "ignorance and papal superstition," which they depicted as enemies to liberty.[65] As we saw above, this Upper Canadian attitude is consistent with the broader British tradition in which, as Linda Colley has argued, British identity and nationhood became defined in opposition to the supposed tyranny of neighbouring Catholic nations; thus, British identity by the 1830s had become synonymous with the defence of Protestantism and a Protestant sense of liberty.[66]

The fact that liberalism still had culturally specific appeal in Upper Canada meant that Protestant Dissenters were the main advocates for liberal policy changes in the first half of the nineteenth century. This tendency is most observable in the liberalization of church–state policies, which ruptured the longstanding notions that the state had a divine mandate to propagate church institutions and that the church establishment formed the basis of the social order.[67] In place of this older paradigm came the liberal laissez-faire approach to religion in which churches were required to seek out and retain the voluntary support of individual patrons (also called "voluntarism").[68] Canadian historians such as Michael Gauvreau have already credited Protestant Dissenters for pioneering the liberal-voluntarist model of religion that demanded the individual's freedom of association with the faith of their choice.[69] These ideas were simply alien to the majority of Anglicans and Catholics, whose church hierarchies had historically been embedded in the state and enjoyed exclusive sanction in their respective communities. Indeed, even outside of church–state issues, it is not difficult to see the unique enthusiasm with which many early Protestant Dissenters advocated other liberal principles (e.g., free trade, home rule) throughout the nineteenth century.[70] Even 150 years after Locke's writings, liberalism in British North America continued to hold appeal almost exclusively within Protestant culture.

What is equally striking, and equally indicative of the cultural component of early Canadian liberalism, is how often Protestant liberals believed they *failed* to achieve their aims. In 1878, Goldwin Smith observed that not only was Catholicism still the established church in Quebec, but that its hierarchy was increasingly able to exert considerable influence on federal politics by directing its adherents' votes.[71] Presbyterian Rev. Stuart Acheson lamented that, despite past victories, at century's end Ontario was right back where it started with church–state relations. From Acheson's perspective, Dissenters had been outvoted and outmanoeuvred politically to entrench a new form of church establishment, namely the state-funded, church-run separate-school system. Whereas their predecessors fought to rid themselves of the clergy reserves, Acheson said, later governments had passed school laws whereby "religious communities may still be supported by the public funds as they were in the corrupt days of the 'Family Compact.'"[72] In the minds of these Dissenters, their longstanding voluntarist vision for church–state relations had failed due to political compromises with Catholic leaders.

The disillusionment of many Dissenters towards liberal compromises by the 1870s reveals exactly what first attracted Dissenters to liberalism: it was a *means* to advance their faith and their culture. The idea of a free market of religion in which individuals chose which denomination to support seemed to promise a scenario in which the true faith would naturally outperform false rivals. False versions of Christianity, as Dissenters believed Anglicanism and Catholicism and other state-supported churches to be, would no longer have what they perceived to be an unnatural advantage through state support. Reformer John Rolph in 1837 captured this sentiment perfectly:

> I will not endow [religious] error. Nor will I legislate against it, because I heartily believe that the divine truth contains within itself all the necessary elements for its own achievements … Remove all artificial obstructions, and light dispels the darkness wherever it shines. But if, invading the empire and prerogative of Heaven, you endow this darkness, and give it legislative locality and habitudes, you, more or less, obstruct the genial ray and eclipse the firmament of truth.[73]

Liberal politicians continued to draw on this line of thinking for decades to come, with George Brown arguing in 1851 that "pure religion will prosper for better if left dependent on the voluntary contributions of the Christian people than when pampered by the State."[74] On a visit to Ottawa in 1877, the British Congregationalist Edward Miall likewise argued that voluntarism was necessary to secure "man's right to serve the Almighty in accordance with the dictates of his own individual conscience; and hence," he said, he was "against the civil power being in any way used to further the projects or the interests of any ecclesiastical party or body."[75] Thus, when liberal politicians in the mid- to late nineteenth century decided to appease Catholic voters by abandoning aspects of *voluntarism* in favour of *state accommodation*, they defeated the very culturally specific purpose for which Dissenters had initially embraced the liberal paradigm regarding church–state relations in the first place.

Second, liberalism changed in order to appeal to non-Dissenting political allies. What the Protestant Dissenters noted as failures to fully separate church and state Ian McKay has explained as "bargains with liberal hegemony" that were necessary to integrate peripheral groups such as Catholics into the liberal order.[76] Indeed, these church–state compromises distinguish Canada's liberal order from that of the United States and other Western liberal democracies.[77] Protestant Dissenters were not interested in the supposed long-game strategy behind such compromises, but decried them as shameful concessions of principles designed to buy the Catholic vote. For example, when Liberal Prime Minister Alexander Mackenzie appeased Catholics by including a provision for separate schools in the North West Territory Bill of 1875, the Protestant liberal newspaper editor Robert Sellar accused him of "keeping in power by an alliance with the Hierarchy."[78] Sellar saw church–state compromises as undermining the "very backbone of Liberalism," which he said rejected special privileges for "any unduly favored section."[79]

Whereas the Dissenters' existence outside of traditional church–state alliances led them to pursue disestablishment and voluntarism as strategies to propagate their faith, the opposite was true for Catholics whose faith had long been nurtured in the bosom of the state. Indeed, Catholics had good reason to be leery of supposedly secular institutions, which they perceived to be designed to undermine their faith. For example, in the 1840s and '50s Catholics accused Protestant volunteers in the non-denominational orphans' asylum system of using their positions to proselytize to Catholic-born children.[80] Catholic thinkers like Thomas D'Arcy McGee came to envision what historian David A. Wilson called "a kind of Catholic domino theory" in which Protestantism inevitably led to liberalism, which led to revolution and socialism.[81] At the same time, the Catholic hierarchy in Rome embraced ultramontanism, which insisted on papal supremacy in civil affairs. With Pope Pius IX himself condemning the separation of church and state and other liberal ideas in his Syllabus of Errors, Catholic leaders in Canada began to follow suit; in 1871, a handful of Catholic journalists and clergymen known as the *Programmistes* began urging co-religionists to vote against liberal policies like separation of church and state, secular marriages, and secular education.[82] Given fears of Protestant influence and direct warnings from Rome, many were sometimes hesitant, if not hostile, vis-à-vis liberal ideas; liberalism often appeared to them to be a code word for Protestantism.

As an alternative to liberal voluntarism, then, Upper Canadian Catholics in the 1840s began to demand state accommodation for their faith such as separate schools and (until 1854) grants from the clergy reserves. The clergy reserves, a large swath of land originally set aside in 1791 for the support of the Church of England, had in 1840 been extended to offer state financial support to four denominations, including the Roman Catholic church. The effect was a kind of "multi-headed establishment" that elevated no single church, but allowed four to draw from state coffers.[83] The first state-funded separate Catholic schools in Upper Canada emerged in the 1840s under the leadership of Bishop Michael Power of Toronto,[84] and a decade later his successor, Bishop Armand-François-Marie de Charbonnel, began in 1852 to call for Catholics to refuse to support or attend the common schools.[85] His agitation led to the School Bill of 1853, which set up a separate Catholic school system in Upper Canada intended to be on a par with the minority "Protestant" (non-denominational) school system in Lower Canada. The bill incorporated separate school boards to handle their own funds, while exempting Catholics from taxes for common schools.[86] Notably, this law (and later additions) would have failed if left entirely to Upper Canadian members, but passed with a majority from Lower Canada combined with its Upper Canadian allies in the united legislature.[87]

Contrasting the Catholics' demand for state accommodation with the Dissenters' demand for voluntarism makes clear that liberalism was not universally transferable in nineteenth-century Canada. British-Canadian Protestants considered their own religion compatible with modern progress, freedom, and liberalism in a way that Catholicism simply was not.[88] Protestant liberal Charles Lindsey, for example, wondered what would happen if Catholics ever became politically dominant again in Canada, and was not optimistic: "If those who make loud profession of these dogmas [ultramontane Catholicism] could grasp in their hands the whole political power of the country, what guarantee would remain for the maintenance of the rights and liberties of the rest of the population?"[89] Lindsey's concerns were based on his decades of political experience in Upper Canada and the words of prominent anti-liberal Catholic leaders.[90]

Simply put, Catholics started out on the periphery of the early liberal order, which therefore had to convince them of its value in maintaining their own interests. Compromises in the form of state accommodation became the central strategy towards that end.

Third, liberalism failed to supersede collective religious interests with its individual-based paradigm. Some liberal leaders convinced themselves that the old religious divisions would soon disappear once they agreed to allow state accommodation for Catholicism. With a spirit of great optimism and reconciliation, the former Liberal leader George Brown stated in 1871, "All the vexed questions that caused the separation have been settled and swept away, and now all are free to act together for the advancement and prosperity of our country, and to treat all men alike, without regard to their religious opinions."[91] The celebration was premature. Only four years later, the issue of separate schools (which Brown had referred to as "settled forever")[92] surfaced *again* during debates in Parliament regarding the North West Territory Bill of 1875, which the governing Liberals resolved with further state accommodation by including a clause allowing for separate schools.[93] Indeed, the supposedly "settled" issue would surface several more times that century.[94]

Liberals had underestimated the persistence of the religiously based politics of collective identity, and consequently found themselves ruled by it. For most of the 1850s and '60s, it was the Conservatives under John A. Macdonald who had secured the Catholic vote, and private correspondence between Sir John and Catholic leaders reveals the extent to which they treated Upper Canada's Catholics as a voting bloc to be put into play when needed.[95] In the years after George Brown reached out to Catholics in 1871, it was increasingly the Liberals who were, in the words of Conservative Alexander Galt, "now basking in the sunshine of Episcopal favor."[96] As a result, Liberal leaders were increasingly unwilling to advocate positions, even liberal ones, that could upset Catholic leaders. When one of his cabinet ministers publicly condemned ultramontanism in Quebec in 1875, Alexander Mackenzie confided in private that he "cannot object to the sentiments but the time was ill chosen. We cannot govern without a large following from Quebec and any aggressive act is seen to lose it for us."[97] By the 1880s it was not the Liberals, but Ontario's Conservative party, under William Ralph Meredith, that challenged further state support for separate schools. Meredith said in 1889 that "the thunderbolts of a great Church were discharged against me, and Roman Catholics from one end of the province to the other were summoned to cast their votes against me."[98] The fact that Ontario Catholics in 1889 voted *Liberal* to defend their collective church–state interests indicated that the Liberal party's transformation was then complete.

Cultural-historical theory can help explain why collective religious interests were more enduring than nineteenth-century liberals were willing to admit. As the cultural historian William McNeill has emphasized, one of the strategies groups tend to employ to consolidate social cohesion is to define their group through contrasts with the outsiders who served as its historic enemies.[99] Through sermons, public celebrations, and anniversary commemorations, Canadian religious groups constantly reinforced their identities by retelling stories of past conflicts and triumphs against outsiders. For example, upwards of two and half centuries after the fact, Toronto Protestants continued to celebrate Guy Fawkes Day (5 November), burning in effigy the Catholic terrorist who narrowly failed to blow up Westminster Palace (Parliament) in 1605.[100] Furthermore, within the broad umbrella of Protestantism, some denominations told stories that reinforced their distinction from other Protestants. For example, in 1862 Canadian Congregationalists met to commemorate their separation from the Church of England two centuries previous. Speaking to his Hamilton audience, Rev. William Fletcher Clarke sought to demonstrate "that we have a history of which we have no reason to be ashamed" and to inspire his fellow Congregationalists "to stand where our nonconforming forefathers stood."[101] Clarke understood that to avoid dissolution and / or absorption into a larger body, his community required clear lines of separation, and a justifiable foundation for that separation.[102] Thus for Clarke and other Dissenters like him, an appeal to the feuds of centuries past was not simply gratuitous provocation, but a necessary strategy for maintaining his group's existence amidst religious pluralism.

Canadian Catholics were similarly reluctant to abandon collective interests and historic animosities. Quebec's ultramontane Bishop Bourget explained Catholic political involvement as a strategy of self-preservation in early 1876, saying, "Modern Liberalism pretends that religion should not leave the sacristy, nor go beyond the limits of private piety. But the Pope declares that Catholics can only efficaciously defend their rights and their liberties by actively mixing up in public affairs."[103] Like the Orangemen's periodic shows of force, Catholics occasionally defended their collective interests through violent extra-legal means. For example, there were several instances throughout the nineteenth century when Catholic protesters shut down anti-Catholic speakers,[104] and on one occasion in December 1875 a Catholic mob allegedly burned down a Methodist church on the previously Catholic-majority Oka First Nation reserve.[105] Actions that Protestants understandably interpreted as violations of their freedoms of religion and speech must have seemed to some Catholics defences against Protestant aggression – and vice versa.

The persistence of collective-identity politics was the great tragedy of the neutral-liberty perspective, which had promised a fresh start through the equal treatment of everyone as individuals before the law. As Lord Dufferin argued in his farewell entreaty, the "traditions of animosity and ill-will and the memory of ancient grievances" had no place in Canada, which he described as "a stainless paradise, fresh and bright from the hands of its maker."[106] And yet these traditions of animosity persisted. Even the most optimistic nineteenth-century liberal thinkers found themselves struggling against recurring inter-group conflict. The man of the "sunny way" himself, Wilfrid Laurier, reflected in 1887 on the relationships between religions, regions, and cultures within Canada since Confederation, and he admitted that "the prejudices of race and creed have increased in bitterness" due to conflicts such as the recent Northwest Rebellion of 1885. The purpose of Confederation, he said, was "to bring the different races closer together, to soften the asperities of their mutual relations … *But are the divisions ended?*"[107]

Despite Laurier's optimism, his poignant question warrants reflection for historians of religion and liberalism. The pages that follow examine the clash between liberal ideals and the religious divisions in nineteenth-century Canada. The central argument of this study is that although Protestant Dissent animated and shaped the early liberal-reform movement in Upper Canada, its perspectives were ultimately pushed out of the Liberal party in order to appeal to a wider electorate. The making of Canadian liberalism itself demanded the taming of inherited group identities and the ancient feuds that they harboured, but throughout the nineteenth century this liberal dream was still far from fulfilment.

Sources and Structure of the Book

I undertook the primary research for this study in a series of archives in Ottawa and Toronto in 2016 and 2017, later conducting additional research using microfilm available through the holdings of the University of Calgary. Major primary sources at Library and Archives Canada included a vast body of private correspondence between leaders of the Liberal party during Alexander Mackenzie's government (1873–78), and the earlier writings of several other politicians such as long-time Liberal-Conservative / Liberal parliamentarian Sir Richard William Scott, PC, of Ottawa. The Archives of Ontario, located at York University in Toronto, gave me access to the collections of William Lyon Mackenzie and the related Lindsey family, Congregationalist minister John Roaf, James Hervey Price, Charles Clarke, and long-time premier Oliver Mowat. The Dundas Museum and Archives enabled me to examine the rich diaries of the devout evangelical reformer James Lesslie and that of several of his family members. Additional sources were available through the United Church of Canada Archives and the Lambton County Archives. Through the University of Calgary's Taylor Family Digital Library, I was able to gain access to a wide array of published nineteenth-century materials in print or through the CIHM microfilm collection, including several useful historical newspapers such as the *Colonial Advocate,* the *Constitution,* the *Examiner,* the *Globe,* the *Irish Canadian*, the *Leader,* and the *North American.* My study also draws on a breadth of research by other scholars of Canadian history, particularly those who specialize in religion or politics in the nineteenth century, with occasional supplementary material by British and American scholars as well.

This book is organized chronologically and is divided into five chapters, plus the introduction and conclusion. Chapter 1 begins in 1828 with the election of the first reform-party majority in the Upper Canada legislature and ends with the Upper Canada Rebellion of 1837. Drawing much of its support from the evangelical Dissenters, the first reform-dominated legislature was reviled by critics as a "saddle-bag parliament," invoking the image of Methodist itinerant preachers on horseback.[108] The chapter explains how the reform party emerged as a coalition by relying heavily on Dissenting concerns as its rallying cries and most consistent source of support. With Dissenting culture at the centre of the movement from the beginning, reformers naturally drew on Dissenting meanings to explain the many roadblocks they encountered when advocating for democratic reform through the 1830s. The chapter culminates in the Toronto rebellion led by the radical journalist and fellow Dissenter William Lyon Mackenzie in December 1837. Even during the uprising itself, Dissenting culture provided a primary means of interpreting Canada's political struggles and of recruitment to the rebel cause.[109]

Chapter 2 begins with the aftermath of the rebellion and ends with the victory of Robert Baldwin in the "responsible government" election of 1847–48. In either direct or indirect response to the rebellions in both provinces, this decade saw a restructuring of governance, including the Union of the Canadas with a united legislature of forty-two seats each for Upper Canada / Canada West and Lower Canada / Canada East, responsible government (executive branch accountable to the elected legislature, instead of to the British viceroy), and a public-school system. Church–state relations were reconfigured, with separate Catholic schools and clergy-reserve funds to multiple denominations. With the rebellion's leaders in exile, the early union period saw the rise of the moderate Baldwinite reformers, who built coalitions across religious and sectional lines. However, many Dissenters such as Isaac Buchanan and George Brown began to express concern about the increased political influence of Catholics in the united legislature. Their sense of political vulnerability only amplified when the horrifying Irish famine brought unprecedented numbers of Irish Catholics to Upper Canada. In this context, reformers began to speak explicitly about religious demographics in the colony and the failures of the church establishment in Ireland. After the election of 1848, Dissenting voters soon grasped that Baldwin did not share their desire for a speedy end to the clergy reserves or separate schools, moves that would risk upsetting his Catholic allies in the legislature and executive. Thus, after a decade of relative liberal unity under Baldwin's leadership, the stage was set for a major schism between the proponents of neutral liberty and the supporters of Protestant liberty.

Chapter 3 captures the height of inter-religious animosity and liberal anti-Catholicism in the 1850s, closing with the Reform Convention of 1859, wherein Oliver Mowat proclaimed his frustration with the "Baneful Domination" of Catholic Quebec over Ontario. Following the success of the Clear Grits and other anti-Baldwin liberals in the 1851 election, Dissenters continued to organize and push back against church–state advocates, helping to press the conservative-led coalition to secularize the clergy reserves in 1854. This decade also saw a consolidation of the Catholic system of separate schools, despite Upper Canadian reformers having a majority of their own section's seats for much of the decade. Throughout this time, the liberals were clearly divided between the supporters of Francis Hincks, whose expression of neutral liberty emphasized economic opportunity over cultural concerns, and those of George Brown, who became the unparalleled champion of Protestant liberty. Despite notable electoral success throughout the 1850s, however, the Brownites had been repeatedly outmanoeuvred by coalitionists, culminating in the "Double Shuffle" of 1858, in which George Brown's sole chance at serving as premier was swiftly terminated (after two days). By the late 1850s it had become clear to Upper Canadian liberals that the main barrier to their political self-determination was "this alliance of Roman Catholic bishops who command the votes of three-fourths of the people of Lower Canada." Thus, in 1859, Brown declared that the only way out of their position at the mercy of Catholic legislators was to end the legislative union with Lower Canada through the introduction of a federal system for British North America.[110]

Chapter 4 covers the reform cause through the Confederation debates of the 1860s and ends with the hanging of Thomas D'Arcy McGee's convicted killer Patrick James Whelan in 1869. The chapter examines the increased inter-religious conflicts of the 1860s, including that deriving from additional Catholic separate-school bills, debates about immigration and religious demographics, and the religiously charged Fenian invasions of 1866. Building on the work of other historians who have explained the secular-materialist motives for Confederation, this chapter adds that Upper Canadian liberals also advocated it as a means to separate from Lower Canada and thus to achieve a form of Protestant self-determination. Furthermore, we see how conflicting religious identities continued to defy the logic of neutral liberty, culminating in the high-profile murder of the former Irish nationalist Thomas D'Arcy McGee. Despite the lofty rhetoric about a restart in Protestant–Catholic relations after Confederation, discussions during the trial of Patrick James Whelan again demonstrated a disjuncture between politicians and judges' desire to neutralize religion from public life and average Canadians' public assertions of their collective religious identities.

Chapter 5 traces the transformation of the Liberal party under both Ontario Premier Oliver Mowat and Prime Minister Alexander Mackenzie away from Protestant liberty and towards neutral liberty, and ends with Mackenzie's election defeat in 1878. As a devout evangelical Dissenter himself who had been active in the reform party since the 1850s, Mackenzie was something of a pioneer for evangelicals in federal government. However, the necessity to unify an infighting caucus and retain Catholic votes made him extremely reluctant to rock the boat on church–state issues. Although private correspondence reveals his severe distaste for ultramontanism and all church–state connections, in practice he did nothing to oppose these forces. Meanwhile, at the provincial level the Liberal party under Oliver Mowat was also beginning to directly solicit the Catholic vote. Both leaders took their cue from George Brown himself, who decided in 1871 to reach out to Catholics when it appeared that the Liberals had the opportunity to form government in Ontario. At the end of the decade, both the provincial and federal manifestations of the Liberal party had explicitly rejected the voluntarist heritage of their five-decade relationship with Protestant Dissent, and had instead campaigned on free trade in an attempt to appeal to a wider audience.

The aftermath of this five-decade period of sectarian political struggle was a thoroughly transformed Liberal party and a modified version of Canadian liberalism. Whereas Upper Canada's liberal leaders in the 1830s had openly stated that they did not want taxpayer money to support what they perceived to be false versions of Christianity (Catholicism and Anglicanism), by the 1870s liberals had rebranded themselves as friendly to all faiths and willing to silence members of their party who continued to raise the "No popery" cry. By the following decade, the Liberal government of Oliver Mowat was willing even to increase state funding for church initiatives to appear "progressive."[111] In order to seal this transformation, liberals stripped their ideology of its previous Protestant connotations and accepted church–state compromises. Dissenting narratives about true believers standing up to church–state persecution were replaced by more neutral invocations of ancient feuds fading away in order to allow the peaceful coexistence of religions. Despite Lord Dufferin's hope for the coexistence of various groups within Canada's "stainless paradise," however, such a paradise contained its own forbidden fruit. Indeed, the persistence of collective-identity politics as fuelled by competing interpretive patterns and international currents had threatened the defining myths of Canada's liberal order before it even began. The following pages explain how the persistence of inter-religious "ancient feuds," and the resultant competition between Protestant liberty and neutral liberty as different ideas for how to manage such feuds, contributed to the origins and transformation of Canadian liberalism.

1

Revolt against Wicked Rulers

The Rise of Reform, 1828–1837

William Lyon Mackenzie's campaign announcement for election to the legislative assembly appeared in several issues of his weekly newspaper, the *Colonial Advocate,* throughout the winter of 1827–28. Amid commitments to advocate for public-works projects and to serve "the cause of the people," Mackenzie included a striking statement about religion: "I have ever been opposed to ecclesiastical domination; it is at enmity with the free spirit of Christianity; and nations which have bowed to its yoke, are become the dark abodes of ignorance and superstition – oppression and misery. That corrupt, powerful, and long endured influence which has hitherto interfered with your rights and liberties, can only be overthrown by your unanimity and zeal."[1] The immediate context of this statement pertains to two religion-related controversies that had become election issues – namely, the proposal for a state-funded Anglican university and what to do about ongoing state support for the Anglican church in the form of the clergy reserves.[2]

To explain Mackenzie's rhetoric as an isolated appeal for a specific policy, however, is to miss the broader trend of invoking religious concepts in discussions of "liberty" in nineteenth-century Canada. As this chapter demonstrates, Mackenzie and his contemporaries often used explicitly religious concepts from Protestant Dissenting culture to explain their ideals for government. This firm reliance on religious concepts carried over into Mackenzie's recruitment for the Upper Canada rebellion of 1837, in which he increasingly came to believe and teach that the Bible itself justified what he called "revolt against wicked rulers."[3] Indeed, references to "ecclesiastical domination" and related concepts were not incidental, but central, to the ways in which early Upper Canadians understood liberty.

The principal argument of this chapter is that the liberal movement in Upper Canada, and consequently the colony's main expressed ideology of liberalism, began in the 1820s and '30s with the self-conscious purposes and perceptions of Protestant Dissent. Ian McKay suggested that historians of Canadian liberalism address what he called "actually existing liberalism" rather than "flights into high theory."[4] Instead of examining what liberals ought to espouse or what a liberal society ought to look like in theory, this chapter proposes that the liberal movement operated in Upper Canada in a cultural context shaped by Protestant Dissent. When Mackenzie spoke about "the free spirit of Christianity," he clearly meant the Dissenting tradition. How could an Anglican in Upper Canada or a Catholic in Lower, for example, whose respective church institutions were then actively and historically unified with the state, agree with Mackenzie that nations with an established church inevitably "become the dark abodes of ignorance and superstition" antithetical to "rights and liberties" and that such establishments must be "overthrown"? These notions simply did not come naturally for an Anglican who weekly sat in the pew of a church itself "established" in Upper Canada, if less clearly so than in Britain.[5]

With church–state relations featuring so prominently and heatedly in political discourse, denominational differences shaped colonists' political engagement. The minimal information available about voting patterns reveals a strong correlation between religious affiliation and political party. Indeed, George Emery wrote that "ethno-religious differences were *the chief influence* on voters' party preferences."[6] In the 1830s (and for much of the century), conservatives attracted consistent support from Anglicans, Catholics, and British Wesleyans, and liberal reformers routinely appealed to the Dissenters such as Baptists, Congregationalists, episcopal Methodists, Presbyterians, and Quakers.[7] Although this situation would evolve over time, the liberal movement in Upper Canada was designed by and for Protestant Dissenters.

The Upper Canada rebellion of 1837 fits directly within this interpretation. As this chapter demonstrates, William Lyon Mackenzie and many of his supporters were stirred to action in 1837 by the belief that their faith and liberty were under threat from colonial authorities. Indeed, Mackenzie consistently stoked these anxieties in order to recruit Protestant Dissenters and argued that it was a "bible duty" to overthrow tyrannical rulers.[8] This interpretation reorients a body of scholarship that has downplayed or overlooked religion, an absence noticed recently by others.[9] Some historians, such as Albert Schrauwers and Robynne Healey, have laid crucial groundwork by examining the Quakers' role in the 1837 rebellion, but they concentrate on that one denomination.[10] This study suggests that the Quakers were but one part of a wider appeal to Protestant Dissenters during the rebellion.

Historians have offered a myriad of interpretations to explain "why fifty-year-old farmers with property to protect and a family to support would take up arms against a powerful imperial government."[11] Earlier historians such as Gerald Craig suggested that the farmers were simple young men easily "duped" by Mackenzie.[12] While less dismissive and offering a more thorough analysis, Colin Read and Ronald Stagg still argued that Mackenzie fomented rebellion among folks only seeking reform.[13] One more recent trend is to examine the international influences, such as that of the Jacksonian United States, whose "market revolution" and the political ideas of the radical Democrats had parallels in Canada.[14] The role of churches in this exchange has produced some fruitful works, such as J.I. Little's examinations of the American influence on churches and loyalism in the Eastern Townships of Lower Canada.[15]

As this chapter examines below, the early Upper Canadian elites worried frequently about the influence of American clerics, not without reason.[16] Of course, the connections between Upper and Lower Canada in 1837 also played a role. Alan Greer advocated analysing the two rebellions in tandem, and even suggested that by late 1837 "Mackenzie sounded more and more like the leader of a Lower Canada solidarity campaign."[17] Benjamin T. Jones similarly emphasized the similarities between the two colonies in his study on their civic republicanism: the rebel cause was "neither French nor English; it was a battle over the spirit of the British constitution."[18] Michel Ducharme also put the two Canadas together, placed them within a wider transatlantic movement for republican liberty, and attributed violence to an irreconcilable ideological division between "republican liberty" and "modern liberty" in the colonies.[19]

While historians now tend to take seriously the rebels' concerns and ideology, lumping Upper Canada together with other polities may overlook the role of religion and culture. Although rebels in both Canadas shared a common enemy (the unaccountable executive), and even found inspiration from each other's actions,[20] their motives were very different and culturally specific. Alan Greer's study of French Canadians' habitant culture shows how their reform movement differed fundamentally from Upper Canada's Anglo-Protestant rural reformers.[21] Indeed, many of the Lower Canadian rebels experienced a "disengagement from religion" due to the Catholic clergy's disapproval of their rebellion,[22] while, as this chapter explains, Upper Canadian rebels often doubled down on their religious rhetoric – a contrast that reveals just how Protestant Dissent harmonized with their rebellion. Unfortunately, the strategy to hypothesize a common struggle for "republican liberty" risks boiling the conflict down to somewhat intellectual concerns about the relationship between the legislatures and the executives, an approach that Michel Ducharme admitted favours the language of elites.[23] To truly understand what motivated farmers in Upper Canada to pick up their pitchforks and march on Toronto, we must analyse how their own distinct worldview and experiences shaped their views of the state. Upper Canadian reformers (and later, the rebels) interpreted and responded to the political crisis of the 1830s in terms of Protestant Dissent. This chapter explains how the distinct meanings of Protestant Dissent were foundational to the reform movement and the rebellion.

"Saddle-bag Parliament": The 1828 Election

The 1828 election for Upper Canada's legislative assembly was a monumental victory for the political movement then beginning to unify around the term "reform." For the first time in the colony's four decades, members critical of the appointed executive council (cabinet) would dominate the elected assembly.[24] In addition to representing the ascendancy of the reform party, however, the 1828 election illustrates the central role of religion in the colony's politics. So entwined was this election with religious divisions that one critic called the new reform-majority assembly a "saddle-bag parliament," after Methodist itinerants on horseback.[25] Indeed, the three main election issues that year – the Anglican university charter, the alien or naturalization question, and the clergy reserves – each helped forge a lasting relationship between Dissenters and reform. Whereas the clergy reserves remained a persistent wedge issue for decades, this section focuses on the university charter and the alien question. Using William Lyon Mackenzie's *Colonial Advocate* as its main source, it illustrates the extent to which the reform triumph in 1828 represented a political victory for Protestant Dissent.

The university charter was the rallying issue for Dissenters in the summer of 1828. Many believed that a state-funded Anglican university – King's College – in York (later Toronto) would mean the ascendancy of an established church, as anticipated by church officials like Anglican archdeacon John Strachan. He argued that it would help to foster the colonists' "attachment to the British Monarchy and to the Established Church."[26] As one might imagine, this goal was anathema to many Dissenters. James Wilson, a Methodist reform MLA from Prince Edward County,[27] argued in the assembly that "this charter if allowed to go into operation would aggravate the minds of the people of the country, to think of a college, an university, erected and endowed at the expense of 9–10ths of the inhabitants and diametrically opposite to their views and wishes."[28] In February 1828, an assembly committee chaired by reform leader Marshall Spring Bidwell had met to discuss the university charter. The committee rejected the proposal partly because it saw the scheme as part of a broader attempt to make Anglicanism the official state religion, worrying "that it was the intention of His Majesty's Government to incorporate the church of England or any other church with the Government as an appendage of the state."[29] Although the college had received a royal charter from King George IV in 1827, followed by the promised endowment of 225,944 acres of crown lands, the Dissenters' opposition delayed construction until 1842.[30]

While some Anglicans also opposed state funding – and two committee members were Anglicans[31] – political opposition to the measure was largely crafted by and targeted towards Dissenters. For example, the committee's report expressed concern even at the expansion of Anglican numbers in the colony. In addition to leading dangerously close to church establishment, the committee warned, "the effect of establishing this University, will be ultimately to make the greater portion of the population of the province, members of the Church of England." In contrast, the report praised the Methodists' "christian zeal and benevolence" for spreading "our holy religion" throughout the sparsely populated colony in its early days.[31] Reformers expected no such "christian zeal" from an Anglican university: as one anonymous author wrote, "If the charter of that literary monopoly, the university, shall be suffered to go into operation … the inevitable consequence will be an extension of the reign of bigotry."[32]

As for the alien or naturalization bill so contentious in the 1828 election campaign, it, though explicitly a question of nationality, contained a notable religious subtext. The executive attempted to disenfranchise colonists who were born in the United States or were U.S. citizens at some point after 1783, when the loyalist migration began after the signing of the Treaty of Paris recognized American independence. Beginning as an attempt to disqualify a former U.S. citizen, the reformer Barnabas Bidwell, from serving in the legislative assembly, the alien controversy developed into a broader question about loyalty and naturalization.[33] Loyalty was a recurring theme in Upper Canadian politics, especially after the War of 1812, wherein many British-born colonial leaders believed the American-born colonists should be regarded with some suspicion.[34] In 1825, Attorney General John Beverly Robinson drafted a naturalization bill that he claimed would protect both the political and property rights of American immigrants, but reformers pointed out that it implied possible disenfranchisement. The British government eventually proposed that former American citizens could be naturalized if their names were registered and they took a special oath of allegiance, a stipulation that reformers also rejected vehemently and petitioned against. London responded by blocking Robinson's proposal and allowing the assembly to come up with a new one.[35] Before the summer election, in May 1828 the reformers drafted and carried their own bill that automatically naturalized all colonists who had lived in the colony before 1820, and subsequent arrivals could become naturalized after seven years of residence and an oath of allegiance.[36]

But the resulting alien controversy tapped into a longstanding concern about the colony's American-dominated religious culture. In 1828, Robinson expressed concern that the colonists had been "placed under the guidance, even in spiritual matters, of preachers from a foreign country… The preachers from the United States, being naturally attached to their own country and its laws, inculcate sentiments at variance with our constitution."[37] This concern hearkens back to the colony's earliest days, when British leaders began to notice the proliferation of American-based itinerant preachers. Early tory legislative councillor (member of the upper house) Richard Cartwright, a devout Anglican, had warned back in 1806 that evangelical "fanatics" were likely spreading republican sentiments in the colony.[38] Archdeacon John Strachan revived this concern in 1825 when he accused the Methodists of disloyalty, spurring a public war of words with the young Methodist preacher Egerton Ryerson.[39] It was not merely the Methodists' connection to the United States, but also their evangelical beliefs and emotional style of worship, that troubled Strachan.[40] Indeed, although American origin was the main target of the alien bill, some tory commentators saw it as an opportunity to target all potentially seditious elements, whether American or British.[41] With clergymen like Strachan and Ryerson becoming public figureheads for debates about loyalty and naturalization, it was only natural that the question of American loyalty ran parallel with that of evangelical loyalty. Thus, even though the alien bill itself targeted national origin, it was part of a broader debate about the cultural direction of Upper Canada, wherein religion played a significant role.

With the beleaguered university charter and naturalization issue fresh in colonists' minds, reform politicians approached the election with confidence. A poem in the *Colonial Advocate* depicted the Tories Strachan and Robinson lamenting their impending loss, with the university charter and the alien bill taking the blame. As the caricature of Strachan is depicted as saying, "Our schemes are all laid low / Thy Alien Bill, My college craft / Have work'd our overthrow."[42] Reformers simply needed to rally the right voters to the polls in July. Dissenters, the people most likely to be concerned about Anglican ascendancy, would of course be their natural targets.

Dissenting churches seemed to respond well to the reform message, and many lent their support. Methodist Egerton Ryerson, for example, appealed to Dissenters to come together in opposition to John Strachan's church–state ambitions. Ryerson noted that similar bills in Britain were "completely counteracted by the united efforts of Dissenters; and if Dissenters in this Province will pursue a similar course, [Strachan's] unparalleled measures, will likewise fail."[43] Some Methodist itinerant preachers helped to spread reform petitions throughout the countryside.[44] Some churches hosted reform meetings, as at a Lutheran church in Fredericksburg.[45] Several Dissenting clergymen joined with reform politicians in the lead-up to the election to publicly condemn arrangements like the clergy reserves and the Anglican university charter. The Baptist minister Alexander Stewart and the Methodist elder William Case, for example, joined a litany of reform politicians' responses expressing what Case called an "aversion to any thing like an ecclesiastical establishment."[46]

Reformers could harness the Dissenters' support because they understood and spoke to the Dissenters' shared worldview and value system. Their rhetoric appealed to four central Dissenting themes: millennialism, open denominations, anti-clericalism, and voluntarism.

First, millennialism was based on Dissenters' interest in biblical prophecies regarding the end of time. In an open letter to Strachan, Ryerson suggested that a church establishment would lead to something akin to the reign of the Anti-Christ. Invoking the imagery of "the beast" in the Book of Revelation, Ryerson warned that "an ecclesiastical establishment begins to show itself here, and the iron claws of the beast are about." Quoting Methodist leader Charles Wesley, Ryerson referred to established churches as "purely evil, 'Tis Babel, Antichrist, and Pope, and Devil." More than merely giving Anglicans the edge in an otherwise-friendly competition for parishioners, church–state ascendancy meant a threat to religious liberty for Ryerson and his supporters. Upper Canadians were "exposed to the most imminent danger, and [we] feel it our duty to give the alarm, before ourselves and our posterity are forever bound in chains."[47] Whether or not Ryerson intended to be partisan, this kind of high-stakes millennialist rhetoric pushed Dissenters to vote for reformers who promised to oppose church–state measures.

Second, Dissent's emphasis on the conversion experience, rather than on church-centred ordinances, downplayed denominational boundaries. This concept of open denominations, embraced by many Dissenters and less commonly by Anglicans, accentuated the tory–reform divide during the 1828 campaign. Although low-church Anglicanism was more flexible on this point, high-church adherents, like John Strachan, saw orthodox ordinances and liturgy as essential for salvation and exclusive to their denomination.[48] By contrast, most Dissenters embraced the evangelical concept of loose boundaries between denominations and balked at dependence on a particular ecclesiastical "system" for salvation. They used this concept to depict Anglicans as too controlling or narrow in their faith. One poem published in the *Colonial Advocate*, for example, caricatured an Anglican clergyman as condemning all non-Anglicans to hell: "Ah! pity your soul, for without our church pale / If you happen to die, to be damn'd you can't fail / ... Ah pity your soul!

come be of our sect / For then you are safe, and may plead you're elect." Invoking the Old Testament, the author compared the Anglican faith to "a levitical bride." Even this seemingly minor doctrinal difference invoked the Dissenters' perennial fear of persecution by a state church, with the poem caricaturing the Anglican perspective: "Come along with us ... and be of our sect / And we'll bind all dissenters by the heads and the neck."[49] Dissenters attributed the same exclusivity to Catholics, generating ammunition even for political disagreements. For example, in an argument with the Catholic fellow reformer Francis Collins, colonist James McMillan spoke of open denominations in a personal jab at Collins's faith: "Neither do I wish to monopolize Heaven to the sect to which I belong, to the exception of others, believing it sufficiently spacious for the whole human family."[50] Whether as a critique of Catholics or of Anglicans, the concept appealed to Dissenters, who used it occasionally to disparage political opponents.

Third, anti-clericalism engendered a critical stance towards the established clergy. It had perhaps the greatest appeal to Dissenters during the 1828 campaign, largely because John Strachan's church–state proposals had made him their highest-profile enemy. Despite the handful of Anglican reformers, Dissenters depicted Anglican imagery and doctrine as inherently corrupt and hypocritical. In one poem published during the campaign, the anonymous author invoked Jesus' rebuke of the Pharisees in the Gospel of Matthew to condemn Anglican clerical positions:

Wo to ye! Scribes and Pharisees
Ye hypocrites of all degrees
And shovel hutted Hectors
Archdeacon, vicar, priest, or dean
From prelate proud to hireling mean
Ye 'church and state' directors.[51]

William Lyon Mackenzie's writings are rife with anti-clericalism, and he accused Strachan "and his brother priests" of being "tools in the hands of the English dignitaries, and [they] only want POWER."[52] Reformers sometimes presented themselves as merely opposing "ecclesiastical supremacy" and claimed to respect aspects of Anglican tradition.[53] However, the wider body of their rhetoric often seemed to conflate Anglican doctrine and institutions themselves with church–state corruption.

Finally, voluntarism meant simply that churches should be supported solely by voluntary contributions, not by the state. This concept obviously came into play in an election revolving around church–state relations. The thorough separation of church and state might look secularist today, but in the nineteenth century it was in fact wedded to Dissenting culture. The arguments for voluntarism rested on a Dissenting understanding of the church's "purity," with even politicians such as Marshall Spring Bidwell stating in 1828: "As the [clergy] reserves now stand they detract more from the purity of true religion than they add to its riches."[54] These expressions of voluntarism also explicitly rejected the Catholic and Anglican doctrine of their bishops' apostolic succession from Christ. Whereas many Anglicans believed that their church derived its authority from an unbroken chain of succession tracing back to the original twelve apostles and that it therefore deserved special sanction from the state,[55] many Dissenters believed that this link was corrupted during the reign of the Roman emperor Constantine. Therefore, Christianity must seek its "purity" in the pre-Constantine version of the church, which the Dissenters characterized as voluntarist, rather than via apostolic succession.

Ryerson appealed to this concept in an open letter to Strachan, condemning the church–state union, which he called the "antichristian invasions on the apostolic purity and simplicity of Christ's holy religion, in the days of Constantine and his successors." Invoking the biblical parable of the foolish man who built his house on sand, Ryerson argued that churches resting on state support were "built upon sand, which the current of truth speedily washes away, and sweeps into deserved ruin." This doctrinal point had clear political implications, as Ryerson called directly for Christians to oppose church–state alignments. Just as he believed true Christians would have opposed Constantine, Ryerson declared, "Equally bound is every patriotic christian, to oppose similar encroachments and corruptions, at the present time, and in this Province."[56]

In July 1828, Upper Canadians went to the polls and elected a reform-majority assembly. Throughout the campaign, the reformers pitched themselves either explicitly or implicitly as champions of Protestant Dissent. Mackenzie had presented himself as fighting on the side of the colonists in their "laudable endeavours to obtain a mild efficient and liberal government, and to cast off the yoke of ignorance and superstition with which they are now attempted to be enshrouded."[57] Once the election was over, the *Colonial Advocate* celebrated the victorious reformers who would fight "for great and fundamental principles" and would be exemplary in "asserting and maintaining the unassailable rights of men and of christians."[58] Thus, the rise of the reform party in 1828 was wedded to Dissenting concerns and culture, and Upper Canadian reformers would build upon this foundation in the years to come.

"Dominion over … our very souls": Religion in the Fight for Self-Rule

Despite their historic success in 1828, reformers still had an uphill climb ahead. Although they would revise the alien bill and delay implementation of King's College, the idea of an encroaching church establishment escalated due to three public issues: the clergy reserves, state funding for a Methodist university (Upper Canada Academy, later Victoria College), and the rectories crisis of 1836. Additionally, the early-to-mid-1830s saw frustration as their reforms were repeatedly thwarted by the unelected executive.[59] When faced with such barriers, many reformers saw not only a constitutional problem but a spiritual one. For example, in a sermon of 1834 the Quaker leader and reformer David Willson (Children of Peace) blamed "the national churches" for erecting "the pillars of bad government."[60] He presented the existing church–state alliance as not truly Christian and said that the colony had to return to biblical principles based on the "humility and mercy" of Jesus: "Good government does not consist in form or system … but in the established principles of the Son of God."[61] Reform supporters consistently employed this kind of rhetoric vis-à-vis governance and liberty. This section examines the liberal reform party from the 1828 election to Mackenzie's *Seventh Report of Grievances* in 1835 to illustrate how the movement's religious connections only deepened during this tumultuous era.

Despite the reform party's interest in a variety of issues ranging from banking to land management, the struggle for colonial self-governance preceded everything else. As Paul Romney explained, reformers often saw their plight through a stark dichotomy of "liberty" and "tyranny," casting their political opponents as foreign appointees who continuously denied the colonists self-rule.[62] By contrasting this view with the Tories' perspectives, Romney suggested that both sides generally viewed the other as a kind of alien: the reformers saw Tories as foreign (British or British-aligned) oppressors, and the Tories perceived reformers as foreign (American or American-influenced) rebels, each side struggling for control over the colony.[63] The myth of alien oppression, as Romney put it, was reinforced by a contrast of material wealth, in which the colony's farmers were often saddled with debt and struggled to turn a profit. Meanwhile, the well-connected state officials, bankers, and merchants profited from the farmers' financial dependence on them.[64] Bryan Palmer examined the role of economic disparities in the political divisions of the 1830s, proposing that reformers often portrayed themselves as "workingmen," as contrasted with the tory "parasites" who ran the colony without their democratic consent.[65] Thus reformers often prioritized greater autonomy, claiming that replacing the exclusive and appointed ruling clique, known as the "Family Compact," with elected representatives was the necessary prerequisite to all other reforms.

Underlying these external contrasts of material holdings and status, the reformers' myth of alien oppression was reinforced by a spiritual component. According to one anonymous contributor to the *Colonial Advocate* in December 1829, British administrators had sought "dominion" over "our very souls" by using state resources to prop up an established church: "The persons who represent Great Britain here, are greedily grasping the dominion over our judiciary, our finances, our lands, our liberties; nay even our very souls. – Our happiness both here and hereafter, must, it seems, be placed in their safe keeping, to be doled out to us, as they see fit!"[66] In contrast with state favours for the Anglican church, some Dissenters believed themselves to be treated as second-class people. The unnamed author continued, "Our ministers and elders *shall* continue to wear the badge of inferiority, notwithstanding every effort of our houses of assembly on their behalf."[67] These Dissenters saw not only a *procedural* injustice (i.e., the executive branch overruling the assembly), but also a *spiritual* and *cultural* one. Not only did the British authorities deny Upper Canada a fuller measure of self-rule, but they did so in ways that violated the religious sensitivities of the colonists.

To illustrate how Protestant Dissent influenced reform in the 1830s, we can consider three biblical terms that surfaced in reform rhetoric:

hireling, Pharisee, and leaven. First, "hireling" was a derogatory term applied to suggest that state-funded clergymen were loyal ultimately not to the Christian faith or to God, but only to the money and to the state. The term comes from chapter 10 in the Gospel of John, where Jesus contrasts himself, as "the good shepherd" who is willing to give his life for his sheep, with the "hireling" who is paid to tend to the sheep but flees at the first sign of danger and leaves the sheep to be scattered by wolves.[68] In 1832, the Methodist *Christian Guardian* used this terminology to criticize churches that accepted state funds: "That kind of loyalty which can be either bought or sold is not worth having. What dependence can be placed upon a *hireling* either in politics or religion?"[69] The reformer William Lesslie (brother of James Lesslie, discussed in chapters below) recorded in his journal some cynical thoughts about a tory meeting in 1832 in which a Catholic bishop – the Scottish-born Hon. Alexander McDonell of Kingston – reportedly gave a speech praising the executive council. Lesslie said that the prelate spoke only because he was one of the government's paid "hirelings" (a legislative councillor): "£600 per annum from the Government is surely worthy of a Courtly address."[70] Thus the concept of the hireling combined both anti-clericalism and voluntarism: established clerics were not to be trusted *because* they were paid by the state.

Second, reformers used the term "Pharisee" in similar contexts, as a slur against Anglican and Catholic clerics, but with different connotations. The Pharisees were an ancient sect of Judaism regularly featured in the New Testament, and whose representatives appear as antagonists to the first-century Christians. The Gospels portray them as conspiring to "destroy" Jesus, often accusing him of spiritual errors, including blasphemy and breaking the Sabbath, and asking him questions designed to entrap him.[71] In chapter 23 of the Gospel of Matthew, Jesus lambastes them as frauds who appear righteous while being inwardly corrupt: "Woe unto you, scribes and Pharisees, hypocrites! For ye are like unto whited sepulchres, which indeed appear beautiful outward, but are within full of dead men's bones, and of all uncleanness."[72] The reformers sometimes associated established clergymen with Pharisees to paint them as hypocritical elitists void of the true faith. For example, Quaker David Willson said that state support for select churches had enabled "almost the full reign of the Pharisee. Every priest has got on the sheep's clothing, but has not obtained the lamb's heart." He further referred to these people as "Pulpit gentry" and suggested that they were growing rich with "tribute money" from the state.[73]

Finally, some reformers employed the biblical concept of "leaven" to represent the corrupting effect of state support for churches. The term originally refers to an additive used to make bread rise, and one of its earliest biblical references relates to Passover, in which Moses prescribed unleavened bread for the Israelites during and after their escape from Egypt.[74] In New Testament usage, leaven came to symbolize doctrinal impurity: "Then Jesus said unto them, Take heed and beware of the leaven of the Pharisees and of the Sadducees," which is explained later to mean not literally "the leaven of bread, but of the doctrine of the Pharisees and of the Sadducees."[75]

Upper Canadian reformers invoked leaven occasionally to describe the corrupting nature of church–state alliances. For example, in a legislative committee meeting on the clergy reserves in December 1836, a reform MLA named Mr Park (probably Irish-born Thomas Parke from Middlesex) declared, "Never did a government offer a bribe to ministers of the church without a corrupt and deceitful motive ... A little leaven leaveneth the whole lump, and small sums granted to them by government would only increase their avarice."[76] That particular wording, "a little leaven leaveneth the whole lump," comes from two of the epistles of Paul.[77] Reform MLA John Rolph (Norfolk) invoked the concept to argue for secularizing the clergy reserves rather than distributing them to additional denominations, suggesting that state support was inherently corrupting for any church: "The payment of one church by the state is thought of dangerous tendency. How much more alarming is the proposition to pay four? ... To add the leven [*sic*] of the state to one church is bad; to add it to four is fearfully worse."[78]

In the lead-up to the assembly election of October 1830, necessitated by dissolution following the death of King George IV on 26 June, Dissenting clerics continued to advocate for reform, and Dissenting issues continued to be the party's major rallying points. In an article for the Methodist *Christian Guardian,* later reprinted in the *Colonial Advocate,* the author encouraged readers to vote solely on "Religious Privileges" and education. Although other issues would surely come up, "the great interests of religion ... compared with these, are like the sun to the surrounding planets – like the soul to the body – like life to the animal system – like sight to the eyes."[79] Mackenzie also emphasized religious concerns, warning voters: "Your liberties, your religion, your civil and political rights are still in jeopardy!" As an example of injustice, "Education is in the hands of a particular sect – The bishops and priests of three religious denominations are openly pensioned out of the proceeds of the public lands."[80] When the results started to come in at the end of October, revealing victories for some reformers such as Jesse Ketchum (York, later Toronto) and Mackenzie (York), they were lauded for "their devotedness to the sacred principles of civil and religious liberty."[81] Many reformers were not so fortunate, however, and the party lost its majority.[82]

Just over a month after the election, reformers resumed pressure on church–state issues by organizing meetings and petitions through a twenty-three-person committee called the "Friends of Religious Liberty." Gathering first in a Presbyterian church in York in December 1830, the group included many of the colony's leading reform voices, such as Robert Baldwin, W.W. Baldwin, Jesse Ketchum, James Lesslie, William Lyon Mackenzie, and Egerton Ryerson.[83] They offered the usual voluntarist resolutions, stating that all Christian denominations ought to be equal before the law, that clergymen should not occupy positions of political power, that the proceeds of the clergy reserves ought to be assigned to general education, and that the charter of King's College ought to be modified to "exclude all sectarian tests."[84] The main order of business was to collect signatures for a petition to end state aid for churches. By March 1831 it had received about ten thousand signatures to send to England, where the radical MP Joseph Hume would present the case to the House of Commons at Westminster in October 1831.[85]

The voluntarists imagined that state neutrality towards churches would enable a more genuinely Christian society. The logic was that colonists, if left to their own devices on an even playing field, would voluntarily support the churches that best served their spiritual needs, and that the Catholic and Anglican churches would cease to have an advantage over the Dissenting faiths. Ryerson hoped that Upper Canadians would embrace "the zeal of real Christianity" if they could "put an end to the abominations of Church and State union in Canada."[86] The voluntarists who disparaged the plan to use state funds for the Anglican-run King's College certainly did not desire that the colony's higher education should be a bastion of atheism. Indeed, one commentator described a scenario in which "every denomination of professing christians" would build their own seminaries adjacent to the state-funded university, "in order that divinity students may have the benefit of its classes, in conjunction with their religious studies in their respective theological seminaries."[87] This kind of Christian education, right down to the elementary level, was seen as necessary for the colony's well-being. The *Colonial Advocate*, for example, reported on the Sabbath School Union Society, whose purpose was to raise money for children's religious education in the York area. In addition to teaching literacy and providing free access to books, the society believed itself to be part of a broader effort to plant "the seeds of eternal life" in the colony's children – "a foundation of such instruction is laid, that upon which the superstructure of religion may be safely built."[88] Voluntarists also usually offered biblical justifications, saying, for example: "The New Testament expressly forbids the employment of the sword, as a means of enforcing belief in the doctrines of christianity."[89] Understood correctly, the voluntarist movement encapsulates the idea of liberty that had emerged in the colony by the 1830s: for reformers, the voluntary *means* were an essential part of their liberalism, and so were the Christian *ends*.

In late 1831, the reformers faced a couple of public challenges that reinforced the religious basis for the colony's political divisions. First, in September, when representatives of the Methodist Episcopal Church issued a good-natured address to Lieutenant-Governor John Colborne stating that they wished to work with the government to promote public morality and "pure religion," Colborne responded coldly and dismissively. He told them that their preachers had been interfering in politics and that he was concerned about the American influence within their denomination.[90] Second, in December, Mackenzie was expelled from the assembly in a move that he suspected was orchestrated in part by John Strachan. The official reason was that his newspaper's critiques of executive-council members were allegedly libellous.[91] Mackenzie believed the timing had been selected to neutralize his opposition to a banking bill making its way through the assembly, which allowed the Bank of Upper Canada to print £1.2 million in additional paper currency, and which Mackenzie had intended to delay and to thwart if possible by adding amendments in committee.[92]

Even though the clash started over a non-religious matter, Mackenzie still suspected the work of the Anglican clergy in his expulsion. In his address "To the People of Upper Canada," Mackenzie called out

Strachan by name and added that his opponents had heeded the "counsel of those turncoat ambitious and busy opponents of the people, who wear the convenient garb of apostles of the meek and lowly Jesus."[93] Both instances only served to rile up the reformers and make them more dedicated to their cause. Indeed, after two or three thousand supporters gathered in the cold for a pro-Mackenzie rally, he was re-elected to the assembly in early January 1832.[94]

Two months later, on 23 March, religious divisions again came to the forefront in a violent clash – the "York Riot" – between reformers and Tories, the latter described by the reform press as Roman Catholics.[95] The historian Carol Wilton explained that the Catholic bishop McDonell had recently criticized Mackenzie, which she said was the reason why tory demonstrators cheered when they passed by the prelate's home (in York, where he served on the legislative council). Otherwise, her account of the disturbance did not mention religion.[96] The basic outline of events may be summarized as follows: when Mackenzie and a group of supporters met at a York courthouse for a public demonstration against the government, they were met by pro-government counter-demonstrators. When Mackenzie's adherents attempted to move to a new location to speak to a crowd of people from a wagon platform, the counter-demonstrators reportedly followed them, pushed the wagon, and assaulted the speakers before leaving. They then raised an effigy of Mackenzie and marched it throughout York before burning it. To top it all off, they smashed the windows of his *Colonial Advocate* office.[97]

The reform press clarified the religious element of the incident. For example, the *York Courier* described the religious divisions in this attempt by the "Catholic Body … to beat down the Protestants of York."[98] According to the *Colonial Advocate*, a "catholic party" disrupted the reform demonstration by throwing stones and calling the reformers "damned heretics." The reporter estimated the anti-reform crowd included "nearly two hundred persons of the Roman church." The article named a few of the known rioters, mentioning each person's Catholicism when known. Although the author later clarified that "several liberal catholics" supported the reformers, the majority of the Catholics reportedly "acted as they did … entirely owing to their priest and bishop, whose influence over them is truly surprising." The author seemed shocked that Catholics would turn against them because reformers had long been "firm friends to catholic emancipation" and had "never uttered a syllable against the catholic faith." Yet, despite the reformers' supposed good will, the late events had apparently been orchestrated along religious lines. Thus, the author concluded, the Catholic involvement "proves the power of the priesthood over their hearers to be far more dangerous and extensive than we had before had any conception of."[99] Although the reformers under George Brown would later acquire a reputation for their clashes with the Catholic hierarchy (see chapters below), these reports indicate that such political alignments along Protestant–Catholic lines were already emerging in the early 1830s.

Two events in the autumn of 1833 affected the Methodists' role in the reform movement: their own union with the conservative-leaning British Wesleyans and Egerton Ryerson's defection from reform. Since 1828, Canadian Methodism had undergone a series of changes: independence from the American conference, the internal Ryanite schism, and the beginning of a union with the British Wesleyans. Independence was granted in 1828, after several decades under the U.S.-based Methodist Episcopal Church.[100] The following year, the new church set up the *Christian Guardian* and selected Egerton Ryerson as editor. While the Canadian Methodists had long been associated with the reform movement, especially with leaders like Ryerson openly supporting reform policies, British Methodist leaders did not approve.[101] As early as July 1832, British Wesleyan Missionary Committee representative Robert Alder had met privately with Lieutenant-Governor John Colborne to discuss government grants for Methodist missions in the colony and their mutual concern that Canadian Methodists had succumbed to American influence or, as they put it, "Yankeeism."[102]

Merely months later, Alder began talks between the British Wesleyans and Canadian Methodists to discuss unifying the two groups. Commenting in August 1832, Ryerson admitted that the idea had generated "strong anxiety" for Canadian Methodists. Still, he found Alder's "modest respect and caution" reassuring and expressed the hope that further discussions would promote "the glory of God and the good of humankind."[103] Ryerson then resigned from the *Christian Guardian* and departed for a year-long trip to England, where he would take part in merger discussions. In his parting comments, he reminded readers of his ongoing fight "against the introduction into this country of an *endowed political* church" and assured them that the *Guardian* would continue to exemplify and protect these "principles and morals."[104]

The new editor was James Richardson, a committed voluntarist and reformer. He was also a devout evangelical who had been raised Anglican but joined the Methodist church after a conversion experience at a camp meeting in 1818.[105] Richardson valued Methodism's independence from the state, a position he reiterated many times during his year as editor. Whereas other churches had succumbed to the "evil" of church–state alliance, Richardson wrote in the summer of 1833, the Canadian Methodists remained committed to voluntarism: "Our church adheres to the precepts and example of her Divine lawgiver in the mode of supporting her ministers, as in every thing else." He wrote approvingly that "the people of the province among whom we labor … have hitherto voluntarily and cheerfully contributed to our wants."[106] Like other voluntarists, Richardson also made it clear that state grants to multiple churches would not be any better than having a single favoured church. The problem was not the inequity of such support but its existence at all. Indeed, he expected the Methodists to reject any state grants if offered: "We hope and trust that should any such tender be made it will be promptly but respectfully refused."[107]

In the autumn of 1833, the union between the Canadian Methodists and British Wesleyans was finalized, an arrangement that Todd Webb argued was essentially a British takeover.[108] The historian Goldwin French detailed the extent to which the British Wesleyans immediately began to act behind the scenes to redirect the Canadian Methodists away from their hardline voluntarism and public entanglement with reform. In correspondence between Robert Alder and John Colborne, the British Wesleyans promised to "influence" the Canadian Methodists, and Colborne promised to approve additional state grants to the church. Indeed, British Wesleyan leaders explicitly instructed the Canadian Methodists that the *Christian Guardian* must cease to criticize government grants for churches.[109] Following the union's ratification, the *Guardian* reported in October 1833 that the church had been granted £1,000 for missions and that the new British leaders had advised them to avoid "the mere politics of this world, to render for Christ's sake, all due obedience to 'the powers that be.'"[110]

While this anti-reform direction was emerging at the institutional level, Ryerson's personal political views were shifting as well. Although he had been a figurehead of the reform movement since his feud with Strachan in 1826, his negotiations with the British Wesleyans in England reshaped his political views. Following his return and the announcement of the union, he was reinstated as the editor of the *Christian Guardian.* That same month, his "Impressions made by my late visit to England" compared the piety of British Tories, whigs, and "radicals." To the surprise of his readers, he concluded that the Tories most often acted "from religious principles" and best represented the "sterling virtue of the nation."[111] The description seemed opposite to the experience of colonists who associated the Tories not with "sterling virtue" but with the unaccountable elites that frequently disparaged and insulted their evangelical faith. Thus, the article provoked a series of outraged letters from reform supporters, and Ryerson spent much of the following months defending his positions and reassuring his readers that he still believed that "there ought not to be any State Church or State Churches in Canada."[112] The controversy reveals just how crucial the reform movement had become to Methodists and other Dissenters in the colony.[113]

The main reason for Ryerson's political change appears to be his exposure to a non-Christian side of Britain's radicals. Clearly the British MP Joseph Hume, who had advocated for the reformers in the House of Commons,[114] did not live up to Ryerson's expectations for Christian piety. Hume "has no influence as a religious man; has never been known to promote any religious measure or object as such, and has opposed every measure for the better observance of the Sabbath." Rather, Ryerson suspected that the "radicals" had aligned themselves with "infidel" elements of British society[115] – all the more shocking given the close connection between reform and religion that he had long witnessed, indeed nurtured, in Upper Canada. He had also mingled extensively with the inner circle of Wesleyan conservatism, including the notorious tory Jabez Bunting.[116] Unlike his brother George Ryerson, whose meetings with the British Wesleyans in 1831 had left him disgusted at their seeming deference to the established Church of England,[117] Egerton had apparently enjoyed a comparatively positive experience with his Wesleyan hosts.

Very few Canadian Methodists followed their church leaders' political shift. Long after Ryerson's "Impressions" article in 1833, most of them continued to affiliate strongly with the reform movement. In fact, voting records indicate that the supposedly united Methodists were still divided politically throughout the 1830s. In the 1836 election, for example, Methodists who would later side with the British Wesleyans in the 1840 schism voted tory, and those who would ally with the Canadian Methodists chose reform.[118] Based on this voting record, Paul Romney concludes: "This makes Ryerson's abandonment of Reform in 1833 look less like leadership than an astute change of horses."[119] This division is also apparent in the controversy surrounding the Methodists' Upper Canada Academy. Though originally funded by voluntary contributions, the academy replaced two of its most outspokenly voluntarist committee members and applied for state funds in 1834. Methodist donors withdrew their contributions in protest.[120] James Richardson, who had served 1832–33 as editor of the *Christian Guardian*, protested by withdrawing from the Wesleyan Methodist church and joining the smaller, independent Methodist Episcopal church in 1836.[121]

Following Ryerson's comments on British politics in October 1833, William Lyon Mackenzie added the newly united Methodists' leaders to his long list of political enemies. He argued that Ryerson had become "degenerate" and had joined the ranks of "apostate priests." He defended Joseph Hume, whom Ryerson had singled out as irreligious, asking his readers whether "the Methodists of Upper Canada had already forgotten Mr. Hume's persevering and disinterested efforts to purify religion in this colony, by sifting it from the dross of state connexion?"[122] A year later, while still in the assembly, Mackenzie helped to establish a "Committee on Grievances" and used his new authority to summon and interrogate the most influential men in the colony. Based on these interviews, in April 1835 Mackenzie published and distributed 2,000 copies of a compilation of findings, which came to be known as *The Seventh Report of Grievances*.[123] The issue of church establishment featured in the text, and Mackenzie did not spare the Methodist leaders the sort of criticism he had long levelled against the ruling tory Family Compact. Beginning in 1833, the report said, the Methodists had become part of the "Ecclesiastical Establishment" along with the Roman Catholic and Anglican churches, a change that Mackenzie described as "very singular," given their history. Despite the Methodists at one time actively criticizing government policy, Mackenzie noted, "since, however, a share of the public money has been extended to, and received by them; there seems to have been established a mutual good understanding."[124] His implication was clear: he believed the Methodists had been bribed to stop criticizing the government.

Religion was not the only source of political discontent in the 1830s, but it was the most persistent and the most sensitive one. In the words of historian Gerald Craig, opposition to church establishments was "the one unvarying constant in Upper Canadian politics."[125] After rallying around Dissenting concerns for the 1828 election, reformers continued to build on this foundation. Their liberal positions of voluntarism and separation of church and state were designed not merely to ensure an even playing field for its own sake, but also to foster a more genuinely Christian society through voluntary contributions to Christian initiatives. Despite the reformers' subsequent losses in assembly elections, unresolved issues surrounding the King's College charter, the clergy reserves, and state funds for missions all kept Dissenters active in the political conversation through petitioning and the press.

The reformers' goal of colonial self-rule was made all the more necessary by their conviction that they were governed unjustly by an "alien" power that had utter contempt for their religious traditions, an impression inadvertently confirmed by the impolitic comments of John Strachan and John Colborne. This alien power appeared to be gaining ground, even winning over the Methodist church, just as it accepted the state funding it had once shunned. Quaker David Willson said in 1834 that the colony was witnessing "almost the full reign of the Pharisee." But this could not last. Willson went on to prophesy, "These tottering towers are preparing for a fall, and Church and State measures will be greatly affected with it."[126]

"Is not revolution in such case a bible duty?": The Upper Canada Rebellion

The events that followed the release of the *Seventh Report of Grievances* steadily escalated tensions that culminated in the 1837 rebellion. The Colonial Office in London's Whitehall took Mackenzie's document rather seriously, fearing it could fuel sentiments for colonial independence; Lieutenant-Governor John Colborne downplayed it and was dismissed,[127] and his final order reawakened the ire of Dissent. In a closed-door meeting in January 1836, Colborne granted fifty-seven (later reduced to forty-four) new rectories for the Church of England – a land grant totalling 21,000 acres.[128] For Dissenters, the "rectory crisis" appeared to aggressively reassert Anglican power. Politicians began to speculate aloud in the legislature about the executive council's tyrannical church–state pretensions. Reformer John Rolph, for example, warned that "an act might be passed establishing a new religion in Upper Canada, protected by penalties to be inflicted upon all non-conformists, just as infidelity was proclaimed in France."[129] One Methodist preacher even reported in June 1836 that "everywhere the rectory question meets us, and I am compelled to believe that while a vast majority are devotedly loyal, yet many of our gracious sovereign's best & most affectionate subjects would almost prefer revolution to the establishment of a dominant church."[130] It was exactly that preference for revolution, perhaps a mere overstatement in 1836, that Mackenzie would come to count on in his recruitment for the rebel cause.

The rectories crisis of 1836 reawakened the Dissenting Protestants' worst fears about the excesses of church establishment. Reform supporters meeting in the village of Keene worried that the rectories would "thus introduce into this young colony the greatest evil of the mother country, a dominant church and government paid priesthood, with the full ecclesiastical powers of the Church of England."[131] Some colonists began to spread rumours that the government was about to impose an Anglican tithe.[132] Mackenzie's new newspaper, the *Constitution* (1836–37), provided them a platform. Apocalyptic themes and imagery became rampant in both the paper's news reports and its creative content. For example, in October 1836 it introduced a poem as describing "the probable effects of Tory misrule" and warned of an imminent, tyrannical state church:

> Of every mother's son he frames the best,
> T'establish Satan's rule, and spread the pest,
> Whose Stately Church I think I see it stand,
> Proudly ascendant o'er the ridden land;
> . . .
> For soon the *Priest – the Overseer* – the King –
> Will claim their share – yea, every pleasant thing
> . . .
> Our farms laid waste, our rights all overthrown;
> Nor shall the fool be found to claim his own,
> If now they speed to put Mackenzie down.[133]

This prophesied implementation of "Satan's rule" is an example of the moral absolutist rhetoric leading up to the 1837 rebellion. The political controversy was increasingly depicted as a struggle between good and evil. For example, in late 1836 the *Constitution*'s story "Birth and Reign of Kings" depicted church establishment as part of a literal satanic plot. Written in the style of a biblical vision, the anonymous prose depicted seven kings being seduced by "the serpent," drinking blood before an inverted crucifix in a dark room, and plotting "to quench Liberty." To secure their reign, the kings decided they must "abolish the religion of Christ": "It is his religion that is our destruction." Most notably, they destroy Christianity by paying priests to do their bidding: "Let us gain over to us the ministers of Christ with wealth, and honors, and power. And they will command the people, on the part of Christ, to be subject to us in all things, whatever we may do, whatsoever we may ordain."[134] Thus, the voluntarist conclusion was that church establishment was not only akin to bribery but, indeed, part of a broader satanic plot to destroy simultaneously true Christianity and "liberty" itself.

This conflation of liberty and Christianity was not incidental, but rather a longstanding, defining feature of Upper Canadian reform. To align the state with a particular church or churches, one author said in 1830, violated "the religion of Jesus" and represented "a step towards tyranny and the destruction of the nation."[135] Similar rhetoric was also featured in commentary on the charter of King's College, which warned that the school's Anglican exclusivity was "a greater piece of despotism than even Oxford itself."[136] Reform MLA Thomas Parke suggested to a legislative committee in December 1836: "The payment of PRIESTS is a most powerful engine in the hands of an unjust government, whose object generally is to sustain itself by the aid of religion. The Almighty has never placed his church in the care of man, never delegated his power to any government."[137] As we see below, this traditional association of true Christianity with liberty, and church establishment with tyranny, would help Mackenzie justify attempting revolution.

Three events that followed the rectories crisis of early 1836 illuminate the pre-rebellion breakdown in trust: the reformers quitting the executive council in March 1836, the perceived fraud of the June 1836 election, and the introduction of Lord John Russell's Ten Resolutions in March 1837. At first, the new lieutenant-governor, Francis Bond Head, who arrived in Toronto in January 1836, signalled his friendliness to reformers by appointing in February 1836 two reform leaders, John Rolph and Robert Baldwin, to the executive council. However, this friendly demeanour did not last. When the lieutenant-governor clashed with his advisers he did not hesitate to replace them with tory stalwarts. When reformers in the assembly denounced the dismissal and voted to withhold funds for general operations, Head dissolved the assembly and called a new election for June.[138] Head himself actively campaigned against the reformers and made considerable effort to smear them as republicans who would "ruin this country" if elected.[139] The reformers were decimated, a result they ascribed to violent voter intimidation and bribery at the polls.[140]

Despite the governor's attempt to make the 1836 election about loyalty versus disloyalty, the role of religion cannot be overstated. In June 1836, William Ryerson wrote his brother Egerton, "There would be very little cause for doubt or fear as to the results, were it not for one of the last acts of Sir John Colborne's administration, in establishing and endowing nearly sixty Rectories … The result can only be attributed to that unjust and most unpolitic act."[141] Another brother, John, suggested that the dissatisfaction with Head derived from his insensitivity to local religious sentiments: "He takes good care to let every one know that *he* esteems every day alike, travelling on Sabbaths the same as other days. Indeed he seems to have no idea of religion at all, but is purely a man of pleasure. His popularity will soon be upon the wane if he does not mend in these respects."[142]

To add insult to injury, the reformers' formal complaints about election fraud were met with indifference and even mockery. Egerton Ryerson actually played a role in that hostile reception while in England from November 1835 to June 1837. In his autobiography, he recounted being secretly present at Westminster in September 1836 when Joseph Hume was introducing the petition on behalf of the Upper Canadian reform MLA Dr Charles Duncombe (Oxford),[143] who had travelled to England and was (though no mention of this point from Ryerson) reporting allegations of fraud in the 1836 election.[144] Ryerson prepared counterpoints about Canadian politics for William Ewart Gladstone, then a young conservative MP, who immediately gave the House a critique of Hume's comments. According to Ryerson, the whole exchange "kept the House in a roar of laughter at Mr. Hume's expense for more than an hour; the wonder being how Mr. Gladstone was so thoroughly informed on Canadian affairs. No member of the House of Commons seemed to be more astonished and confounded than Mr. Hume himself."[145] The tone of mockery towards Duncombe's petition suggests that these politicians were more interested in discrediting the "radicals" than in actually hearing their grievances. They were not only ignoring a cry for help, but shutting the door to another of the colonists' few remaining peaceful avenues for redress.

With elections allegedly rigged against them and their petitions laughed down at Westminster, reformers like Mackenzie and Duncombe began to see few remaining constitutional options. In March 1837, the final door closed with Home Secretary Lord John Russell's Ten Resolutions, which reaffirmed rule by executive decree in the Canadas.[146] Over the next few months, Mackenzie began to speculate in print about whether the neighbouring Lower Canadians might seek to overthrow "their Downing Street Tyrants."[147] By September, he was clearly thinking strategically about the strength of his own potential forces vis-à-vis Britain's: "The whole physical power of the government ... redcoats and all, is not equal to that of the young men of one of our largest townships," and reminding his readers that the ice-bound St Lawrence would keep Britain's "agents" from arriving in the colony for five months.[148] Although he would not directly announce the idea until the start of December, Mackenzie had already begun to plan a revolution in Canada.

Mackenzie's religious justification was clearly articulated by November 1837. In the final issue of the *Constitution* before he led the Toronto rebellion, he argued: "Governments are not mere social compacts, they are ordained of God." Thus, when men in power turn against their ordained purposes, he reasoned, God "puts it into the minds of virtuous and heaven fearing men to sweep away injustice and oppression." He credited godly inspiration for the Glorious Revolution of 1688, the American Revolution of 1776, and the defeat of Napoleon Bonaparte, and proposed that these were all examples in which righteous men "lifted up the sword and the spear in his [God's] strength, and relying on his all powerful arm to support religious and civil rights." Crucially, Mackenzie made the case that the colonists of Canada now faced a similar violation and should follow suit: "Is not revolution in such a case a bible duty? Is not the whole scripture, given for our use and example, full of authorities for revolt against wicked rulers? We know that it is."[149]

When Mackenzie issued his call to arms on 1 December 1837, his target audience was clearly the Protestant Dissenters whom he had courted politically over the past decade. Promising them compensation of hundreds of acres of land from the clergy reserves, he called supporters to put down their oppressors "in the name of that God who goes forth with the armies of his people, and whose Bible shows" that tyrannical authorities should be overthrown. His appeal specifically condemned the "Roman Catholic and Episcopal Bishops and Archdeacons" who were "bribed" by the government and expressed his confidence that "God has opened the eyes of the people to the wickedness of these reverend sinners." Ultimately, Mackenzie promised, a successful revolution would allow them "to establish free institutions founded on God's law," so "He who commands the winds and waves will be with us."[150] The document repeatedly emphasized the proposed uprising's spiritual mission and spiritual justification. Given the broader religion-based political controversies, and rebel recruitment appealing to Dissenting concerns, Protestant Dissenters made up the majority of the participants.[151]

The aftermath of the failed rebellion also reveals the event's religious meaning for the participants. Awaiting trial in Toronto jail or Kingston's Fort Henry, many rebels carved inscriptions into small wooden boxes for loved ones should they be executed or exiled. Many used variations of "Civil & Religious Liberty," and some condemned the clergy reserves or church establishments.[152] One imprisoned rebel, a Quaker named Jesse Cleaver, dreamed: "O when will tyrants cease to reign, the priests no longer preach for gain, and kings and emperors quit the throne and let the church of God alone."[153] These few sources capture the meaning of the rebellion in the participants' own words; the limited evidence available suggests that the spiritual significance that Mackenzie so frequently invoked in his speeches, newspapers, and call to arms itself resonated very deeply with the young men who marched on Toronto.

Historiographical debate about 1837 has addressed a variety of angles, not all of them easy to summarize.[154] For this study, however, the most relevant scholarship may involve its significance for the colonies' ideological development. Benjamin T. Jones, for example, argued that the rebellion was a civic republican attempt to restore a sense of public virtue and an adherence to "the common good over individual gain."[155] Jones acknowledged the Christian rhetoric in Mackenzie's call to arms, which "clearly took for granted that Christianity would be the foundational civic religion and a source of identity and morality."[156] However, since faith may not have animated all reformers, he proposed that we interpret such rhetoric as a particularly Christian expression of the civic republican tradition.[157] Jones sought to detach the reformers and rebels from Lockean liberalism, based on individualism and "negative rights" (what the state *may not* do, such as inhibit free speech), and ground their ideas within the communitarian or civic republican tradition, exalting the common good and "positive rights" (what the state ought to do, such as promote virtue and community).[158]

But Jones's non-liberal interpretation of the rebels invoked a later, narrow understanding of liberalism. For example, he wrote: "There is little in the liberal tradition that endorses communalism or an emphasis on the common good."[159] However, as this chapter seeks to demonstrate, the reformers wanted Upper Canada to be both liberal (with the state playing a limited role in church affairs) *and* a virtuous Christian society. Perhaps this study's disagreement with Jones relates to means versus ends: the reformers expected that liberal voluntarism and separation of church and state would facilitate a more genuinely Christian society. Communitarians or civic republicans may have agreed with Protestant liberals about the ideal *ends* of Christian civic virtue, but been more likely to accept an established church imposing religious conformity if the common good required it. Indeed, as William Westfall explained, many Anglican leaders believed an established church was necessary to promote a common sense of virtue and loyalty, a prescription that clashed with the reformers' voluntarism.[160] The Protestant Dissenters who made up the majority of Upper Canadian reformers wanted to limit the state's power in church affairs because they believed a powerful church–state alliance would inevitably persecute them; yet they still expected that such limitations on the state would encourage "the zeal of real Christianity."[161] Jones believed that "individual freedom and non-interference" stood in opposition to "religious zeal" and Christian virtue,[162] but the Upper Canadian reformers did not.

Michel Ducharme similarly scrutinized republicanism and liberalism, though in different terms, summarizing them as "republican liberty" and "modern liberty," respectively. For him, the rebellions of 1837 represented a final showdown between these two versions of liberty, and the loyalists' victory signalled the defeat of the rebels' republican liberty and the rise of modern constitutionalism in Canada.[163] Ducharme acknowledged that the churches' involvement in these debates needed further study, but he believed the reformers' concerns about religion had little to do with "liberty or state legitimacy."[164] However, as this chapter has shown, Mackenzie believed that the colonial government had lost its legitimacy precisely because it had failed to live up to its obligations to God. In his words, "Governments are not mere social compacts, they are ordained of God." Thus revolution against "wicked rulers" was a "bible duty," and he trusted that "a strength greater than his will be given him" if the colonists acted for "the great cause of his country and of human kind."[165]

The centrality of religious meanings to the ideological clash of 1830s' Upper Canada suggests we revise the dichotomy of individualistic liberals versus communitarian republicans. Whereas Ducharme argued that republicanism "allowed one to appeal successfully to the people as the source of all legitimate authority, and in so doing to challenge the established order,"[166] Mackenzie, as we saw above, appealed simultaneously to "the people" and to the Bible.[167] Even when he cited republican sources like the deist and American revolutionary Thomas Paine's *Common Sense* (1775–76), he pointed out that Paine had been a Christian at the time of writing: "The author, although afterwards led away by the example of French Philosophy, expresses himself throughout with the most reverential deference for the scriptures of truth, and the revelations of Christianity."[168] In Mackenzie's drafted constitution of November 1837, the first four articles strictly separated church and state, and the preamble promised to safeguard "the blessings of civil and religious liberty to ourselves and our posterity."[169] In this context, "Protestant liberty" may be a more appropriate designation for the vision of Upper Canada's reformers and rebels in the 1830s.

For William Lyon Mackenzie and many of his followers, the attempted revolution of 1837 was explicitly Christian, and religion spurred their decision to take up arms for colonial independence. The Dissenters' apocalyptic vision of church–state tyranny made drastic action an imperative, and their absolutist rhetoric about good versus evil rendered compromise undesirable, so their well-established religious communities thus provided ample grounds for recruitment. In the ominous ending to the prose narrative "Birth and Reign of Kings," faithful Christians fight back against the satanic forces conspiring against liberty: "And it was said to a just one, at that moment watching and praying before the cross, Thy day draweth nigh: worship, and fear nothing."[170] Although Ryerson himself had abandoned the radical cause, many remaining Dissenters took seriously his dire warning in 1828 that church establishment was a "most imminent danger" that must be opposed "before ourselves and our posterity are forever bound in chains."[171] Raised in the traditions of Protestant Dissent, the Upper Canadian rebels of 1837 interpreted the actions of the colonial government as threatening their "Civil & Religious Liberty" and took up arms to prevent the apocalyptic outcome they envisioned.

Conclusion

The controversies surrounding church–state relations in Upper Canada consolidated most Protestant Dissenters behind the reform banner and empowered them to shape liberalism in the image of their faith. Reform's first major electoral victory in 1828 created a "saddle-bag parliament," and the Dissenters' concerns and biblical rhetoric dominated political discourse throughout the 1830s. Although the Canadian Methodists' re-organization and new leaders in 1833 discouraged such close ties to the reformers, the general members' political allegiance did not shift. Indeed, their palace revolution reinforced Dissenters' contempt for state funding of churches, particularly as large payments preceded the church leaders' new condemnation of the reform movement. Voluntarist reformers had long warned against a "bribe to ministers of the church," which might make Christianity a mere tool of the ruling elites.[172] Reformers demanded instead a separation of church and state in order to make Upper Canada a truly Christian society.

A turning point in the reform movement came with the rectories crisis of early 1836. Many Dissenters interpreted the lieutenant-governor's grants as a step towards a full church establishment, which they associated with despotism and the persecution of their faith. When legal appeals were repeatedly thwarted, some of the desperate reformers began to consider outright rebellion. William Lyon Mackenzie appealed to the Bible and magnified fears about a malevolent church establishment, which helped rally supporters to his cause. Although the rebellion was defeated, its religious rhetoric and context exemplified the extent to which the concerns of Protestant Dissent had become entwined with the liberal reform movement and with the concept of liberty itself.

2

Judgment upon Babylon

The Early Union Period, 1838–1848

William Lyon Mackenzie's promise of a new government founded on Christian principles did not materialize in 1837. The rebellion was defeated, and its leaders fled to exile across the U.S. border. The rebel headquarters at Montgomery's Tavern on Yonge Street, in the town of Eglinton (now fairly central in today's Toronto), was set ablaze as a symbol of total loyalist victory. Loyalist forces then moved on to the Quaker settlement at Sharon (home to the Quaker offshoot Children of Peace) and threatened to burn down its iconic temple.[1] Although worshippers convinced the militia to spare it, its singling out shows how contemporaries associated particular religious affiliations with the rebellion. When government officials inquired into the rebellion's causes, religious grievances emerged as central factors. Indeed, Methodist Egerton Ryerson wrote to Colonial Secretary Lord Normanby in May 1839 to recommend that the government address the clergy reserves, which Ryerson argued had "fomented discord; emboldened, if not prompted, rebellion."[2] When the new governor general, Lord Durham, published his report on the causes in 1839, he wrote that in Upper Canada the "question of the greatest importance raised in the course of these disputes, was that of the disposal of the clergy reserves."[3] Whatever solution the authorities concocted, it would have to confront the colony's religious divisions.

The failure of the rebellion also forced a partial reset of the reform movement. Reformers had to soften their message and image in the light of the stigma of disloyalty.[4] Indeed, with prominent reform leaders such as Mackenzie, Bidwell, and Rolph fleeing to the United States, the power vacuum attracted moderates such as Robert Baldwin, Francis Hincks, and James Hervey Price.[5] Yet the failure of 1837 did not eliminate the Dissenting culture that had nurtured the radical reformers. Some outspoken Protestant Dissenters – such as the Baptist James Lesslie, the Methodist Jonathan Scott, and the Quaker David Willson – acquired prominent positions and continued to advocate for the same issues. Newcomers from Britain, like Congregationalist John Roaf and the Presbyterian father-son duo Peter and George Brown, quickly became leading voices.[6] Church–state controversies still dominated in public disputes among Methodists (whose 1833 union with the British Wesleyans collapsed in 1840) and Presbyterians (who produced a Canadian manifestation of the Free Church of Scotland following Scotland's Disruption of 1843). Just as the Sharon temple survived while Montgomery's Tavern burned, so the culture of Protestant Dissent persisted even with its old political champions in exile.

The uneasy fit between the new, moderate, Baldwinite leaders and the "radical" Dissenting base is an underlying theme of this chapter. Historians often associate the 1840s with Robert Baldwin's celebrated legacies – especially in his ruling reform–*rouge* coalition of 1848–51 with Louis LaFontaine – of biculturalism and responsible government (in which the executive branch of government is accountable to the elected legislative assembly, instead of chosen by the British viceroy),[7] but prominent Dissenting reformers had different priorities. As James Lesslie, the editor of the reform newspaper *Examiner*, wrote in 1848, the "question of questions" in the colony was "securing the repeal of the Act relating to the Clergy Reserves, and the abolition of the Rectories … all others being comparatively of minor importance."[8]

Baldwin's inability or unwillingness to secure these priorities would eventually be his downfall. Shortly after he helped to achieve responsible government in 1848, the reform party split between the Baldwinites and the "Clear Grits," who desired more democratic changes[9] and defeated Baldwin in his own riding in 1851.[10] Dissenters had certainly supported Baldwin and responsible government, but as the reform defector Isaac Buchanan wrote in 1844, "Mr. Baldwin knows that he does not represent the feelings of Upper Canada … except upon that one vital principle, the theory of Responsible Government."[11] Considering the party's later split, Buchanan's observation has some merit. Some historians have depicted the 1840s as a turning point for Canadian liberalism, with Baldwin's generation as a moderate constitutionalist break from reform's more radical and "civic humanist" past.[12] The Dissenters' unease with Baldwin represents a continuity between the pre- and post-rebellion reformers. Within this larger context, Baldwin appears more as an exception in the reform movement than its natural representative.

This chapter explains how liberal reformers navigated the delicate circumstances of the post-rebellion era and proposes that, despite the leadership's veneer of moderation and inter-religious cooperation, the priorities and narratives of Protestant Dissent continued to simmer beneath the surface. For the period of 1838–48, we examine three themes. 1) *Union with a Catholic colony*: Durham's recommended union of the Canadas forced a Protestant Upper Canadian reform movement to work with Catholic allies, ultimately heightening Dissenters' anxiety about religious demographics and their political prospects. 2) *Transatlantic Dissent:* with a rise in international communication and British immigration, Dissenters increasingly saw themselves as part of a great transatlantic struggle to defend "liberty" against the threat of church establishments. 3) *Millennialism*: during the millennialist fervour of the 1840s, Dissenters harnessed beliefs about biblical prophecy to interpret the perceived advances of church establishments, including the extension of the clergy reserves to multiple denominations. These three themes, corresponding to each of the sections below, illustrate aspects of the Dissenters' continuing influence on liberal reform.

Despite, or perhaps because of, the political complications of the early union period, Dissenters continued to articulate their political concerns in religious terms. Indeed, their narratives and values continued to claim ownership over the liberal vision for Upper Canada. As this chapter highlights, Dissenters cited biblical prophecy and past persecutions to remind each other of the high stakes, to reinforce their group commitments, and to encourage collective political action. Whereas some religious leaders advised moderation and cooperation with old rivals,[13] several public voices of both Dissent and reform pushed on with the fight for a liberal vision that included removing religious endowments and reducing rivals' influence. Although the period complicated and set back the Dissent–liberal platform, this chapter reveals how liberals continued to build on earlier religious and cultural foundations.

"This Suicidal Act": Legislative Union with a Catholic Colony

The Durham Report of 1839 included a recommendation that would alter Upper Canadian politics for the next three decades: a legislative union of the Canadas. For British administrators, this represented a step towards the ultimate cultural and linguistic assimilation of French Canadians into British colonial society.[14] Some reformers like Robert Baldwin expected coexistence rather than assimilation and embraced the union as the beginning of a bold new bicultural experiment.[15] Several Protestants, however, were not so confident that their own culture would thrive in the new union. For example, one Protestant politician, tory MLA John Gamble (First York), warned that the Act of Union was "suicidal" and certain "to subject the protestant population of the Canadas, to a majority of members in the united Legislature, of the Roman Catholic persuasion."[16] Each colony would have forty-two seats. Such concerns were simply dismissed as "Puritanical" bigotry, and the union went ahead without much delay. Over the next decade, however, liberal leaders like Peter and George Brown came to believe that they were living out a scenario very similar to that which Gamble described, wherein Protestant perspectives were simply overpowered by Catholic votes in the legislature. Although it was not always apparent during Robert Baldwin's time as reform-party leader throughout the 1840s, the idea of a Catholic advantage in the united legislature would become one of the driving concerns of Upper Canadian liberal reform over the following three decades.

The union shifted antagonists for the Dissenters: reform leaders had originally imagined the Anglican hierarchy as the priestly organ supporting the Family Compact,[17] but the union made some Dissenters see Catholicism as the greater threat to their political aims. As Todd Webb has explained, the Dissenters had always based their critique of Anglicanism on older anti-Catholic sentiments, regarding Anglicanism as "diluted popery" masquerading as Protestantism.[18] Indeed, the 1840s' growth of England's Tractarian (or Oxford) movement – in which Anglican clergymen reasserted apostolic succession and salvation as available only through the sacraments of the established church – renewed the Dissenters' concerns about the Church of England's closeness to Rome.[19] Although critiques of Anglicanism did not disappear,[20] they soon became secondary to concern about direct Catholic influence in the united province. Liberal newspapers such as the *Banner* and the *Examiner* frequently reported on Catholic–Protestant conflict in Lower Canada, clearly sympathizing with their co-religionists and warning about Catholic hostility to religious liberty. For example, when an Irish Catholic mob prevented a Protestant preacher from speaking in Montreal in 1845, Peter Brown retorted that the Catholic religion itself had "trampled the rights of conscience under foot" and had inflicted "a deep wound on our religious liberties."[21]

At the same time that Protestant Upper Canada found itself in legislative union with Catholic Lower Canada, its own Catholics began to increase in number and visibility. In Toronto alone, their share of the population rose from 16.8 per cent in 1841 to 25.8 per cent in 1851 due in large part to Irish immigration.[22] Upper Canada's growth overall was slower but steady, as Catholics made up 13.3 per cent of the total in 1842 and 16.3 per cent in 1848.[23] Catholics began to visibly assert their presence through the building of cathedrals: Notre-Dame (1842–46) in Ottawa, St Mary's (1842–48) in Kingston, and St Michael's (1845–48) in Toronto.[24] Catholics began to exert their political muscle by demanding separate schools; by 1850 there were eight in operation at public expense.[25] As Brian Clarke has explained, the Catholic church's assertiveness, including its push for separate schools and renewed appetite for imposing neogothic cathedrals, indicated its new ultramontane direction.[26] Although Dissenters may not yet have been familiar with ultramontanism, this movement asserted papal supremacy over civil affairs and would affect Catholic–Protestant relations in Canada for the rest of the century.[27]

The increased interactions between these two great branches of Western Christendom within the new union of the Canadas did not necessarily endear them to each other. Political leaders who advocated for union had hoped it would "unite the people within them in one common feeling."[28] However, negative perceptions deeply ingrained through tradition and upbringing continued to inform their contacts and exchanges. For example, the evangelical John Lesslie (brother to James Lesslie) wrote in his diary in 1842 about attending a lecture by a Roman Catholic priest at his local Mechanics' Institute, and he recorded with incredulity that the priest "attempted to show that the period of *the dark or middle ages were ages of light*!"[29] British-Canadian

Protestants strongly associated their own traditions with liberty and reason, and Catholicism with tyranny and superstition; as one contributor to the *Banner* put it, Protestants were engaged in a "war of antagonist interests" against "ignorance and papal superstition," which had no place "amidst the light and liberty of the nineteenth century."[30] Beyond the relatively harmless day-to-day distaste for one another's faiths, increased interaction in the 1840s also launched a decades-long series of violent inter-religious riots.[31] Despite optimism from some political leaders, Canada's new bicultural experiment began with less than resounding enthusiasm.

Despite Protestant–Catholic hostility in several corners of the united colony, the new reform leader Robert Baldwin was attempting to lead his party in a more conciliatory direction. As a moderate reformer and a high-church Anglican, he had risen to party leadership following the exiles of stalwarts like Bidwell and Mackenzie.[32] At a time when charges of disloyalty were common, he emerged as a safe and moderate choice.[33] With their beloved firebrands gone, the reform party chose more reserved leaders like Robert Baldwin, Francis Hincks, and James Hervey Price. A major theme of their leadership was working with the mostly French and Catholic reformers of Lower Canada under Louis-Hippolyte LaFontaine. From the beginning, Baldwin made overtures to Roman Catholics, personally abjuring the "oath of supremacy" (a relic of Henry VIII's reign), which renounced papal authority in British dominions – a vow surely offensive to his new Catholic allies.[34]

Under Baldwin's leadership, much of Upper Canadian reform initially welcomed Durham's recommendation for union with Lower Canada. Durham's report, after all, had single-handedly restored a sense of legitimacy to the post-rebellion reform movement by endorsing responsible government, so some reformers, despite hesitations about the union, managed to cast such cares aside to become the most enthusiastic Durhamites.[35] In December 1839 and January 1840, reformers and other colonists met in townships around Upper Canada to declare their support for uniting the colonies.[36] Although the reform press acknowledged some disagreement, it strongly implied that opposition was a marginal position, not taken seriously at the meetings. For example, a report on several gatherings in the Home District stated: "Petitions against the union were introduced in some of the townships, but they were indignantly rejected."[37] A meeting in Whitchurch even noted that they had "learned with surprise and regret that petitions are in circulation against the Union of the Provinces" and had been "thrown under the table"; it further resolved that the union was "best calculated to promote the happiness & prosperity of these distant appendages of the British Crown."[38]

The most vocal opposition to the union in 1839–40 was motivated chiefly by religious and cultural differences. J. Toronto, a pseudonymous writer to the *Examiner*, asserted that the union "places the Protestant population of both the Canadas under a legislature virtually Roman Catholic," and John Elmsley of Toronto, a legislative councillor and recent Catholic convert, argued that "no sufficient grounds now exist for a re-union of these Provinces" because they contained "two people so dissimilar in every respect."[39] MLA George Rykert's (Second Lincoln) lengthy critique expressed cynicism towards cultural assimilation: "The two races [English and French] are almost as destitute and foreign to each other in feeling, as they were three quarters of a century ago. And yet we are told by hon. members, give us the union upon any terms, and we shall soon make good members of society, and good British subjects of every one of them."[40] Some critics explicitly weighed the supposed economic benefits against the perceived cultural cost. For example, John Gamble (First York) invoked the biblical story of Esau and Jacob to suggest that his fellow Protestants who hoped for financial gain in the union were "bartering away [their] birth right for a mess of pottage."[41]

By contrast to this initial skepticism, moderate reform leaders were generally eager to court Catholic allies in the new legislature. It was Baldwin who refused the "oath of supremacy" and insisted that French Canadians be included in the cabinet.[42] It was Baldwin who proposed in 1843 that the capital city of the united province be moved from Kingston to Montreal, as a gesture of goodwill and an acknowledgment of past wrongs against French Canadians.[43] It was Baldwin who suggested legislation designed to restrict processions by the ultra-Protestant Orange Order, and proposed to ban members of the Orange Order from holding public office.[44] And it was Baldwin's close colleague Francis Hincks who drafted the first bill to create Catholic separate schools in Upper Canada in 1843.[45] During one legislature debate in 1845, Baldwin was even brought to tears as he spoke remorsefully of past Protestant aggression against French Canadians.[46] Whether the reformers' wooing of Catholic allies succeeded, however, is doubtful. French Canadians were on the whole less interested in Baldwin's progressive vision than in securing their own cultural and linguistic interests within the union.[47]

Despite the new Catholic-friendly face of the Upper Canadian reform leaders, the old religious hostilities continued to brew beneath the surface. Liberal journalists followed the example of recent Scots Presbyterian immigrant Peter Brown, who continued to call out the "exclusive and intolerant spirit" of "Popery and High-Church-of-Englandism" and argued that Catholicism and Anglicanism were "essentially the same in substance."[48] For dedicated Dissenters like Brown, it did not matter that his party leader was an Anglican or that their party's great new hope was a successful alliance with Roman Catholics – what mattered was the ancestral warnings regarding Catholicism's supposedly tyrannical nature. Dissenters continued to assert their heritage as champions of liberty against the historical tyrannies of the established church, reminding each other that their cause was worthy and required defensive action. For example, in discussing a proposal for Jesuits to administer education for some First Nations, Peter Brown warned readers that it was just the beginning of Jesuit encroachment: "Canada is destined to be sacrificed, if the Protestant feeling of the country is not aroused."[49] At the same time that Baldwin was weeping in the legislature in penitence for Protestant crimes, some of the key voices in his party were rousing some of the old "Protestant feeling."

This fundamental division between reform leaders and the Dissenting base led to some public disagreements, especially the defection of Isaac Buchanan. A businessman and devout evangelical Presbyterian, Buchanan had been elected as a reformer MLA in Toronto in 1841, but became disillusioned with his leader's perceived coziness with Catholics and published a series of tracts against him in 1844.[50] In addition to suggesting that Baldwin had insulted the loyalists and was leaning republican,[51] the tracts accused him of selling out his fellow Upper Canadians to Lower Canadian interests: "While neglecting every well-known feeling of Upper Canada," Buchanan wrote, he had dared "to dignify every prejudice of Lower Canada with the name of feeling." He warned that that province would never reciprocate such generosity.[52] As a result of Baldwin's "infatuation," he added, "the population of Upper Canada had their most vital interests most *glaringly sacrificed* by him."[53]

Although Buchanan emphasized the sectional nature of his concerns, religion was a major part of the critique. His biographer Douglas

McCalla acknowledged his subject's sincere religious beliefs and his role in the Free Church of Scotland, but he summarized his controversy with Baldwin as disagreement over responsible government.[54] Despite such distinctions, religion was central to Buchanan's critique. He himself explained, "My object and the object of the Reformers, was solely to do away that incubus on the young energies of the province – an irresponsible High Church Oligarchy."[55] He suggested that the reform leader had forgotten this original goal and was actually helping to perpetuate "the High Church Oligarchy" in Upper Canada.[56] He gave no specific examples; indeed, Baldwin opposed the proposed Anglican exclusivity of King's College and stood up to his own church leaders to do so.[57] However, Buchanan was perhaps invoking the specter of Catholic state–church encroachments, such as the separate schools introduced the previous year due to Baldwin and Hincks's initiative.[58] Whatever his reasoning, he argued that yielding significant ground to any church establishment would lead to rebellion much like in 1837. He believed that "the more immediate cause of the late rebellion" was that colonists resented "all the favours and patronage of the colony being heaped upon the extreme and bigoted High Church faction"; if Baldwin allowed such patronage to continue, he suggested, he invited attempted "revolution" again.[59]

Living in exile in New York, the disgraced Mackenzie wrote to Buchanan to express support: "I tried long and vainly what you are now endeavouring to accomplish." He connected particularly with the religious dimension of his critique: "You seek for men believing as you and I were taught to believe on religious questions, equal rights with other men who adhere to the Church of England." Yet Mackenzie's letter was pessimistic. Years in exile, with very few old friends visiting or offering support, as well as his ruminations on the nature of power in Upper Canada, had left him bitter and disillusioned. He warned Buchanan: despite your efforts, "you do not succeed. Men in power in the colonies … stand ready to oppose you – and actually claim credit for superior loyalty for so doing."[60] Although Buchanan likely had no sympathy for Mackenzie – he opposed forgiving the 1837 rebels[61] – the rebel leader's letter suggests that at least some reformers noticed and appreciated Buchanan's attacks on religious patronage and influence.

Some Dissenters defended Baldwin against Buchanan's attacks, but none of them challenged Buchanan's points about church establishment or Lower Canadian influence. Rather, they countered only his suggestion that Baldwin was a rebel sympathizer. For example, the Quaker leader David Willson made no mention of religion or sectionalism:

> Could we believe his thoughts are true,
> Our Council is a rebel crew
> And they're disloyal to the bone,
> And aliens to the British throne[?]
> We know the truth he does despise
> And few now on his pen relies.[62]

One anonymous letter to the editor of the *Examiner* likewise objected to Buchanan's insinuations of disloyalty, defended Baldwin for his "consistency as a Reformer," and recommended that reformers continue to stand "shoulder to shoulder" in order to fight for responsible government.[63] Buchanan expected reformers to defend Baldwin in this way, suggesting that the majority of them were willing to turn a blind eye to their leader's state–church concessions as long as responsible government remained on the table.[64]

The Protestant Dissenters' anxiety about perceived Catholic influence was exacerbated by the Irish famine of 1845–47, which sent unprecedented numbers of Catholic migrants to Upper Canada.[65] In early 1847, Dissenters responded with great sympathy and charity, and meetings throughout the province promised to collect relief aid and to facilitate Irish migration to Canada.[66] The pro-migration arguments usually included a mixture of charity and the hope for economic benefit for Canada. As one meeting in Toronto resolved, not only was it a moral obligation to "generously come to the aid of our suffering countrymen," but the migrants would certainly "add to the wealth, strength, and safety of the colonies of the empire."[67] In February and March 1847, Peter Brown publicly advocated for migration to Upper Canada as the best means of addressing the famine: "Permanent relief can only arise from an extensive emigration, and the sooner Government sets about it the better."[68] The basis of Brown's argument later evolved from moral to economic, to suggest that Canada would benefit because the migrants would become hard workers: "A crushed peasantry would be at once converted into hardy and independent yeomen."[69]

The Dissenters' initial charitable reaction was quickly replaced, however, with a profound concern about religious demographics. By May 1847, Peter and George Brown had both backtracked: "We are convinced, after a very careful examination of [the migration scheme's] contents, that it cannot be carried into effect … It proposes to send two millions from Ireland, all of one religion, and to gather if possible from the United States all the natives of the same faith (the Roman Catholic), and to set[t]le the whole in one District of Canada. It is not a scheme of emigration, but of colonization. Ireland is to be transferred to Canada, and to take possession of it."[70] The summer brought tens of thousands of destitute and often diseased migrants into a colony simply not prepared to process so many arrivals. James Lesslie, the editor of the reform newspaper *Examiner* and devout evangelical Dissenter, wrote to Mackenzie to describe the "great suffering and wretchedness" in Toronto, concluding: "We are being made sharers in the calamities proceeding from the misrule of unhappy Ireland."[71] Articles in the *Examiner* decried "the prevalence of disease and death among the poor emigrants who have arrived and are still crowding in upon our shores." All the while, the migrants' religion remained subtly in the background: one article mentioned that on 12 August "the last rites of the Romish Church had been administered to about 150 of the dying."[72]

The famine migration also reinforced Dissenters' negative perceptions of church establishments. If Ireland had not been allocating millions of pounds to maintain its established church (Anglican), James Lesslie reasoned in a letter to Mackenzie in March 1847, those funds could help alleviate the nation's poverty. For Lesslie, this misallocation was the best way to explain Ireland's "wretchedness," in "a fertile land with a hardy population."[73] In an *Examiner* editorial he argued that the Church of Ireland "should be compelled to disgorge its vast revenues to provide bread for the starving millions" rather than "compelling the Colonists to feed and nourish the dying and famishing outcasts of tyranny and oppression."[74] Some Dissenters, initially charitable towards the migrants, decided that they had been swindled into accepting the burdensome consequences of church–state mismanagement.

What had started as a decade of optimism for a revived reform party, ready to set aside the blemish of 1837 and participate actively in the bicultural experiment of the united province, had by 1847 begun to show signs of severe strain. Not only did Baldwin and Hincks's gestures of goodwill to Lower Canada appear to be uni-directional, but mass migration from Ireland seemed to leave Upper Canadian Protestants vulnerable to "colonization" at the hands of a foreign faith. By the end of 1847, Peter Brown predicted that if some political leaders had their way, and if they did not counteract church–state arrangements like the clergy reserves, "Canada in a few years after will be the most priest-ridden country on the American Continent."[75] The union had forced Upper Canadian liberals to think beyond their colony's immediate religious dynamics, previously focused on Anglican–Dissent relations, to that of the wider jurisdiction. The result was an increased spotlight on Catholic–Protestant relations, which would become an obligatory obsession for Canadian liberals in the decades to come. Despite initial optimism, the changing political and demographic contexts of the early union period ultimately helped to foster the Protestant Dissenters' growing sense of cultural vulnerability.

"Rebels on both sides of the Atlantic": Dissenters in a Transatlantic Struggle

Just as Upper Canadian reformers began to see themselves as under threat at home from Catholic influence and church–state sympathy in the new union, so too were they concerned about the perceived ascendancy of these forces abroad. In the 1840s, Upper Canadians took notice of several international events that seemed to jeopardize their cause: for example, Britain's Graham Factory Bill (1843), which would secure Church of England control over children's education, till then operated voluntarily in some regions by Dissenters like the Methodists,[76] and the Maynooth Endowment (1845), a massive state grant for the Catholic seminary St Patrick's College, Maynooth, in Ireland.[77] Meanwhile, a growing anti–state church movement in Britain – exemplified by the church–state matters in the split of Canadian Methodists from the Wesleyan Methodist church (1840) and the Disruption of the Church of Scotland (1843) – helped convince Canadian Dissenters that they were part of a broader international community with the same values and goals.

Several recent transatlantic arrivals quickly became prominent public figures in the reform movement in the 1840s. One example is the

Congregationalist Rev. John Roaf, who had immigrated to Toronto in November 1837, mere weeks before the outbreak of the rebellion. As a pastor in Wolverhampton, England, Roaf had developed a reputation as an evangelical who advocated for causes like anti-slavery and had even served on the election committee for Whig candidates in his constituency.[78] Roaf immediately linked up with the colony's reform movement, and even welcomed reform party leader Marshall Spring Bidwell and his wife as "occasional members" of his congregation at Zion Congregational in Toronto.[79] After the rebellion, Roaf wrote to the exiled Bidwell in December 1837 to encourage him to remain firm in his opposition to Lieutenant-Governor Head and the colonial government.[80]

Roaf made his own stand in February 1838 when he refused to participate in a state-sanctioned "Day of Thanksgiving" to celebrate the rebellions' defeat.[81] The fact that the celebration was billed as a state-enforced day of worship is what offended Roaf as a Dissenter. Head's decree had stated that loyal subjects should "send up their Prayers, Praises, and Thanksgivings to the Divine Majesty" in order to "avoid His wrath and indignation."[82] Roaf replied, "The Lieutenant Governor bears the commission of the Queen – but not that of Christ ... Spiritual allegiance to him would be treason to Heaven."[83] Over the next two decades, Roaf would become one of the colony's leading voices against the clergy reserves and any other government action that fostered what he called "churchism."[84]

Roaf's seamless transition from Britain's reform movement to Upper Canada's is indicative of the transatlantic nature of mid-nineteenth-century Dissent and liberalism.[85] Several 1840s' newcomers would follow the same pattern. For example, the young Alexander Mackenzie quickly took an interest in Canadian politics after arriving from Scotland in the spring of 1842, engaging in heated arguments at work after expressing his opposition to the clergy reserves.[86] Dissenters were able to adapt so seamlessly because extensive communications across the Atlantic enabled them to see themselves as part of a worldwide struggle of good against evil, of liberty against tyranny, and of true against false religion. As fellow Scottish immigrant Peter Brown noted in 1845, "The world apparently consists of two grand divisions; the supporters of the *Establishments*, and of the *Voluntary* principle," and through this lens he derived conclusions about political controversies in Ireland,

England, Scotland, and Canada.[87] International news reports such as those included in Brown's *Banner* kept Dissenters informed about what Brown called the assaults of "Anti-Christ" upon "the Christian world."[88] This constant flow of international news helped to bond a large, transatlantic community of Dissenters, despite great physical distance.[89]

The Disruption of the Church of Scotland in 1843, and the formation of the Free Church of Scotland, resonated in Upper Canada. This development followed a decade of disagreement in Scotland over the state using the civil courts to decide matters that many church leaders deemed "spiritual." The conflict came to a climax on 18 May 1843, when the elderly minister Thomas Chalmers led over 400 Presbyterian ministers and about 40 per cent of the church's members out of the Church of Scotland. The following year, twenty-three Church of Scotland ministers in Canada also led their congregations to form their own branches of the Free Church in Canada, a number that grew to 158 by 1861.[90] The Free Church became the spiritual home for several major liberal reformers, including Peter and George Brown and Isaac Buchanan. Although the Free Church rejected some aspects of voluntarism, accepting government endowments for churches, its overall belief in greater separation of church and state meant that many adherents were "on the Whig / Liberal side in politics."[91] For people like the Browns, the Disruption of 1843 helped to fuel political polarization along religious lines in Upper Canada just as it did in Scotland. As Michael Gauvreau explained, "Because in Scotland religious and social inequality formed the central axis of politics, Peter Brown naturally conceived of evangelical conviction as a political weapon to be immediately deployed to fight Tory principles in church and state."[92]

The Canadian Methodists in the 1840s also experienced a series of internal conflicts that included a transatlantic component. After the controversial unification of the Canadian and British Methodists in 1833, the British church leaders had hoped to redirect the Canadians away from their longstanding criticisms of the clergy reserves and other state supports for churches.[93] However, Canadian church leaders continued to denounce the clergy reserves and even issued a public resolution in 1837 that labelled them "in direct violation of those principles of civil and religious liberty."[94] During a visit to Canada in 1839, British Wesleyan Robert Alder reaffirmed his support for the established church and persuaded the Canadians to rescind their previous resolutions against state funding. Subsequent disagreements emerged over government aid for missionary activity among the Indigenous peoples, along with other government grants, and by 1840 both sides realized that the shaky union had to end.[95] These two branches of Methodism operated separately until both sides' struggle to increase membership made them open to another union in 1847.[96] By that time, many British members had begun to soften their support for church establishment to a degree acceptable to the Canadians. One reason for this softening was the ascendancy of the high-church faction within the Church of England, particularly the Tractarian movement, which in 1842 had directly condemned Methodism.[97] Thus the Canadians and British Wesleyans' shared aversion to the Tractarians (and the threat of "popery" that they represented) helped to facilitate the 1847 re-union.[98]

The critics of Dissent and reform grasped the international dimension of these twin movements. For example, one conservative tract published in Britain in 1840 depicted a correspondence between a John Steady in England and his brother in Canada regarding the "rebels on both sides of the Atlantic," and the siblings marvelled at "what a close family resemblance there is between them everywhere."[99] They noticed the tight connection between religion and politics for these "rebels," which they saw as hypocritical: as one put it, "What a mockery and contradiction to rebel against the 'powers that be,' which are 'ordained of God;' … and then call themselves Christians, and lovers of their country!"[100] One even suggested that political agitators were simply pretending to be Christians in order to obtain preaching licences, solely to advance their political cause under the auspices of religion.[101]

In reality, the crossover of religion and politics was not as deceptive as the Steady brothers imagined. As in Upper Canada, in Britain several devout evangelical preachers found that their religious beliefs led them to take an active interest in political matters. For example, Joseph Rayner Stephens was born in Edinburgh to a family of devout Methodists, became a Methodist preacher himself, and like many Canadian Dissenters came to oppose the church establishment. When the issue brought him into conflict with the Wesleyan leaders, he resigned from the church in 1834.[102] Decades earlier, Alexander Kilham was a Methodist preacher in Sheffield who, on being expelled from the Wesleyan church for being a "Paineite" liberal, went on to form the Methodist New Connexion and advocate for democratic reform.[103] The conservative Steady brothers did not understand how a sincere Christian could come to dissident political conclusions or oppose the "powers that be," which stance they believed to violate biblical precepts.[104] But as Rev. John Roaf explained only months after his arrival in Canada, "The very Apostles that tell us 'to be subject to the higher powers,' refused to obey Magistrates and Emperors in things spiritual, and died as martyrs to maintain a simple fidelity to Christ."[105] On both sides of the Atlantic, sincere adherence to the Dissenting tradition became a justification to challenge government policy.

One British political cause that resonated on both sides of the Atlantic in the 1840s was Chartism and related reform efforts such as "complete suffrage." The Chartists advocated a number of social and economic changes, but rallied around their six-point People's Charter, which called for universal male suffrage, a secret ballot, annual parliaments, abolition of the property requirement for MPs, salaries for MPs, and equal electoral districts by population.[106] Although the Canadian reformers and rebels did not advocate for these particular changes, some contemporaries believed the two sides to be the same in spirit. Indeed, the conservative Steady brothers saw a direct line across the Atlantic from the Upper Canadian rebellion of 1837 to the Chartist movement in Britain, which emerged formally in 1838: "All this [rebellion] has vanished from Canada, but has just sprung up in England – the old principles under a new name … You may ask what witchcraft has deceived them. They call it CHARTISM."[107] There is evidence that some British Chartists took inspiration from the Canadian rebellions, such as the Yorkshire shoemaker Abram Hanson, who said in January 1838 that British reformers should "imitate the example of the Canadians, and be united in their demand for their rights."[108] The transatlantic influence went both ways, as some Upper Canadians would later take inspiration from the Chartist movement to form the more overtly democratic wing of the reform movement known as the Clear Grits in 1849.[109]

The British reform movements of the 1840s contained a wide range of expressions, from radical to moderate and from working to middle class. Although many Protestant Dissenters in Britain were attracted to reform causes, they did not widely embrace Chartism in its entirety. Rather, as historian Malcolm Chase has explained, many middle-class Dissenters in the early 1840s were hesitant to take on the "Chartist" label, but often exercised "cautious support for at least the principles within *The People's Charter.*"[110] A good example was Congregationalist minister Edward Miall, who was also the editor of the *Nonconformist* and a well-known advocate for disestablishing the Church of England. His newspaper wrote positively about several Chartist initiatives, including universal manhood suffrage, but preferred the term "complete suffrage" rather than "Chartist."[111] The Quaker Joseph Sturge, who wrote a series of political articles with Miall on complete suffrage, founded the National Complete Suffrage Union (NCSU) in 1842. This more moderate version of the Chartists was open to incremental reforms and sought to unify the middle and working classes, but still advocated much the same kinds of reforms. More radical Chartists like Feargus O'Connor viewed the NCSU's incrementalism with suspicion, and treated it as a competitor to his own National Charter Association (NCA). However, the gap between these two groups was not always so pronounced; for example, the first NCSU conference affirmed every plank of the Chartist platform and was even attended by grassroots members of the NCA.[112] Although the majority of Dissenters were more likely to be attracted to the NCSU, their desire for sweeping reforms overlapped consistently with the wider Chartist movement.[113]

While the six-point Chartist platform itself contains no mention of religion, several British historians have noted the influence of Dissenting themes in ways strikingly similar to Upper Canadian politics. For example, animosity towards the established church was a rallying point for both. Just as William Lyon Mackenzie had accused the Anglican hierarchy of being a "furious political demon,"[114] so too did Chartists regard the Church of England as the "immoral handmaiden of a corrupt political order."[115] Indeed, so important was this issue to the Chartists that when spokesman Patrick Brewster came out in favour of the established church, his fellow Chartists accused him of being a government spy.[116] The physical space of the Anglican parish itself became a site of contention for Chartists to convey their message more directly. From July to September 1839, Chartists organized a series of sit-ins at Church of England parishes all over the country.[117] They generally announced in a local newspaper the date of the demonstration and then wrote to the parish priest to request he speak on certain biblical texts that related to their cause, such as one about proper treatment of the poor or the hypocrisy of religious leaders.[118] On the prescribed morning, the Chartists would often make a spectacle of marching to the church, singing hymns and holding banners, and then file in before the regular parishioners arrived. In many parishes, pews were paid for and assigned to particular members and families, so these sit-ins usually resulted in heated exchanges between the Chartists and the pew's owners![119] Some of Mackenzie's followers in Upper Canada similarly converted the Church of England into a site of political protest, in one case by locking the Anglican minister V.P. Meyerhoffer out of his own church in Markham.[120]

As in the Upper Canada rebellion, the Dissenting Protestant faith provided a powerful set of rhetoric and meanings that Chartists used to challenge government policy and to stir supporters to action. For example, Michael Sanders has examined the use of hymns written by Chartist supporters and sung at Chartist rallies throughout Britain, which had been compiled as the *National Chartist Hymn Book,* to illustrate the close relations between Protestant Dissent and Chartism.[121] Many hymns contained anti-clerical rhetoric that, like the Upper Canadian reformers, blamed the establishment clergy for most of their grievances.[122] Several emphasized the idea that God would soon overthrow tyranny and restore liberty, whether through divinely sanctioned human agency or through sudden divine intervention.[123]

Messianic and millennialist themes were prevalent in Chartist rhetoric. For example, the Methodist minister and Chartist spokesperson Joseph Rayner Stephens likened the disenfranchised Britons to the biblical Israelites who withstood the evil forces around them while awaiting God's promised deliverance.[124] In one sermon in 1839, Stephens paraphrased Jesus to situate Chartism at the cusp of "a very great change, a very awful change, and perhaps a very sudden change."[125] Heralding a moment both revolutionary and apocalyptic, Stephens cryptically told his followers to light their lamps and follow the bridegroom into the marriage supper.[126] For audiences familiar with Stephens's biblical references, the sermon was a bold assertion that their movement was divinely sanctioned and even correlated with the Second Coming of Christ.[127]

Even though the Chartist reforms did not become widely accepted in belief or practice in Canadian politics until much later, Dissent shaped political activism in both jurisdictions, suggesting a deep cultural kinship that spanned national borders. This transatlantic context affected the engagement of Dissent in Upper Canadian liberalism in the 1840s. Dissenting British immigrants such as Peter and George Brown,

Alexander Mackenzie, and John Roaf all moved to Upper Canada with preconceived notions about church–state relations, Protestant–Catholic relations, and God's expectations for human governance. Theirs was a supernatural biblical worldview that forged the cultural touchstones for an international community, offered imperatives that stirred them to political action in a new land, and provided the narratives that fashioned their understanding of liberal ideology.

"Babylon is Fallen": Millennialism and Church–State Relations

The Dissenting worldview that had energized Chartism and anti-state–church sentiments in the old world was just as alive in the hearts and minds of colonists who took up the liberal cause in Upper Canada. Although they faced different political issues, like separate schools and the clergy reserves, recent arrivals from the British Isles and even those with a less immediate claim to British lineage could face these issues by drawing on a common Dissenting Protestant cultural heritage. For example, in an election speech in 1840, reformer John Armstrong of Zorra invoked his Scottish Presbyterian roots to legitimize his political platform. He called on voters to remember the "blood of our ancestors who fought and died in defense of their religious rights" against "a dominant Episcopal Church." Such a legacy "ought to stimulate us on this side of the ocean to … maintain our civil and religious rights as our fathers did before us."[128] Even though reform leaders' attitudes towards religious culture changed about 1840 due to the union, the prevalence of similar, culturally specific appeals throughout the decade suggests a cultural continuity with the reform movement of the 1830s.

Upper Canadian liberal political rhetoric in both decades often drew on one of two kinds of Dissenting narratives: persecution and millennialist. 1) *Persecution narratives*: confessional retelling of actual historical events in which Dissenters were targeted for their beliefs. Such accounts emphasized their predecessors' resilience under perceived church–state tyranny, whether under the Stuart monarchs as Armstrong's election speech implies, or occasionally more ancient precedents like the early Christians under the Roman Empire. They were often meant to invoke sympathy for Dissent or to warn of what could happen if church establishments were to become powerful again.[129] 2) *Millennialist narratives:* the application of symbolic meanings from biblical revelation to contemporary events. Such extrapolations invoked a supernatural order that Dissenters perceived to underlie human history, offering believers not only a means of interpreting past and current events but also a kind of roadmap for what was expected to happen in the future.[130] Both kinds of narratives also contributed to the increased anti-Catholic rhetoric of the 1840s, as Protestants regularly depicted the Roman Catholic church as a historically persecuting force and as the prophesied "Anti-Christ" and "man of sin" described in Revelation.[131] Though drawing on differing source material, these two narrative forms were complementary, and both reinforced group identity and offered direction for collective political action.

This section focuses on one political issue of the 1840s, which many Dissenters interpreted through the lens of persecution and millennialist narratives: the clergy reserves. As we saw at the start of this chapter, in the aftermath of 1837 several prominent public figures noted the reserves' role in inciting public hostility towards the colonial government.[132] The authorities reacted by trying to appease those excluded from the clergy reserves by offering them their own share of the benefits. Whereas in 1791 clergy-reserve payments went only to the Church of England, later they included the Church of Scotland, and in 1840 they added the Roman Catholics and the Wesleyan Methodists. Upper Canada had created what Curtis Fahey called a "multi-headed establishment."[133]

Although this new direction was more inclusive, the decision missed the point of what made the clergy reserves so controversial to most Dissenters in the first place. When the government suggested this idea earlier in 1837, reformer John Rolph had objected, "The payment of one church by the state is thought of dangerous tendency. How much more alarming is the proposition to pay four?"[134] When word of this proposal again circulated in early 1840, the *Examiner* mocked the idea as inviting "the curse of perhaps a dozen state churches" on the colony and pointed out to its majority Protestant readership that it would be "including of course Roman Catholics." Surely, it commented, such a division of power and resources among the "priests" would ultimately mean bidding "farewell to the liberties of the people."[135] As the Dissenters had made clear time and time again, their main objection was not that their own churches were excluded from state support, but that such state support for churches existed at all.

The notion that church establishments of any kind threatened the colonists' liberty was based on the Dissenters' understanding of history and of prophecy, wherein the state church was inherently corrupting and persecuting. In the summer of 1840, when the Anglican editor of the *Church* newspaper argued that Dissenters enjoyed more freedom in a country that had an established church, the Methodist editor of the *Christian Guardian*, Jonathan Scott, replied fiercely: "Almost every page of ecclesiastical history assures us in characters of blood, that when such an establishment has had its full play, it has produced confusion, and bondage, and martyrdom."[136] Scott published a series of articles asserting that state support for churches had been inherently corrupting of religion throughout Christian history: "Have not ministers been made for the church by the world, Popes by Emperors, in opposition to the desire of the church? Have not our own Bishops been created and annihilated by Kings – often wicked, perhaps infidel Kings?"[137] Peter Brown offered similar appeals to history to support his own voluntarist position, going beyond the usual Stuart-era narrative to ancient Rome. Brown wrote that Protestants ought to "cast their retrospect to the days of Constantine, and find that all the blood which has been shed since that time for religious opinion, was owing to some sect being established, and having the sword of persecution put into their hands, or employed on their account."[138] Through such narratives, Dissenters positioned themselves as heirs to a legacy of righteous resistance to corrupt state power. Even when these writers claimed to express "no political opinion,"[139] their point was clear: Dissenters ought to oppose church establishments as their predecessors had done.

To these historical precedents, many Dissenters added the sanction of biblical revelation. Millennialist themes were particularly relevant to public discourse in the 1840s because of emerging millennialist movements such as Joseph Smith's Mormonism and William Miller's Adventism. By the early 1840s, Mormon millennialism had called several hundred Upper Canadians to gather at "Zion" and follow church leaders in sequence to Ohio, Missouri, and Illinois.[140] The Adventist movement proposed the literal return of Christ to Earth in either 1843 or 1844, based on Miller's calculation of the symbolic "weeks" and "days" of biblical prophecies in Daniel and in Revelation. An Adventist camp meeting in the English-speaking Eastern Townships of Lower Canada attracted thousands of people in 1842, and the message spread to Upper Canada through a series of Adventist publications in Toronto.[141]

Although the two movements remained peripheral in Upper Canada, they stimulated discussion about millennialist themes among the wider population.[142] The Congregationalist John Roaf, for example, responded with extensive teachings on the subject in an 1844 tract. He explained how biblical prophecies had already been fulfilled several times through historical events and suggested what Christians could expect in the near future based on scripture.[143] He disagreed with William Miller principally on when Christ would return in relation to the foretold millennium. Whereas Miller was *pre-millennialist*, expecting an imminent physical return of Christ to judge all humans and inaugurate a thousand-year reign on earth, Roaf and most other Upper Canadian Protestants were *post-millennialist*, expecting the return and final judgment only after Christianity covered the earth.[144]

This distinction affected how Upper Canadian Protestants engaged with the secular world. Pre-millennialists like the Millerites generally believed it impossible for humans to make the world better; rather, the earthly order would only degenerate spiritually and morally until Christ intervened to establish his own kingdom on earth.[145] For post-millennialists, however, the kingdom would occur only after Protestantism and its accompanying social progress covered the world. Thus humans could and should work to advance the kingdom by improving society.[146] Articulating a sense of inevitability and rightness of the cause, post-millennialism inspired many Upper Canadian Protestants to align their society with the "laws of Christ."[147] Thus it encouraged believers to engage actively with public affairs.

Although post-millennialists like Roaf relegated some major eschatological events to the distant future, they still had a strong sense that biblical prophecy was relevant to their own day. Roaf meticulously assigned biblical imagery to contemporary kingdoms, churches, events, and people in ways that added supernatural significance to contemporary politics and inter-religious exchanges. For example, he believed that Revelation's symbolism of a leopard-like beast with seven heads and ten horns, described in scripture as making war with the saints, represented the Roman Catholic church. For Roaf, the descriptions of this beast in Revelation 13:1–10 lined up with past events, such as the beast's "deadly wound" representing the sixteenth-century Protestant Reformation.[148] Some of Roaf's interpretations hit even closer to home by interpreting some biblical imagery as prophetic references to Britain and British dominions. For example, he believed that the Church of England fitted the description of the second beast of Revelation 13:11–18, a two-horned lamb with the voice of a dragon: "This 'lamblike' beast has exercised the power of the first beast in the British dominions – has dictated to conscience, prescribed belief, enforced conformity – has caused many to become in spirit Papistical – or 'to worship the first beast whose deadly wound was healed.'"[149] Indeed, Roaf believed the dreaded Anti-Christ of biblical prophecy was the Roman Catholic church and, for that matter, any Protestant church (including the Church of England) with Catholic-style rituals and priestly authority.[150]

Assigning Revelation's symbols to real-life figures and events, Roaf rendered his own world into a biblical timeframe. Though disagreeing with William Miller about the immediacy of the Second Coming, he believed he knew precisely how the nineteenth century related to the ultimate end of time. Interpreting the seven seals in Revelation 6 and the seven vials in chapter 16 as analogies for epochs of history, for example, he determined that humanity had already lived through the events described in the first through fourth seal and was living out the events of the fifth, in chapter 6:9–11.[151] Roaf described his own epoch as a time of persecution, wherein the papacy was recovering from its earlier "deadly wound" and "the English Church" would direct unsuspecting Protestants towards popish practices.[152] For example, Dissenters worried about Tractarians turning Church of England adherents towards Catholicism.[153] In the same epoch of deception and persecution, however, the true gospel was spreading throughout the world and would culminate in the defeat of false religion.[154] For Roaf, the next great prophetic event was not the literal return of Christ, but rather the defeat of Anti-Christ (Roman Catholicism and its Protestant facsimiles), fulfilling the angel's declaration, "Babylon the great is fallen" (Revelation 18:2).[155] In this worldview, contemporary events and figures each played a role in a great cosmic drama of good versus evil, and were mapped out in biblical prophecy for devout Protestants to decipher.

It is not difficult to see how millennialist commentary like Roaf's (e.g., labelling rival denominations and the governments that support them as "Anti-Christ") could affect both inter-religious relations and geopolitical events. Indeed, sometimes Dissenters invoked millennialist themes to address policy issues like the clergy reserves. For example, as the Presbyterian Peter Brown summarized in 1845, "True Protestants shrink with horror from the State placing itself in alliance with a Church, which they believe to be the Anti-Christ spoken of in the Word of God." Like Roaf, Brown was hopeful about the impending defeat of Anti-Christ, suggesting that "the present British Establishments are soon destined to fall … before the kingdoms of this world shall become the 'Kingdoms of God, and of his Christ.'"[156] To engage in the political battle against church establishments, then, whether opposing clergy reserves or separate schools, was tantamount to taking up arms in the spiritual battle against Anti-Christ.

This cultural backdrop helps explain why Dissenters prioritized religious issues leading up to the Canadian election in January 1848. Some believed that the most important precursor to "liberty" was the separation of church and state, even more than responsible government. As the *Examiner* summarized, "The whole superstructure of our liberties is, in fact, endangered by the existence of this sectarian political inequality, and that danger must be averted by wise and righteous legislation."[157] When campaigning began in December 1847, Upper Canadian reformers billed themselves not only as champions of responsible government, but also as "defender[s] of your civil and religious rights," and smeared their tory opponents as desiring "to have National Episcopacy established in Canada" and to have the colonists "taxed directly or indirectly to support exclusively the teachers of [their] creed."[158]

Indeed, the reform candidate James Beatty in Toronto did not mention responsible government even once in an election pitch published in the *Banner;* rather, he focused on his promise to "resist all attempts at Church domination." He appealed explicitly to the Dissenters' persecution narratives, suggesting that the Church of England would not be content simply to control education and public land, but that some in the church even desired to "put to death those who differed in opinion from them."[159] Although his rhetoric may be unusually inflammatory, it is consistent with the Dissenters' persecution and millennialist narratives, which had long depicted established churches as exercising the kind of tyranny Beatty described.

The Dissenters' vision for liberal reform in Upper Canada in the 1840s valued responsible government as one part of a more holistic, culture-driven political change. They promoted both responsible government and free institutions in the same breath as they called for "genuine religion" to counteract "gross superstition" and "political priests."[160] They wanted an end to church–state privilege as a means to curb the tyrannical tendency of their rival faiths' church establishments, a notion culturally rooted in Dissent's driving narratives. Unlike Baldwin's Catholic-friendly political strategy, their liberalism did not reach out to people of other faiths but counteracted potentially illiberal aspects of those faiths. Throughout the 1840s, Dissenters wrote about Catholics and high-church Anglicans as obstacles to freedom who were always either scrambling for government handouts for their church (i.e., through the clergy reserves or education endowments) or scheming so that "the days of darkness must once more overspread the world."[161] In the 1840s, even with a high-church Anglican (Baldwin) leading the reform party, Dissenters continued to assert that their own faith (or "genuine religion") had a unique claim over civil and religious liberty. Indeed, as Peter Brown put it, "To maintain free institutions is part of religion."[162]

Despite the resounding liberal victory in the 1848 election, Dissenters found their pet issues absent from co-premier Robert Baldwin's list of priorities. In a letter to Mackenzie in exile, James Lesslie noted a certain "timidity" to the reformers under Baldwin's leadership.[163] Of course, this timidity was due to the fact that Baldwin's reformers relied on Lower Canadian support in the united legislature. When the Baptist minister J. Winterbotham of Brantford wrote to MLA James Hervey Price (South York) to ask about the clergy reserves, Price's response was blunt: "Think my dear sir for a moment … Who have we to convince? The Lower Canadians." Price believed that the Lower Canadians would always vote together to sustain their own collective religious interests, and any attempt by the Upper Canadian liberals to separate church and state would end Baldwin's decade-long alliance: "If my fears are realized the French will join the Tories and protect their own religious endowments by not interfering with ours." As Price also understood, this answer was not satisfying to those Upper Canadian "fiery spirits" who wanted longstanding grievances resolved right away.[164] Political change, like the millennium, would keep the Dissenters waiting a little longer.

Conclusion

The early union period initiated three major political changes for Dissenters in Upper Canada. First, the union required Dissenters to work across religious lines in Catholic-majority Lower Canada. Although reform leader Robert Baldwin embraced this new reality by advocating greater Catholic representation in government, approving state funds for Catholic schools, moving the capital from Kingston to Montreal, and offering tearful apologies for Protestant wrongs, such actions were alien to most Upper Canadian reformers. Indeed, many of his Dissenting supporters continued to view Catholicism as incompatible with their Protestant notion of liberty. Their sense of demographic vulnerability was only exacerbated by the tragic outcomes of the Irish famine of 1847, which sent unprecedented numbers of Catholics to Upper Canada and led some Dissenters to believe they were bearing the brunt of church establishments' failures and mismanagement.

Second, the rise of church–state controversies abroad helped Upper Canadian Dissenters to imagine themselves as part of a transatlantic movement. Several newcomers, such as Peter and George Brown, Alexander Mackenzie, and John Roaf, brought with them a religious culture that helped them blend almost seamlessly into their new environment and quickly become leaders in Upper Canada's reform movement. And third, the millennialist fervour of the 1840s stimulated Dissenters to revive their own interest in biblical prophecies, which became, along with persecution narratives, a powerful way of engaging with contemporary inter-religious relations and political issues. Seeing the political world through this lens, Dissenters were unwilling to compromise on issues like the clergy reserves, whose extension to four denominations did absolutely nothing to settle the controversy.

The liberal vision for church–state relations that Dissenters advocated was driven in large part by their historical vision of past persecutions and their prophetic vision of millennialism. However, they shared a legislature with people who did not possess the same inter-generational memories of persecution at the hands of a state church, nor the same interpretation of the biblical beasts, seven seals, and seven vials that had provided a roadmap for their world. Thus, even with the liberals' historic victory in the 1848 election, the realization of church–state separation still appeared impossible. As James Hervey Price had admitted, the political power of Catholics within the union meant that any discussion of removing religious endowments was tantamount to political suicide. Biblical prophecy may have promised their eventual victory, but in the meantime their vision appeared to be thwarted by voter demographics and sectional imbalance. With the rise of the Clear Grits and the leadership of George Brown, removing these barriers would become top priority for liberals in the years that followed.

3

Baneful Domination

The Later Union Period, 1849–1859

Celebrations of reform victory in the 1848 election rapidly faded into disillusionment. About a year into the new ministry's tenure, Dissenters began to raise concerns over the Baldwin government's "procrastination" on promises like the liberalization of King's College, the secularization of the clergy reserves, and the dismissal of Egerton Ryerson from his post as superintendent of the public schools.[1] By the spring of 1850, longtime Baldwin supporters had become positively mutinous. The emergent reform newspaper *North American* declared that "the country has been so shamefully duped and betrayed by the 'honest' Robert Baldwin, and the 'honest lawyer,' James Harvy [*sic*] Price," primarily because of their inaction on the clergy reserves.[2] Religion ultimately lay at the heart of this disillusionment, as member of the legislative council (upper house) Adam Fergusson exclaimed, "The protestants of Canada West would never be contented with the present state of things."[3]

Indeed, the Protestants of Canada West soon had their opportunity for revolt. When Robert Baldwin ran for re-election in the riding of North York in 1851, the voters rejected him by a large margin.[4] The political turmoil that followed Baldwin's fall from grace produced the breaking apart and ultimately the reorganization of the reformers under George Brown's leadership. The years 1851–54 saw the party divided between the Hincksite moderates (led by Francis Hincks, Baldwin's successor), some independent reformers, the Brownites, and the Clear Grits (many of whom eventually rallied around George Brown).[5] This schism was based on a handful of disagreements, including debates about the extent of democratic reform needed (the Clear Grits demanded an elected governor, elected upper house, and universal manhood suffrage),[6] but the most immediate division involved religion. Hincks, like

Baldwin, believed in avoiding hot-button religious issues to maintain the coalition with Catholic MLAs, so disavowed Brown's faction for "raising a religious party cry." As one Hincks supporter summarized, "The Reform party is partially split up … An element has been introduced into politics which should be confined to the pulpit."[7] For the Hincksites, Brown's agitation on religious issues amounted to nothing more than "bigotry."[8] For the Dissenters, however, the Hincksites had repeatedly compromised liberal principles in order to appease Catholic leaders – they were too willing to "bow the knee" to "these priests of baal" for the sake of political expediency.[9]

Protestant discontent with Baldwin and Hincks's governing practices not only disrupted the reform party, but also anticipated the breakup of the United Province of Canada. As we saw in chapter 2, Upper Canadian reformers had initially approached the new union of 1841 with hope that they could work with Lower Canada to achieve the reforms they desired. In 1844, defector Isaac Buchanan had been a lone voice when he began to warn that Baldwin had "most glaringly sacrificed" their own section's interests to the other's.[10] By 1850, however, an increasing number of Upper Canadian reformers agreed that their leaders had sold them out, that the union was rigged against them, and that a separation of the Canadas was the only way forward. One reformer's editorial in 1850 summarized the centrality of religion: "The people have formed a very decided opinion of the injustice and insult involved in the principle of State endowment to churches … Should it turn out that the French portion of the Government stand in the way, then we predict an approaching dissolution of the Union."[11] Separation became more and more popular throughout the decade, and the new Liberal party included it in its platform in 1859.[12]

Canadian politics in the later union period (1849–59) correlated with an escalation in Protestant–Catholic tension at home and abroad. In 1850, the Roman Catholic church re-established, after more than three hundred years, its episcopal system in England and Wales by appointing an archbishop and several bishops. This move came to be known as the "Papal Aggression," in part because it went ahead against the advice of Lord John Russell's government.[13] Reform newspapers in Canada reprinted British editorials that blamed Britain's broader tolerance for "popery" in universities and in the established church itself.[14] At the same time, the continued popularity of the Oxford (or Tractarian, or

Puseyite) movement threatened to move the Church of England closer in doctrine and practice to the Roman church. The Methodist preacher William McClure warned a Toronto audience in 1850 that Tractarians were "now making rapid strides in the Church of England" and were preaching against Dissenters in ways that worried him: "Made known from the pulpit, and from house to house, was that … the children of all who were married, and baptized by dissenters, were neither, *legitimate,* nor *christians.*"[15] Looking from abroad at these developments, well-informed Upper Canadian Dissenters were increasingly on the defensive.

At home in Canada, Protestant–Catholic tensions were amplified by two main political issues. 1) *The continuation of the clergy reserves*: although the reformers had made the secularization of the clergy reserves a centrepiece of their platform since the 1820s, a series of barriers kept this issue at play until 1854, when the conservative-led coalition sought to undercut their momentum by resolving their pet issue. Until that time, Dissenters often interpreted the government's inaction as evidence of "the influence of Catholic principles and priestly intrigues in our civil affairs."[16] 2) *Separate schools*: in 1852, Bishop Armand-François-Marie de Charbonnel of Toronto called on Catholics in Upper Canada to refuse to support the public-school system and insist on state support for a separate Catholic system.[17] This agitation reinforced religion-based political divisions and encouraged religion-based political activism, as one commentator noted: "Success is predicated on their [Catholic] united action. Let the Protestants learn and practice the same policy."[18] Outside of the legislature, the Protestant–Catholic tension manifested itself in two fatal religious riots: Toronto's Gavazzi Riots of 1853 and Montreal's St Patrick's Day Riot of 1858.[19] Nearly two decades after the new Province of Canada was supposed to "unite the people within them in one common feeling of attachment to British institutions,"[20] opposing religious identities remained a perennial source of conflict.

Through all of these controversies in the reform party and in Protestant–Catholic relations in general, one can detect a process of soul-searching in early Canadian liberalism. Questions about the limits of tolerance, religious diversity, and identity politics all came to the fore in this tumultuous period. While all sides appealed to liberal dichotomies such as liberty / tyranny and tolerance / bigotry, liberal commentators applied these concepts in competing ways. For example, was it a violation of religious liberty for a Protestant speaker to publicly condemn Catholicism in Montreal – or for a Catholic crowd to silence that speaker? The answer may have been obvious to Dissenting evangelicals, whose existence had always depended in part on open criticism of other religions. However, as this chapter's treatment of the Gavazzi controversy illustrates, public opinion was very much divided on how best to ensure religious freedom in a bicultural society.

Amid this struggle for the soul of Canadian liberalism, the idea of Protestant liberty – reinforced through evangelical theology, voluntarism, and persecution narratives – remained a powerful contender. For many Upper Canadian reformers, the belief that liberty was possible only in Protestant societies continued to challenge the bicultural presumptions of the Baldwinite / Hincksite liberals. In the words of an editorial from 1851, "Popery is seated in our land … and liberty cannot strike its roots into such an affected soil, cannot derive nourishment without the dews and sunshine of heaven; cannot shoot up into an atmosphere so tainted with corrupting pestilence."[21] Indeed, this chapter proposes that Upper Canadian reformers found themselves increasingly drawn to this Protestant-centred version of liberalism throughout the 1850s. Disillusioned by two decades of perceived inaction by moderate reformers like Baldwin and Hincks, many had by 1860 turned to politicians like George Brown, who explicitly spoke to Protestant concerns and appeared to care very little about offending would-be coalition partners in Lower Canada.

By the end of the 1850s, most Upper Canadian reformers had accepted that they lived under the "baneful domination of Lower Canada" and that the only solution was a "separation of the existing union between Upper and Lower Canada, and a confederation of the two with the North West territory."[22] Thus, power in the reform party shifted from the conciliatory Baldwinites, who believed it was possible to work across religious and sectional lines for common aims, to the Protestant-conscious Brownites, who had come to see inter-religious alliances as counterproductive. Unlike Baldwin's bicultural dream, Brown's vision for liberalism required an amicable divorce from Catholic-majority Lower Canada.

This chapter follows the reform party's development from the start of the Dissenters' disillusionment with the Baldwin–LaFontaine government in 1849 to the party's official advocacy of Confederation in 1859 as a means to escape the "baneful domination" of Lower Canada. It traces the rivalry between the Hincksite and Brownite wings and explains how each side's approach to religion helped forge liberal ideology in Canada. In particular, it highlights debates about church–state relations and freedom of speech in the wake of inter-religious violence and political turmoil. Also, building on the work of Paul Romney, who emphasized the legislative separation of Upper from Lower Canada as a key component of Confederation,[23] this chapter explains how religion-based sectional controversies in the 1850s laid the necessary groundwork for the Confederation talks of the 1860s.

"Deeper will be his Perdition": Religion and the Fall of Robert Baldwin

In the spring of 1850, reform editor and devout evangelical James Lesslie sent a foreboding update on Canadian politics to his exiled friend William Lyon Mackenzie: "I think the adm[inistration] have sold us on the question of religious equality, and if so, they are ruined. Every one of them will be hooted, in my opinion, from the Hustings at next election."[24] Later that summer, reformers continued to predict the government's fall: "The tide is already swelling around [Baldwin], and the longer he delays in making for the shore, *the deeper will be his perdition.*"[25] These comments followed a particularly disappointing year for Upper Canadian reformers. Their hopes soared when Baldwin assigned MLA Malcolm Cameron (Kent) to draft and introduce a new school bill in April 1849 allowing students to opt out of religious instruction with which their families disagreed, permitting more localized control over curriculum and over the implementation of school taxes, and subjecting the provincial superintendent's authority to a general board of education responsible to the cabinet. Superintendent Egerton Ryerson, however, denounced the bill and threatened to resign; Baldwin responded by withdrawing Cameron's bill and allowing Ryerson to introduce a more centralizing school bill in 1850.[26] Most troubling of all, by the spring of 1850 it had also become blatantly clear that the Baldwin government was stalling on the clergy reserves.[27] Altogether, it was this longstanding concern about church–state relations that would herald Robert Baldwin's fall from grace for Upper Canadian reformers.

Immediately after Baldwin's election in the winter of 1847–48, Dissenters began to press the new government to eliminate the clergy reserves once and for all. At its annual conference in Toronto in summer 1848, the Congregational Union of Canada West resolved that, since the colony had "obtained Responsible Government and a Liberal Ministry ... the era has come for action – for vigorous and effective action – in order to establish and consolidate our long cherished hopes as to our civil and religious liberties."[28] The year 1848 passed with no action on this front from Canada's first responsible government, however, and the royal speech (speech from the throne) opening the 1849 session did not even mention the clergy reserves. The *Examiner* expressed disappointment: "The country expects at their hands the immediate settlement of this irritating and long vexed question."[29] In response, in May 1850 a group of prominent political and religious leaders from several Protestant denominations met at Knox Church in Toronto to form the Anti–Clergy Reserve Association.[30] Over the next few years, this association would press the government on the issue.[31]

The Dissenters' disappointment in Baldwin began in spring and summer of 1850 to carry a sense of his absolute betrayal. As James Lesslie lamented privately, "All things look ominous of the gathering of what may be the result of the session ... It grieves me to the heart to witness such treachery to a confiding people."[32] Toronto-based poet Rusticus captured the reformers' disaffection:

> Believe me, Baldwin, there is more distress
> Than anger in the words that I express. –
> By Nature gifted to be great and good,
> First in Canadian hearts thou might'st have stood;
> ...
> The people trusted thee, and now behold,
> The trusting people find that 'they are sold.'[33]

One commentator declared that Upper Canadians had been deceived about Baldwin's true opinion on church–state matters: "Had he declared such to be his sentiment before the last election, he would not now hold the *honorable*, but *degraded* position of first Minister of the Crown."[34] Having stood by Baldwin throughout the 1840s in the hopes that he could enable the change they sought, reformers were ruthlessly unforgiving when they came to believe that he had broken their longstanding trust.

When the Baldwin government finally decided to act on the clergy reserves in June 1850, the move was widely condemned as a farce. Rather than asserting the colony's authority over the issue and secularizing the clergy reserves by Canadian legislation, as many reformers had advocated, Commissioner of Crown Lands (a cabinet post) James Hervey Price (MLA for South York) resolved to seek authority for secularization from Westminster. For reform critics, such a course would only tie up the issue for years before establishment members (including Church of England bishops) in the House of Lords would say no.[35] During several days of debate on the Price resolutions, Baldwin and Price made the case that the clergy reserves were "vested rights" under crown authority, that Westminster had legislated on the matter in 1840, and that therefore only it could repeal existing laws. Reformer Malcolm Cameron retorted: "The lands of the Crown in Canada are the lands of the people of Canada; the Crown was merely their trustee" and that therefore the Canadian Parliament could act alone on the matter.[36] In the end, however, the assembly voted to send Price's resolutions to Westminster for its approval.[37] The resolution to the issue would be out of Canadian hands for a few more years yet.

Perhaps the most damaging aspect of this episode for Dissenters was the idea that Robert Baldwin's actions had violated the very principle of responsible government itself. Instead of Canadian legislation being subject to the veto of British viceroys as it had been prior to 1848, some reformers now considered their legislation subject to the veto of Lower Canada. In May 1850, the *North American* had suggested that the Lower Canadian members of the government were attempting to "stand in the way" of resolving the clergy reserves and warned: "Should anything occur to disappoint the people in their interpretation of Responsible Government, during the progress of this measure," the Baldwin–LaFontaine government might lose the support of Upper Canada. The people's interpretation of responsible government, this commentator implied, went beyond its basic mechanics – the composition of cabinet out of elected representatives from the majority party in the assembly. Rather, at a deeper level it meant "the right of the people to self-government." "The people," in this case, meant the voters of Upper Canada, and the threat to their self-government was the political influence of their neighbours in Lower Canada. Upper Canadians, the article continued, "are determined not to be dictated to, nor hindered in their progression by the amalgamation in the Cabinet produced by the Union."[38]

The historian Paul Romney has elaborated upon this sectional-conscious interpretation of responsible government. As he explained, Upper Canada's reformers generally did not see the struggle for responsible government as completed in 1848. Rather, he identifies three distinct waves in a long-term struggle for that goal: 1) the initial struggle for the autonomy of Canada's executive council from Britain, granted to Baldwin and LaFontaine by Governor General Lord Elgin in 1848; 2) the autonomy of Upper Canada from Lower Canada, which reformers sought throughout the Confederation debates of the 1860s; and finally 3) the autonomy of the provinces from the federal government of Canada, taken up by Ontario Liberal Premier Oliver Mowat in the 1870s.[39] From this perspective, explains Romney, "responsible government [of 1848] is a big flop," which "merely replaces the domination of the Family Compact with that of Lower Canada."[40]

Further examination of the religious rhetoric employed during the controversy of spring and summer 1850 makes it clear that many Upper Canadian reformers believed the supposed failure of responsible government to be even deeper and more sinister than Romney acknowledged. Not only had Robert Baldwin violated the sectional-conscious understanding of the doctrine, as his reform detractors charged, but he had also violated, they maintained, a religion-conscious understanding of it. They noted that the main opponents of secularizing the clergy reserves were Catholics and high-church Anglicans. As James Lesslie observed, "The course taken upon the Reserve question strikes every one interested in it with astonishment. I fear there is collusion with the old enemy … to continue the ascendancy of the High Church faction."[41] Commentators were often explicit about their belief that Catholic clerics had orchestrated the government's action: "The people of this portion of the Province, who have for years contended against Church and State connexion, must now be *snubbed*, to please the Catholic Priests of the lower portion of the Province."[42] More than simply blaming sectional imbalance for the perceived failure of responsible government in 1850, Upper Canadian reformers often ascribed this failure to a rival religious faction supposedly hostile to their right to self-government.

The facts that Baldwin himself was an Anglican and LaFontaine a Catholic, previously excused by Dissenters reassured by the men's stated political beliefs, had in the summer of 1850 suddenly become crucial for Dissenters. One letter signed "Young Canada" declared that since Robert Baldwin was "a Puseyite in Theology," he was particularly susceptible to supporting the divine right of kings and "passive obedience" in politics and that the "sentiment of veneration is the ruling passion of Mr. Baldwin's mind."[43] Another commentator in the *North American* similarly declared that Baldwin "is a Puseyite determined to assist the Priests of Upper Canada to keep what they have got." Like many others, this critic drew a direct line from Baldwin's personal beliefs to his policies: "Out of a hundred protestant laymen … who believe the absurd dogma of apostolical succession, ninety-nine will be found to be thorough-paced Tories in politics."[44] In the nineteenth century, the rejection of apostolic succession was one of the defining beliefs that distinguished Dissenters from the Church of England. As the Methodist Rev. William McClure noted in a sermon in Toronto in 1850, "Jesus said to us 'by their fruits ye shall know them' – Puseyism and Popery, say no, but by unbroken succession from the Apostles you shall know them."[45] Thus, the invocation of this doctrine as inherently "Tory" was an implicit signal for Dissenters to be wary of Anglicans and Catholics in politics.

Much like the rhetoric about "judgments upon Babylon" in chapter 2, Dissenters used the latest religious controversy to reiterate their notions of liberty / tyranny through the biblical language of millennialism. In the legislative assembly, Malcolm Cameron argued: "Endowments are remnants of kingly and priestly tyranny, and despotism" and invoked the apocalyptic imagery of Revelation chapter 17, "There are many who may still wish to see the Church with harlot head yet reclining upon the corrupting bosom of the State."[46] After commenting on the government's apparent "treachery," James Lesslie concluded, "These things tell us of the flood of evils flowing from disobedience to God." Lesslie offered hope, however, for "the world's deliverance by the spread of intelligence and truth and the religion of Christ" and the "dawn of the Jubilee of the world Sabbath of rest in the millennium."[47] As much as ever, Baldwin's actions seemed to reinforce the Dissenters' association of their own beliefs with liberty, and their religious rivals' with the very worst kinds of despotism.

The reformers' religious rhetoric suggests the need to reorient the place of responsible government within the longer British tradition of

Protestant liberty.[48] Indeed, Baldwin's error was not only that he seemed to subject the will of Upper Canada to that of Lower Canada, but that by his actions Upper Canadians' very "rights and liberties are thus placed under the keeping of the Priests and Jesuits of Lower Canada!"[49] During the legislative debates on clergy reserves in June 1850, Malcolm Cameron suggested that the failure to secularize them represented a failure of the idea of responsible government as it had been pitched to Upper Canadians. As Cameron put it, Baldwin "seems to forget that his strongest and most successful argument in favor of responsible government was, that it would enable the people to obtain a just and equitable settlement of this question."[50] Such comments suggest that, as important as the principle of self-government was to the reformers, it was never about autonomy for its own sake, but was always part of a broader vision for "civil and religious liberty," complete with checks against the ever-looming threat of tyranny from Rome and Canterbury. Paul Romney brilliantly explained the reformers' insistence that sectional autonomy was a necessary component of responsible government, but it was fundamentally a religious / cultural rift that made these sectional disagreements possible (and so imperative to Canadians).

One year after the controversy, Upper Canadians sealed Robert Baldwin's "perdition." Upon his return from exile in 1849, William Lyon Mackenzie had swiftly joined his former reform colleague James Lesslie in critiquing the "slow-coach" Baldwin government.[51] In April 1851, he won the Haldimand by-election, and by May the old firebrand was standing across the aisle in the legislature and challenging Baldwin face to face.[52] It was he who tabled the fateful bill to abolish the Court of Chancery, and by arguing that the court had served as the basis for costly and unnecessary patronage appointments, he persuaded a majority of the Upper Canadian members to support the measure. Despite the bill's defeat, by thirty to thirty-four, thanks to Lower Canadian votes, Baldwin recognized the vote as Upper Canadian mutiny and resigned in July 1851, though staying on as an MLA.[53]

The final knock-out punch came with the general election in the winter of 1851–52, during which Baldwin sought to retain the Fourth District of York (or North York). Unfortunately for the incumbent, several Dissenting reformers made the clergy reserves the driving issue. In June 1851, the *Examiner* proposed that if "all these Reformers have not the moral courage to pass a bill to settle [the clergy reserves] 'at once and forever' they are utterly undeserving of the trust reposed in them, and should be every where rejected when they shall again appear before their constituents."[54] Likewise, speaking about "the all-absorbing question of religious equality," reform veteran John Rolph declared in October 1851: "*No man should enter the new Assembly unpledged upon this subject.*"[55] Robert Baldwin was the top casualty of the Dissenters' mobilization. A Quaker farmer named Joseph Hartman, one of the rising wave of Clear Grits, challenged him for his seat.[56] On 19 December 1851, the voters chose Hartman with 664 votes, leaving the sitting member with only 142.[57]

Baldwin's fall from favour with his constituents has been overlooked or misinterpreted in some recent studies. John Ralston Saul's dual biography of Baldwin and LaFontaine, for example, overstated the strength of their coalition in 1851 and even suggested that Baldwin's departure had nothing to do with "political reasons." Rather, Saul insisted that his coalition was "perfectly workable" and that the "Upper Canadian fracture was reparable."[58] He further dismissed the defeat in Fourth York, saying that Baldwin "had seemed to lose his senses, running in the December 1851 election for no particular reason, without bothering to campaign."[59] This ignores the mounting discontent among Upper Canadian Dissenters, largely over religiously charged issues such as the clergy reserves and public education. Saul's assertion that the bicultural coalition was "perfectly workable" disregards the fact that by 1851 many Upper Canadians believed they had been sold out to Lower Canada in order to preserve that coalition. Michael Cross's biography of Baldwin, however, acknowledged the chronic disjuncture between Baldwin and his constituents, which Cross attributed to a rural–urban division.[60] Building on his observations, this current study adds the religious dimension; simply put, Baldwin had taken for granted the support of Protestant Dissenters and had underestimated how much issues like the clergy reserves mattered to them.

In the history of the united province's religious–cultural divisions, the collapse of Baldwin's coalition in 1851 plays a crucial part. The episode revealed not only the precariousness of cross-sectional political coalitions, which would come to characterize the later union period, but foreshadowed the threat to break up the united province itself along religious and cultural lines. As a commentator in the *North American* wrote on the clergy reserves in May 1850, "Should it turn out that the

French portion of the Government stand in the way, then we predict an approaching dissolution of the Union."[61] After only four years at the helm, the ruling party had rejected its once-popular leader and fractured due to religion-based sectional discontent. Baldwin's coalition of French Catholics and English Dissenters was "workable" only in so far as both sides were able to see their demands met, but when he was forced to choose between incompatible demands (for example, funding for churches and no funding) its inherent instability became all too apparent.

Church–state relations were paramount for Upper Canadian liberals in the 1851 election. George Emery called religious establishment "the major issue" of the campaign, noting that Dissenting Protestants (Baptists, Congregationalists, Methodist Episcopals, Presbyterians, and Quakers) were most likely to support reform candidates.[62] Reformers such as George Brown campaigned heavily on church–state issues like the clergy reserves and made direct appeals to evangelical Dissenters. Speaking at St Lawrence Hall in Toronto in July 1851, Brown declared that state support for churches was "injurious to the cause of Christ." He perceived a natural relationship between the evangelical "religion of the heart" and separation of church and state, as contrasted with the "priestcraft" that he believed stemmed directly from church establishments: "Tyranny, robbery, and injustice in every shape … have been the fruits of state–churchism in every age; when I observe the degenerating effect which it has ever had on the purity and simplicity of the gospel of Christ, turning men's minds from its great truths, as a religion of the heart, to the mere outward tinsel, to the forms and ceremonies on which priestcraft flourishes."[63] Brown further appealed to the Dissenters' persecution narrative (see chapter 2): "If there never had been any connection between church and state, there never could have been persecution for conscience sake."[64] In particular, he raised the possibility of state-enforced Catholicism in Canada if the establishment principle was carried to its logical conclusion, suggesting that it "would entitle them, nay, make it their duty, to force it down the throats of the others according to the majority of each country … It is clear that [official religion] in Canada would be Roman Catholicism."[65] When Brown triumphed in Kent, a dinner was held in his honour at Port Sarnia, attended reportedly by the local clergymen of several Dissenting denominations (including Congregationalist, Free Church of Scotland,

and Methodist). A banner in the dining hall read: "Reform triumphant over priestcraft! Hurrah for Brown and equal rights!"[66] From the campaign speeches to the victory party, there was no mistaking the fact that a victory for Brown was a victory for Protestant Dissent.

When election results started to emerge in late December 1851, the moderate reformers of Upper Canada, who now rallied around Francis Hincks, were reduced to only eighteen seats of forty-two for the section.[67] Dissenters who had been critical of Baldwin and Hincks during the campaign saw the outcome as a rejection of the "combinationists" who had sold them out on church–state matters.[68] One of Brown's supporters, a young stonemason-turned-politician Alexander Mackenzie, in his upstart *Lambton Shield* newspaper, called the results "truly edifying": "We have seen men at one time high in station, and in whom the greatest confidence was placed by their former adherents, made to kiss the very dust by the all potent influence of public opinion."[69] Upper Canadians also turned their democratic wrath on Commissioner of Crown Lands James Hervey Price, who ended up splitting the vote with other reform candidates and allowing the conservative candidate to win, 648 to 321.[70] Francis Hincks managed to escape the Dissenters' revenge because in Oxford County he faced only a pro-establishment Tory named John George Vansittart. Thus, as George Emery found from poll-book data for Oxford County, the Dissenters apparently preferred a candidate who at least gave lip-service to voluntarism (Hincks) over a high-church Anglican.[71] Despite the loss for many Hincksites, their leader formed government by joining his eighteen seats with Augustin-Norbert Morin's thirty *rouges* from Lower Canada. The Dissenters had flexed their muscles, but a greater battle for the soul of Canadian liberalism had only begun.

"High Protestant Ground": George Brown's Vision for the Liberal Party

Due primarily to disillusionment with the Baldwin–LaFontaine government, the Upper Canada reformers were very much divided during and after the 1851 campaign. The fact that they still controlled the legislature under Francis Hincks's leadership did not diminish the threat of party schism any more than it had under Baldwin. Indeed, the informal division had already lost them seats in 1851,[72] and they knew that more losses loomed if they did not restore party unity. Strategically, some worried that their division could cost them support from coalition partners in Lower Canada. Reformer William McDougall noted in a private letter: "The Tories have been working all sorts of humiliating overtures ... to them [Lower Canadians]. They thought they had the [Catholic] clergy in their mouth, but with the blessing of God we will disappoint them." McDougall suggested that reformers must "let bygones be bygones ... especially in regards to the Reserves."[73]

As would be expected, several prominent Upper Canadian reformers were not willing to do that. In fact, George Brown withdrew the *Globe*'s support for the reform ministry when Hincks decided to endorse Catholic separate schools in Upper Canada.[74] Brown had previously condemned the like-minded Clear Grits as radicals and had run (and lost) as a Baldwinite in the Haldimand by-election in spring 1851,[75] before winning his seat in Kent in the general election later that year. However, once he was sure that the moderates offered little if nothing to the voluntarist cause, he took up the opposition banner with a vengeance. By the autumn of 1851, he and his *Globe* were warning more frequently and explicitly about "Popish influence" in both Canada and Britain and called on all Protestants to do the same: "Most contemptible is that Protestant, who, to gain an election, will succumb to that morbid terror of speaking freely on Roman Catholic claims." Rather than remaining silent for strategic reasons, Brown declared, "there is urgent need for such language being boldly and frequently employed." He recommended taking what he called the "high Protestant ground, in breaking with the French Canadians" on anti-state-church principles.[76] In the coming years, he would further develop a vision for the colony, and ultimately refashion the Upper Canada reform party, based on this uncompromising and unapologetic sense of "high Protestant ground."

Other reformers, of course, recoiled at what they perceived to be Brown's divisive approach that risked driving away Catholics. William McDougall was one of them who disagreed with Brown's assertiveness on religious matters. McDougall was the Clear Grit editor of the *North American* who made an arrangement with Francis Hincks in 1851 to publicly support his government in exchange for Grit representation in the cabinet.[77] Whereas the *Globe* applauded the London reform convention's resolution to abolish separate religious schools, the *North American* warned that this position was "driving the Catholics away from the polls" and "would lead inevitably to the breaking up of the party."[78] The following year, the *North American* continued to lambaste the rival *Globe*'s stance, which "basely seeks to inflame Protestant bigotry, and to cast odium and insult upon the Catholic parent, his Bishop and his faith!"[79] George Brown's high-profile defection over religious questions ultimately helped to make inter-religious relations the defining difference between the Hincksites and non-ministerial reformers.

The reformers' disagreements about religion also touched on a wider ideological battle over the future of liberalism in Canada. With their fundamental disagreements about how best to ensure freedom of religion and freedom of speech, and about whether or not the bicultural united province was workable, Brownites and Hincksites' feud points to a deeper soul-searching in Canadian liberal thought. As Jeffrey McNairn has suggested, historians should examine the arguments and debates among nineteenth-century liberals in order to elaborate a "more pluralized view of liberalism."[80] Though often prompted by practical concerns about party strategy, the divisions also related to fundamental questions about the application of liberal principles in a bicultural society.

Most indicative of this profound divide is the reformers' response to the Gavazzi Riots of 1853. During the public appearance at a Congregationalist church in Montreal by controversial ex-Catholic speaker Alessandro Gavazzi, a former monk and Italian nationalist, a Catholic protest outside turned violent. Accounts vary as to which side initiated violence, but witnesses reported a wide array of carnage from rocks bombarding the church building to a man firing shots from the church doors into the crowd. Both sides ultimately participated in the violence before the 26th Regiment of Foot (Cameronians) intervened on the orders of Montreal's mayor. In the end, ten men died and several more suffered injuries, with victims on both sides.[81]

For some Protestant liberals, the sole blame for the riots lay with Catholic intolerance, and the incident illustrated the threat it posed to freedom of speech. Just days before the event, Gavazzi was met by aggressive protesters in Quebec City as well, about which the *Globe* commented, "This outrage will warn Protestants every where of giving countenance to Rome … Where they have the majority, they [end up] forbidding free discussion."[82] Ironically, free speech in matters of religion was also a major theme of Gavazzi's speech in Montreal. He expressed his gratitude that Canada was "a true British country, – that is to say … a free country," and later contrasted the freedom he saw in the British Empire with the Catholic nations of Italy, Austria, and France. Whereas Protestant-majority England allowed the Irish Catholic priest D.W. Cahill to freely "speak against Protestantism," for example, the former monk declared that in Catholic countries the response to criticism was too often to "endeavor to put down free speech with stones and sticks."[83]

Gavazzi used these examples to advocate a principle that captured the liberal sentiments of many Upper Canadian reformers. Objectionable speech, he said, should be met with counter-speech rather than violence: "If I advance anything wrong in my lectures, discuss it freely or refute it if you can, but confine yourselves to arguments, and let there be no mobs and riots, which furnish the best proof in your Canada of your intolerance, and the best proof that you are ruled by Jesuits and priests." Not long after he made this statement, a crescendo of noise emerged from the protesters outside who were apparently "attempting to break into the church." Following several minutes of confusion, a young man was reportedly carried into the building with a bloody head wound after having confronted the crowd outside. When he was finally able to resume his speech, Gavazzi declared that this violent disturbance supported his argument about "the intolerance of the popish system."[84]

In the days and weeks after the riot, commentaries from Protestant liberals offered their support for Gavazzi's conclusions about Catholic intolerance, with one unnamed man at a town hall in Bowmanville suggesting, for example: "The murders at Montreal are a fair specimen what Protestants may expect from the votaries of Rome, should they ever gain the ascendancy over us."[85] For Brown and his like-minded supporters, and indeed for Gavazzi himself, the Montreal riots were simply the latest in a mounting pile of evidence of Catholicism's incompatibility with liberal values like freedom of speech.

Supporters of Francis Hincks, in contrast, blamed the Gavazzi Riots on the Protestants for abusing free speech. One editorial in the official Hincksite newspaper the *North American* reasoned that all societies have limits on free speech, such as to prohibit slander, and that therefore it was sometimes necessary to restrict offensive speech: "The law which *restrains* the freedom of speech to such limits as the public safety demands, is a good law … *No man has a 'right' to slander* his neighbor." Indeed, the writer specifically condemned George Brown for using his speech "to fan into a blaze the infernal embers of religious bigotry, and to array one million of the people of this Province against the other million in deadly strife!"[86] Orangeville contributor J.C. condemned the riot, but emphasized the speaker's error in "goading them [protesters] on to scenes of violence": "We think it is highly imprudent, if not morally wrong for such men as ex-Monk Gavazzi to lecture on the evils of Rome among a Roman Catholic population."[87] Here we see both Brownites and Hincksites claiming the liberal mantle of "tolerance" and charging their opponents with acting out of "intolerance" and "bigotry." But whereas Brown and Gavazzi ascribed intolerance to those Catholics who sought to use violence to shut down a public speech, the Hincksites ascribed it to the speaker himself, whom they blamed for provoking the protesters.

Moving beyond emotionally charged words like "bigotry" and "intolerance," we can parse out a deeper pattern of liberal thought behind each side's approach. Just as Michel Ducharme distinguished between "modern" and "republican" liberty to assess 1830s' liberalism,[88] this analysis continues to contrast the Brownites' "Protestant liberty" and the Hincksites' "neutral liberty." For the Brownites, the Gavazzi Riots confirmed their longstanding belief that true freedom was possible only in a Protestant society governed by Protestant principles. This perspective carried on from the logic of the reform party's earlier generation, which spoke of the "free spirit of Christianity," as explored in chapters 1 and 2. However, rather than this Protestant-specific rhetoric waning over the decades, as scholars such as Jeffrey McNairn have proposed,[89] it actually became more defined and more explicit by the 1850s. As this chapter seeks to demonstrate, this Protestant notion of liberty competed with neutral liberty for dominance of the Liberal party throughout the later union period and ultimately pushed the party to support the dissolution of the union.

The idea of Protestant liberty, as it developed in the 1850s, continued to include religious freedom for all denominations (including Catholics), but was wary lest any one of them become too powerful. Proponents were concerned especially that some denominations – those deemed "popish," which included some establishment-friendly versions of Protestantism – historically sought after dominance in society, and therefore could not be trusted. George Brown made this point explicitly in an editorial in 1852, "Catholicism is utterly opposed to the free institutions which we have chosen and those which we will alone endure. With all the exertions of the hierarchy, all their subtlety and wiles, they cannot suit themselves to the freedom of thought, the result of democratic institutions. As liberty advances they must decline."[90] Thus, although proponents of Protestant liberty were the most vocal advocates for the separation of church and state, their voluntarist vision did not presuppose a societal blindness towards religion. Indeed, as touched on in chapters 1 and 2, even the logic of voluntarism in Upper Canada was designed to advance the culture of Protestant Dissent. Brown himself drew on Dissenting concepts when he advocated the separation of church and state, saying in 1851 that every man "who seeks peace and the advancement of Christ's cause" ought to oppose the clergy reserves.[91] The *Examiner*, likewise, affirmed the theologically Dissenting basis of its political positions. Coming to Brown's defence for his use of the phrase "high Protestant ground," the journal suggested that the *North American*'s support for the supposedly establishment-friendly Hincks–Morin coalition was unbiblical: "We advise our friend of the *North American* to get a little better 'posted up' in his theology, and he will be less liable to blunder in his application of moral and religious principles to political duty."[92] The voluntarists' embrace of Protestant liberty made them the loudest advocates for the separation of church and state institutions, which actually presupposed a consciously Protestant society.

Despite prescribing voluntarism and the strict separation of the state from religious *institutions*, Protestant liberty demanded that a free society affirm Protestant *culture* in several ways. For example, the compatibility of liberal thought with both temperance and Sabbatarianism illustrates liberals' belief in using the state to reinforce their cultural and religious values.[93] Including the Bible in public schools was more controversial, with some voluntarists advocating the removal of all religion to avoid favouring any one interpretation, while others saw biblical instruction as necessary to prevent "godlessness."[94] Alessandro Gavazzi urged Protestants in Montreal, "The Bible is the natural food of your children ... Consent not to allow the Roman Catholics to take the Bible from your schools."[95] Indeed, many Dissenters believed in integrating faith with civic duties. One article in the *Examiner* suggested that Christians should engage with "politics within the circle of God's truth, and calmly [survey] them under the light from heaven," concluding that every participant in every level of government ought to submit all of their "notions of political right, privilege, power, and duty … to the test of divine revelation."[96] Thus Protestants often pitched their liberal advocacy of the separation of church and state as part of a holistic vision in which their beliefs and values would still provide the basis of a free society.

Such a Protestant-conscious vision, however, was simply not practical for work in the united legislature, and thus the competing idea of neutral liberty became a prominent strain in Upper Canadian liberalism by the 1850s. What had started as a practical necessity, to find common ground between reformers in the two Canadas, had become a defining feature of both the Baldwin–LaFontaine and the Hincks–Morin governments. This version of liberalism advocated a society that would be accommodating to differences in religious and cultural identity, and anticipated the gradual disappearance of inter-religious conflict through increased mutual understanding and compromises. As co-premier Augustin-Norbert Morin said in a speech in Waterloo in 1853, "It was impossible with so many different races of people in the country, that any ministry could get along unless mutual concessions were made."[97] In practical terms, for Upper Canadians such compromises meant abandoning the basic premise of voluntarism and allowing guarantees for state-funded Catholic schools. William McDougall's *North American* embraced such compromises as necessary to help counter the "bigotry" of the Brownites. Commenting on the alleged Protestant indoctrination of Catholic children in a public school in Georgetown, one article noted, "The conduct of such intolerant bigots as those of Georgetown (assuming that they acted as alleged) and that of their colleague the *Globe,* makes us almost despair of working for our Common School system successfully."[98] Rather than ascribing inter-religious conflict to enduring cultural differences between Catholics and Protestants, as Brown did, proponents of neutral liberty downplayed those differences and blamed intolerant individuals who enflamed otherwise-minimal disagreements.

In lieu of a common religious culture, the Hincksite proponents of neutral liberty found common ground in economic concerns such as free trade and railway projects. The Hincks–Morin government achieved two major feats on this front: talks with the United States regarding a trade agreement, which led to the Reciprocity Treaty of 1854, and Hincks reaching out to English capitalists to finance the Grand Trunk Railway between Toronto and Montreal.[99] The cabinet pitched itself as the champion of economic progress, as exemplified by an article in the *North American* that celebrated "a Government which seeks to advance their happiness and prosperity by Railroads, Canals, and other improvements."[100] Hincks's embrace of neutral liberty prevented him from promising a Protestant society with Protestant values, but it did allow him to promise that railways "will double the value of your property."[101]

Although Brown would later attract a reputation (unjustly) for succumbing to "the language of crass economic advantage,"[102] in the 1850s he was actually highly critical of the government for being too materialistic. In 1854, he condemned Hincks and his would-be conservative allies, who, he said, had "bowed the knee to the Baal of the Grand Trunk."[103] So convinced was he of Hincks's prostration to "Mammon" that after Hincks stepped down as co-premier in 1854, Brown led a parliamentary inquiry investigating him on charges of corruption. Although the committee ultimately concluded that he was not guilty, his fierce advocacy for railway interests and his profiting from his own railway investments always made him highly suspect in Brown's eyes.[104] The concern that materialism would corrupt the liberal cause built on earlier criticisms of Baldwin's government, which, as we saw above, accused it of selling out the religious interests of Protestant Upper Canada for the sake of material gain. As the poet Rusticus said of Baldwin, "All nobler motives must subserve his greed / He fawns to all, and sanctions every creed … Denounce materialism while you may / But be consistent where you draw your pay."[105] While Dissenting liberals had always generally been supportive of public works and increased trade, proponents of Protestant liberty believed that Hincks had prioritized such issues at the risk of sacrificing the spiritual or moral integrity of the government.

For Brownites, their disappointment with the Hincks–Morin ministry forced them to rethink their relationship with Catholics in the legislature. Reporting on a town-hall meeting in Bowmanville to address the Gavazzi Riots, the *Globe* noted that some attendees expressed their "disgust and contempt at the conduct of those men (Hincks, Rolph, and their allies from Upper Canada) who basely betrayed their constituents, and in the most barefaced manner lent their influence to build up popery."[106] Months after the conflict, Brown continued to invoke the disturbances to support a new political realignment based on religion, "a union of Protestants, in defence of their rights and liberties."[107] The suggestion was a bold (if politically unlikely) alternative to the ruling Hincks–Morin coalition, a call for a new grouping of reformers and conservatives based on a shared sense of Protestant identity rather than on the historic political divisions of reform / tory.

The ascendant Hincksite reformers seized on Brownite reaction to the Gavazzi affair to present their challengers not only as bigots but as secret tory sympathizers. One month after the riots, the government held a large campaign-style dinner in Waterloo, and the elephant in the room was what one speaker termed "the Brown apostasy." The venue was adorned with several large banners, including one with the caption "The Opposition of 1853," which featured a cartoon of George Brown swimming with a bundle of *Globe* newspapers, while conservative John A. Macdonald stood on a sinking ship, tossing him a rope. At the event, several speakers lambasted the Brownites for causing an unnecessary division. For example, Clear Grit reform MLA David Christie (Wentworth) warned that if Brown succeeded in "[waking] up the Protestant feeling in Upper Canada," the result would be "a breach between the Upper and Lower Canadian Reformers." Hincks himself alluded to the Brownite schism more indirectly: "On one of your beautiful flags I observed the motto 'Union is strength,' and there never was a time when the sentiment was more applicable to the reform party than the present." Mr Drummond (possibly Lewis Drummond, attorney-general for Canada East) condemned Brown's rhetoric about "Lower Canadian tyranny" and suggested that their neighbours, though a "not so progressive people," "would profit by the example of the Upper Canadians, and that all prejudice would soon vanish." Overall, the evening's messages seemed to be: remain united under the Hincksite banner, refrain from upsetting Catholics, and ignore the petty dissensions from Brown and company.[108]

Despite this show of unity and others around the province, the government was in danger from a Clear Grit upset in Upper Canada. In private, even some of Hincks's own supporters expressed doubts about its future. For example, in February 1853 William McDougall wrote to his Clear Grit colleague Charles Clarke about his growing cynicism towards Hincks and deep concerns about the coalition. He speculated that Hincks was planning lucrative work in the private sector if he failed in the upcoming election, and worried that the Brownites would drive people away from "a sound rational, progressive Reform party." But most revealing, despite publicly condemning Brown's religious prejudices, McDougall confided that he was concerned about the role of Catholic leaders in the Hincks–Morin team: "I am no bigot but I dread the influence of Catholic principles and priestly intrigues in our civil affairs." The only way out, he supposed, was to fight for "a separate legislature for U. Canada, & *then* we may triumph. The Catholic element rules & will rule while the present Union lasts."[109] For all of the Hincksites' public disavowals of bigotry, the provincial election of 1854 would show that more Upper Canadian reformers agreed with George Brown than some of them cared to admit.

"The Destiny of the Province": Protestant Liberty v. the Union of the Canadas

Over the next few years, a realignment of political parties and an increase in religion-based sectional tension would eventually lead the Upper Canadian reformers to support dissolving the legislative union of the Canadas. In the 1854 election, the Hincksite reformers suffered major losses in Upper Canada to an emergent alliance of Clear Grits, Brownites, and anti-establishment conservatives. The main issues had cut across traditional party lines, and several Upper Canadian conservatives even pledged to secularize the clergy reserves. As the conservative *Daily Leader* put it, "The old party names, it seems, no longer serve to mark the political distinctions created by the recent election."[110] The subsequent backroom dealing between Hincksites and Allan MacNab's conservatives resulted in a conservative-led MacNab–Morin–Hincks coalition that ultimately restructured Canada's political parties. On the conservative side, the party absorbed the Hincksite element of the liberal reform movement, which was open to some secularization but favoured compromise across sectional–religious lines and actively promoted railways.[111] On the reform side, the realignment ultimately paved the way for George Brown and the Clear Grits to take over what was left of the reform party and fashion it in their own image: emphasizing the sectional interests of Upper Canada, heralding a vision of Protestant liberty, and increasingly in favour of dissolving the union. By the 1857 election, these respective coalitions had more or less solidified into recognizable parties, with Brown and John Sandfield Macdonald (who went by "Sandfield") leading the opposition Reformers against the MacNab-led Liberal-Conservatives.[112]

Religion propelled this realignment. Some historians such as George Emery have suggested that the reconfiguration was about Hincksite coalitionists versus Brownite partyists, who differed on reform involvement in coalitions.[113] However, as Brown had made clear over the preceding year, he was quite willing to work with conservatives if they agreed on a set of key church–state issues. Indeed, he had publicly supported anti-establishment conservatives who opposed Hincks, and had even written to conservative John A. Macdonald after the election to remind him that independent reformers looked to him as an ally on church–state issues.[114] Further, the terms of MacNab's coalition with Hincks and Morin included secularizing the clergy reserves.[115] MacNab could make this reversal only because many Upper Canadian conservatives had taken up the position in 1853,[116] largely in response to George Brown's agitation for a cross-party Protestant coalition. Although Brown and his supporters were ultimately shut out of the coalition that emerged in September 1854, his agitation on church–state questions helped make the coalition possible.

As with most election campaigns in Upper Canada, 1854's began with urgent reminders for reformers to vote along religious lines. As the *Examiner* commented, "The religious questions should every where be held paramount in all others, for by its righteous settlement we prepare the way for a social union and co-operation on great public questions of which now we have little conception."[117] The following week, the paper escalated its rhetoric about Hincks's betrayal of the voluntarist cause, referring to the biblical traitor Judas by calling Hincks's team a "Cabinet of Iscariots."[118] When the election results began to roll out in August 1854, the Brownite reformers and their allies were ecstatic: out of Upper Canada's sixty-five seats (of now 130, evenly split between the two sections), the *Globe* reported Independent Reformers (Brownites) at twenty-nine, about five of them previously conservatives. By contrast, the conservatives totalled fifteen, and the Hincksite ministerialists only twelve.[119]

Despite this victory, it was still not entirely clear what kind of new government would emerge. In the absence of a clear majority across the united province, some sort of coalition would be necessary. Like other Dissenters, James Lesslie had hoped for a religion-based coalition: "Our old lines of political designation will also be removed, and combinations of a moral or political character will be formed."[120] George Brown had hoped to form an alliance with conservatives and even to support a conservative-led coalition as long as it prioritized ending the clergy reserves and separate schools.[121] However, such was not to be the case. Conservative Allan MacNab (Hamilton) privately reached out to Hincks's old Lower Canadian ally Augustin-Norbert Morin and offered to work with him. When Morin confided the offer to Hincks, the two decided to support a conservative-led ministry in exchange for continued representation in cabinet.[122]

For Brownite reformers coming off a groundbreaking victory against Hincks, it was devastating to be outmanoeuvred by his tiny rump of Upper Canadian members. The *Examiner* called it "one of the boldest frauds yet palmed upon the country by Mr. Hincks."[123] Again, it seemed the will of Upper Canadians would be overturned by "Roman Catholic votes to advance High-church schemes … [to] serve the temporary purposes of faction."[124] Not for the first time this decade, rumblings about the unfair legislative union animated the Upper Canadian reformers. One poem, found in James Lesslie's personal scrapbook and dated June 1856, condemned Hincks in colourful terms as a "whited tomb" and a "traitor to Reform" who had allowed himself to "shame thy race" by turning his support to a Lower Canadian coalition: "Condemned by Western Votes – what then? / Thou left thy bench within the den; / Condemned still more – yet back again."[125] The reformers' concerns grew when in early 1855 reformer Joseph Cauchon (Montmorency), known for his close relationship with ultramontane clerics, joined the new cabinet. In expressing concern, the *Examiner* clarified that it was not because he was Roman Catholic, but because he was "the most bigoted and intolerant of that class." Still, the article reminded readers, "So long as the Provinces are united, Roman Catholics must necessarily take part in the administration."[126]

As a condition of the unlikely alliance, the new government proposed a bill to secularize the clergy reserves. Two years after James Hervey Price asked Westminster to grant Canada permission to do exactly that, the British House of Commons had so agreed in March 1853.[127] Still, Hincks had refused to act on it, and eventually postponed the decision until after the 1854 election.[128] MacNab's conservative executive council modified Price's proposals. Whereas reformers had always wanted funds from the sale to go towards common schools, the government offered the proceeds to the municipalities. Also, MacNab's secularization bill included a "commutation clause," a massive lump-sum payment to churches to use at their own discretion.[129] Although the longstanding issue would now finally be put to rest, the achievement was bittersweet for reformers and Dissenters.

Almost immediately after the clergy reserves ended, reformers faced church–state advances on another front: separate schools. Starting in 1843, Upper Canada had allowed separate Catholic schools, which had in 1853 become entitled to a grant from the province to cover costs, in addition to their ability to collect fees from their own members. In May 1855, Toronto's Catholic Bishop Charbonnel issued a request to strengthen the existing system by making it easier to form a new school (only ten students required to receive public funds) and by exempting supporters from the common-school tax. The government obliged, and carried the bill with Lower Canadian votes at a time when many Upper Canadians were away from the assembly.[130]

As would be expected, the new separate-schools measure, and the way it was passed, led to renewed calls for Protestants to unite against Catholic church–state initiatives. If only Protestants would vote together in their own interests, reasoned George Brown, they would be able to deflect such measures: Charbonnel's "very boldness is alarming to all Protestants, and when they are alarmed and banded together as his supporters are, his power is over." The fact that Catholics were a minority using external power to impose their will there made it seem as though they were circumventing the will of the people. Charbonnel, said Brown, "is supported by a power altogether apart from Upper Canada." Thus, Protestants had to organize collectively and reassert their jurisdiction in this area, and only then, Brown said, "shall we save this fine province from becoming the handmaid of Rome."[131] In another article, he decried the bishop as a "foreign priest" who threatened to impose external authority on the colony and make it "a mere Province of Rome."[132] This rhetoric speaks to Paul Romney's point about the perceived failure of responsible government in Upper Canada, a concern that would continue to grow.

Also worrying Dissenters was the reported plan for large-scale Catholic immigration from the United States. In 1855, the Irish Catholic activist Thomas D'Arcy McGee, then an American national, visited Canada to plan a colonization scheme to move hundreds of Irish Catholics to the Owen Sound area. Although lack of funds eventually killed the project, the idea attracted much interest and was discussed at a convention in Buffalo, New York, in February 1856.[133] In response, thousands of Protestants met at St Lawrence Hall in Toronto to condemn the plan. A Mr John Holland proposed that, although it was "an unquestioned right" for *individuals* of any denomination to immigrate to Canada, larger-scale, organized migration was different: "When it became a question of whether masses of a particular description banded together under a foreign power, a foreign religious power, should be brought over here … and when it is said an application will be made to the Legislature for the grant of public money or a grant of public lands to locate them upon, it then became a legitimate object of enquiry for this meeting, whether such a scheme was for the benefit of the Province." Speakers claimed that Catholics were prone to higher rates of crime and poverty. One commented that God was beginning to remove his favour from the British Empire because Britain had admitted Catholics into the House of Commons. One Mr Johnstone invoked Protestant liberty by suggesting that, although Protestant countries like Canada and Britain had offered Catholics religious freedom, "the Catholic hierarchy would settle for nothing less than conquest: They were not satisfied with equality … The old Scarlet Lady is mounted on a beast – she won't walk a foot – she wants superiority – equality will not do for her."[134] Whatever their particular concern, all speakers took for granted that Upper Canada was a free British Protestant colony and that large-scale Catholic immigration would fundamentally alter that reality.

The meeting also raised the topic of cooperation between Dissenters and the Church of England, acknowledged to be uncomfortable yet necessary under the circumstances. One speaker likened the present situation to Irish Protestant divisions in the seventeenth century. Whereas Presbyterians and Episcopalians preferred to "have nothing to do with" each other, he said, both sides came together to fight Catholic forces during the Siege of Derry in 1689: "All divisions [among

Protestants] would be at an end ... When the cry was, Popery is at the gate, there was raised the shout by one and all – 'No surrender.'"[135] Similarly, as has been evident throughout this chapter, politicians such as George Brown who sought to challenge the church–state initiatives of Roman Catholics in the 1850s tended to appeal to voters as *Protestants*, rather than as Dissenters as previous generations of reformers had done. Brown and other liberal leaders would continue this Anglican-inclusive appeal to Protestant identity in subsequent decades, suggesting that the bitter antagonism of Dissenters versus Anglicans in Upper Canadian politics had begun to decline after the settling of the clergy reserves in 1854.[136]

Despite this new will to cooperation, many Dissenters remained skeptical about their new Anglican allies. For example, an *Examiner* article in July 1854 warned that the leaders of "the Romish and Anglican Churches have formed a league, offensive and defensive, against the Voluntaries of Canada."[137] Indeed, according to George Emery, in some parts of Upper Canada most Anglicans still voted tory and most Dissenters still voted reform well into the 1870s.[138] What had changed in the 1850s was not their cultural convergence, as historians such as William Westfall have suggested,[139] but the willingness of some to set those differences aside to challenge "Popery." Still, liberal reformers' new reaching out to Anglicans as a group, unthinkable under Mackenzie in the 1830s,[140] reveals the extent to which Protestant–Catholic tension had replaced Dissent–Anglican tension.

The 1857 election tested the proposed reform alliance of Protestants. Rather than appealing to Protestant interests as he had in 1853–54, however, Brown invoked sectional interests. After a decade of feeling at the mercy of Lower Canadian votes and recently losing power despite a plurality of Upper Canadian seats, reformers considered sectional power ripe for public discussion. "Representation by population" thus became the latest plan to improve Upper Canada's situation in the united legislature. Such a scheme would scrap equal representation – sixty-five seats per section – and allocate seats by population (Upper Canada's had moved ahead of Lower Canada's in the early 1850s). In the lead-up to the 1857 election, Brown published a list of Upper Canadians who had voted against "rep by pop" when he had previously put it forward in the legislature, and declared, "We leave this whole matter in the hands of the Electors of Upper Canada … The decision at the Polls will show whether there is a spark of self-respect left in our country!"[141]

That is not to say that explicit appeals to Protestantism were absent. Indeed, George Brown's election rally at Toronto's St Lawrence Hall featured some of the speakers from the Irish Protestant anti-immigration meeting there the previous year. The aforementioned Mr Holland, for example, offered his enthusiastic support for Brown and outlined the stakes: "In Canada there were two antagonistic principles. There was the priest power on the one side trying to make encroachments upon the rights of the people of Upper Canada, and on the other side there were the Protestants, contending for *equal* rights, and nothing more." "Rep by pop" mattered for Protestants: "Either they must have Representation by Population … or a separation of Upper from Lower Canada ... The Protestants of Upper Canada were determined they would not submit to be ridden over by the Papists of the Lower Province." Holland concluded, "Let us show ourselves to be Protestants, and put Geo. Brown into Parliament – he who has proved himself to be the very Havelock of Protestantism." Brown explained that he did not see the political division as strictly sectarian, suggesting (without providing evidence) that "a great many of the Lower Canadian Roman Catholics were heartily with us."[142] Still, based on his recent rhetoric, one could understand Holland's impression.

The reform platform in 1857 contained additional policy proposals that appealed to Protestants. First, the abolition of separate schools was still central. Brown again rebuked the "abject submission of the present Ministry to the Roman Hierarchy on the school question" and condemned "the teaching of Romanism … as a part of the educational system."[143] Second, though not widely promoted, the platform promoted laws about Sabbath observance. Back in 1854, the conservative *Daily Leader* had denounced a "clear grit" Sabbatarian bill.[144] Now, the *Globe* reprinted the Methodists' calls to "abolish Sabbath labour" in the public service.[145] Finally, Brown promised to vote to incorporate the conservative-leaning Orange Order.[146] The strategy seemed to work: Cecil Houston and William Smyth have suggested that as many as half of Toronto's Orangemen voted for Brown's party, against the order's official endorsement of conservative candidates.[147] Although the liberal reform party was non-denominational, and a prominent leader was the

Catholic John Sandfield Macdonald,[148] appeals to Protestant identity and values continued to inform its 1857 strategy.

The appearance of reform unity in 1857 contrasted with the veritable civil war of the 1854 election, and this united front was aided by Brown's control of much of the province's reform press. He had bought out two rival reform newspapers, James Lesslie's *Examiner* and William McDougall's *North American*, in the first half of 1855. His already dominant *Globe* was now unrivalled in distribution among reform-leaning papers. Many of the Clear Grits still disagreed with him over democratic reforms, such as vote by ballot and election of the governor general. Still, with Brown's sway in the reform press, the emerging, revised liberal party was able to avoid the public infighting that he himself had helped to fuel from 1851 to 1855.[149]

Much as in 1854, the results in 1857 at first looked like a Brownite triumph, but were soon complicated by coalition talks. The Upper Canadian reformers under Brown had increased their seat count to thirty-nine, whereas the Liberal-Conservative ministerialists had only twenty-two. In Lower Canada, ministerialists took thirty-six seats, and Dorion's liberal *rouges* nineteen.[150] Apart from a handful of independents, the two rival groupings – reform and *rouges* v. Tories and *bleus* – each totalled fifty-eight seats. As the Liberal-Conservatives were the incumbents, Governor General Edmund Head invited them to continue with a narrow majority under Premier John A. Macdonald. However, in late July 1858 the opposition proposed to deny Queen Victoria's request to make Ottawa the permanent seat of government. Seeing this motion as an insult to the Queen, several ministers resigned in protest, and Macdonald faced a crisis of confidence. Head offered Brown the opportunity to form government on condition that he put together a cabinet from both sections of the province.[151]

Fast-paced, gestalt-shifting events ensued. Brown met with Dorion to agree quickly on a set of policies and to appoint their cabinet, and he was sworn in as premier on 2 August 1858. However, after only two days in office and minus his new ministers, who had to resign and seek re-election, he now faced a vote of non-confidence, stealthily arranged by John A. Macdonald's Liberal-Conservatives. The new premier was vastly outnumbered, seventy-one to thirty-one (in a 130-seat legislature), and was promptly defeated. Although he advised Head to dissolve the legislature and initiate another election, the viceroy refused and again invited the Liberal-Conservatives to form government.[152] Macdonald reappointed his cabinet members to new positions, making their resignations unnecessary, as less than a month had passed since they left office, and two days later sent them to their old posts – the infamous "Double Shuffle." For the Brownite liberals, the entire episode was a sign of the hopelessly underhanded dealings of the legislature against them. In a public speech in Toronto only days later, Brown lambasted the debacle as "a deliberate plot against the liberties of the people."[153] For Upper Canadian reformers, it proved the last straw.

After a decade of repeated frustration with their prospects in the united province, Upper Canadian reformers began after this 1858 "Double Shuffle" to more seriously consider the existing union. Brown had for several years resisted dissolution, preferring alternative fixes such as "rep by pop." However, in August 1859, he finally conceded that such reforms would never be possible because of Catholic bishops' influence in the legislature. To those reformers who still believed "the present system of government can be worked out," Brown offered a blunt assessment: "To them we commend this alliance of Roman Catholic bishops who command the votes of three-fourths of the people of Lower Canada … and let us ask what hope there is of gaining Representation by Population, or any other measure which will secure us the management of our own affairs." Instead, he suggested that reformers needed "some other remedy which will be complete and final." The alternative he proposed, once followed through, would change Canada's future: "A separation of the existing union between Upper and Lower Canada, and a confederation of the two with the North West territory, are the only measures which will rid us of the baneful domination of Lower Canada, while securing all the commercial advantages of the present union."[154]

For Brown, and for other reformers who had proposed similar solutions, nothing short of divorce would allow them the freedom and autonomy they envisioned. The following winter, reformers met at a grand convention in Toronto, where the party formally adopted the policy of dissolution through confederation.[155] The gravity of the decision was not lost on the attendees; as one editorial noted, the convention's resolutions "will influence the destiny of the province for ages to come."[156]

The idea of Confederation being a divorce between Upper and Lower Canada, rather than a primarily nation-building project, is a notion that historian Paul Romney has done much excellent work to explain.[157] Arthur Silver likewise, focusing on Quebec, emphasized the separation of the united province as a driving force behind Confederation.[158] According to Romney, Upper Canadian reformers believed separation the only way to fulfil their long-held principles of responsible government and provincial autonomy, which they believed had failed under the union.[159] However, to push Romney's conclusions a little further, we should consider *why* these abstract principles mattered so much to Upper Canadian reformers in the 1850s. The present study proposes looking for the answer in inter-religious conflict in Upper Canada, particularly in the notion of Protestant liberty.

Romney's study on Confederation, titled *Getting It Wrong* (1999), overlooks the religious significance of Upper Canadian provincial autonomy because it focuses more on the *form* than on the *substance* of the reform party's goals. For example, in summarizing the party's history, Romney states that George Brown had criticized Hincks's "reluctance to carry out certain elements of the Reform program."[160] Romney's more detailed treatment of this period in chapter 6 of his book mentions that Brown cared about the separation of church and state, but stresses his other reform goals, such as representation by population.[161] To highlight this absence is not to denigrate Romney's insightful study, but to identify an area where we may expand on his conclusions. Indeed, the current study proposes that those "certain elements" that Hincks wanted to avoid – namely, the religious concerns of the reform party's Dissenting evangelical base, such as clergy reserves, rectories, and religious education – explain the sectional controversies of the 1850s and hence the reformers' main impetus to support Confederation in the 1860s.

All the great sectional disputes of the later union period – clergy reserves, separate schools, and representation by population – were based on cultural differences between Protestants and Catholics. This observation may seem simple, even trite, but it reveals a heretofore-unacknowledged dimension of the Confederation scheme as envisioned by Upper Canadian reformers: namely, to allow creation of a truly Protestant society based on the principles of Protestant liberty. For people who believed that their own religious culture was uniquely capable of upholding a free society and free institutions, it became increasingly apparent that they could not pursue their particular vision of liberty if they continued to be subject to Catholic-friendly coalitions in a united legislature. Once free of Lower Canada's "baneful domination," reformers would finally be able to implement, as George Brown put it back in 1852, "the free institutions which we [Protestants] have chosen and those which we will alone endure."[162] While Confederation would eventually come to mean many things to many different people, for reformers in the summer of 1859 it was a proposal borne of Protestant frustration and designed to ensure Protestant self-determination.

Conclusion

In 1858, the English travel writer Charles Mackay visited several cities in Canada, including Toronto, London, Montreal, and Quebec City, and he published his observations the following year in a book called *Life and Liberty in America.* Having met with several politicians during his tour, Mackay desired to comment on the "considerable talk, if not agitation, in Canada in favor of a federation of the North American Colonies." Based on his experience with the English and French in Canada, Mackay was doubtful that such a federation was possible: "Their ignorance of each other leads to jealousies, sufficiently to render their union a difficult achievement … Under the existing circumstances, the best federation which they can establish is the federation of railways."[163] What this visitor did not understand was that the proposed federation was intended to reduce the "jealousies" between Upper and Lower Canada and, indeed, that the united province had already become a "federation of railways." A union based solely on railways and other mutual commercial interests was exactly what provincial leaders like Robert Baldwin, Francis Hincks, Allan MacNab, and John A. Macdonald had counted on when governing a country that was so divided along religious lines. In the 1850s it seemed there was little else besides railways, in terms of culture or religion, that could reasonably ground such a union.

For devout Dissenters such as George Brown, James Lesslie, and their supporters, a union based on railways and compromises was not enough. Such a plan merely allowed "the unrestricted encroachment of Papal authority" and threatened the very liberty of the citizens. As an alternative, Brown and supporters envisioned a consciously Protestant basis for their society, declaring, "To Protestantism, to the

Reformation, the world owes all the liberty and light which it at present possesses, and we are not ashamed of the cause which produces such fruits."[164] They envisioned a polity that strictly separated the state from church institutions, supported a single system of public schools free from "priestly" influence, and affirmed Protestant values by enforcing temperance and Sabbath legislation. They hoped for a society that rejected corruption from the perceived excesses of railway speculation and placed spiritual well-being above "the baal of the Grand Trunk." Throughout the 1850s, Upper Canadian reformers became increasingly convinced that such aspirations were not possible within the existing union of the Canadas and that, in order to escape the "baneful domination of Lower Canada," they had to pursue dissolution of the union through federalism with the North-West and the other British North American colonies.

The later union period facilitated the direct clash between two competing notions of liberty in Upper Canada: neutral and Protestant. Building on Robert Baldwin's optimistic approach to biculturalism in the united legislature, the proponents of neutral liberty envisioned a society blind to religious differences, fostering mutual cooperation through political compromise, and eventually free of inter-religious violence. They blamed the persistence of inter-religious violence on "bigots" like George Brown and the ex-Catholic Alessandro Gavazzi and were willing to curtail freedom of speech in an effort to preserve harmony between competing groups. By contrast, the proponents of Protestant liberty had a more pessimistic view of Canadian biculturalism within the union. They believed that religious differences were deep and determining factors for whether a society upheld freedom or tyranny. They believed that political compromises, in practice, seemed only to be unilaterally yielded up by Upper Canadians and that they, in order to avoid being dominated, had to be *less* compromising on issues like education. They blamed the persistence of inter-religious violence on the Catholic hierarchy's intolerance for alternative ideas and free inquiry and believed that Protestants had to speak up against perceived tyranny even if it risked offending Catholics. Both conceptions of liberty would continue to compete for dominance over Canadian liberalism in the coming years. And both would have much to say about the nature of liberal rights, provincial autonomy, and inter-religious relations in the new Dominion of Canada.

4

Under the Red Cross

The Confederation Era, 1860–1869

After a decade of struggle against the Hincksite reformers, George Brown and supporters had captured the mantle of Upper Canada's liberal reform movement. Under Brown's leadership, the reform party had in 1859 committed itself to a dissolution of the united legislature in favour of a federal union with broader British North America. Just as important, throughout the 1850s the Upper Canadian side of the party had increasingly asserted that true liberty required the stewardship of a dominant Protestant culture to defend against the encroachment of ostensibly hostile foreign faiths. The ancient feuds that had come to define Protestant Dissenters in opposition to their "tyrannical" religious rivals had, through legislative and social clashes with Catholics during the union period, become even more firmly intertwined with the political discourse of Upper Canadian liberalism. Now, on the eve of the Confederation talks, a newly invigorated Liberal party presented a Protestant-conscious plan for its own separate province, for Canadian liberalism, and for the new British North American federation.

This chapter proposes that both Upper Canadian Protestants and Lower Canadian Catholics pursued Confederation in part to protect their respective provinces' religious character. As we saw in the previous chapter, this conclusion builds on the work of Arthur Silver, who argued that Lower Canadians advocated Confederation as a means to secure what became the province of Quebec as a French-Canadian homeland,[1] and the work of Paul Romney, who maintained that Upper Canadian reformers pursued it to secure the future Ontario's provincial autonomy.[2] By focusing on the era's religious context, we can place the two scholars' respective insights into conversation with each other and as complementary halves of the same phenomenon: Confederation split the United Province of Canada along religious and cultural lines.

This study thereby enters the debate about whether Confederation represents centralization or decentralization. The dominant interpretation in the mid-twentieth century was centralization, with Confederation as a nation-building moment that cast the provinces as subordinate to Ottawa. Peter Waite, for example, argued that John A. Macdonald's idea of a strong central government ultimately dominated the British North America Act, suggesting that Ontario reformers did not take up the decentralized position until the "provincial rights" movement years later. Waite proposed rather that George Brown and supporters were so eager for representation by population that they sacrificed most other demands.[3] According to Waite, the Upper Canadian founders advocated federalism in name only, and Macdonald particularly used the term "federal" without ever intending to assign meaningful powers to the provincial governments.[4]

Historians of this mode often depicted George Brown and the Upper Canadian reform tradition as barely influencing the nation's founding. Donald Creighton, for example, downplayed the role of provincial-rights reformers by arguing that Brown was a spent force by 1864. He suggested that Brown's support for the Great Coalition in 1864 represented a softening of his earlier position, "a curious metamorphosis of his character," which he ascribed to his recent marriage to Anne Nelson.[5] Although Brown, he added, still wanted better representation for Upper Canada, by 1864 he planned to leave politics and had lost the will to fight for "his own particular solutions," thus yielding the field to others such as John A. Macdonald and George-Étienne Cartier.[6] J.M.S. Careless gave Brown a more central role in the story of Confederation, but likewise believed that he had ceased advocating for sectional autonomy. For example, Brown began in 1864 to accept that provincial powers should be limited and delegated by the federal government, which Careless explained as expressing his "inherent national aspirations."[7] In these interpretations, the Upper Canadian reformers of the 1860s are either peripheral to the main story, or their involvement is disconnected from their previous decades of advocacy for self-rule, leaving the new union centralized.

By contrast, the decentralization thesis of Confederation found its champions in the aforementioned Arthur Silver, in *The French-Canadian*

Idea of Confederation (1982), and Paul Romney, in *Getting It Wrong* (1999). For Romney, Brown joined the coalition and pursued Confederation not because his commitment to Upper Canada's autonomy softened, but as a means to increase self-governance by ending the legislative union with Lower Canada.[8] Comparing Brown's comments of 1864–65 about federal and provincial jurisdiction with his remarks at the Reform Convention of 1859, Romney argued that Creighton and others had misinterpreted words like "delegated" to propose mistakenly that Brown had changed his mind. Rather, Romney pointed out, he used similar terms and arguments in 1859, and no one questioned that he sought legislative divorce from Lower Canada.[9] Christopher Moore's *1867: How the Fathers Made a Deal* (1997) similarly examined the perspectives of Oliver Mowat, later known for his advocacy for provincial rights as premier of Ontario, in order to underline the reformers' decentralizing intentions. Mowat and other reformers, he explained, had reluctantly accepted centralizing measures such as federal disallowance in order to appease the John A. Macdonald faction, while knowing that provincial powers were so broad and explicit as to render federal disallowance minimal.[10] The decentralization thesis has received additional support recently. For example, Christopher Moore's *Three Weeks in Quebec City* (2015) reiterated that federal disallowance resembled Whitehall's powers of oversight vis-à-vis the colonies, despite responsible government making that option a practical impossibility after 1848, at least in Canada.[11] Similarly, Daniel Heidt's edited collection *Reconsidering Confederation* (2018) argued that most participants sought to advance their own region's autonomy, not to consolidate power at the federal level.[12] While this argument is not new, its continued viability seems to have turned the tide against the centralization thesis.

This study seeks to push the decentralization thesis further by asking *why* Upper Canadian liberals were so keen on self-governance in the first place. Whereas historians have generally accepted that Lower Canada's representatives negotiated for decentralization to secure their particular religious and cultural interests, the notion that Upper Canadians acted on similar interests has attracted relatively little consideration.[13] Indeed, as this chapter examines below, some recent interpretations have arguably overemphasized Upper Canada's secular-materialist interests at the expense of its longstanding religious and cultural concerns.[14] If, as seems clear, its residents frequently brought religious interests into their politics, and as George Brown cited in 1859 the political power of the Roman Catholic bishops as the reason he wanted to pursue confederation,[15] why would they suddenly abandon these concerns at the very moment the Confederation debates began? This chapter explores a series of political controversies in the Confederation era, including immigration, separate schools, and the Fenian crisis, and proposes that the period saw a deepening of religious divisions, which led some contemporaries to believe that Confederation must separate the Canadas along cultural and religious lines, while maintaining a federal union for commercial and military purposes.

Just as Roman Catholics sought to secure their particular religious interests through the British North America Act, many Dissenters affirmed their traditional commitment to making Upper Canada a Protestant society and, through Confederation, ultimately expanded on that vision to imagine God's Dominion extending "from sea to sea." Summarizing his support for Confederation in a speech to the united legislature in February 1865, George Brown declared, "Our scheme is to establish a government that will seek to turn the tide of European emigration into this northern half of the American continent – that will strive to develop its great natural resources – and that will endeavor to maintain liberty, and justice, and Christianity throughout the land."[16] The following year, after the defeat of the Fenian invasions of 1866, the Congregationalist *Canadian Independent* celebrated the triumph of British (and predominantly Protestant) forces: "Canada will be a more christian country under the red cross, than it could ever be under the green flag!"[17] In the Confederation era, as over the preceding decades, the Protestant Dissenters of Upper Canada frequently brought to the table bold ideas about Protestant liberty, identity, and destiny in their colony and in the new dominion.

The notions that Canada would be a Christian country "under the red cross" of the Union Jack and that Confederation would enable the spread of Christianity throughout the northern half of the continent seem to challenge two prevailing perspectives on Confederation and liberal thought: 1) *materialism:* the idea that Confederation and its contemporary expression of liberalism were concerned primarily with secular material interests such as railways, intercolonial trade, and taxes;[18] and 2) *religious neutrality*: the idea that the founders wanted the new dominion to be neutral towards religion in order to encourage the accommodation of religious minorities.[19] In order to support the neutral-materialist interpretations of Confederation, several studies have overlooked evidence of its specifically Christian context. For example, when George Brown's legislature speech of February 1865 was included in a popular compilation of Confederation speeches, the editors understandably shortened it for the sake of space; in doing so, however, they excluded the speaker's call for Confederation to enable the spread of "Christianity throughout the land."[20] Another compilation included the quote, but made no mention of religion in its commentary.[21] This current chapter seeks to restore such evidence to the conversation to reimagine the religious context of the great project. While still acknowledging the founders' secular material concerns regarding taxes, trade, and security, it argues that they also intended to affirm Christianity, a Christianity-infused sense of British identity, and the majority rights of Protestants or Catholics within their respective provincial jurisdictions.

As in previous chapters, this chapter also seeks to explain how Canadians contextualized colonial politics with reference to international and historic events. Outside of the legislative chambers, ordinary Canadian Protestants and Catholics asserted their place in a transatlantic religious conflict that dated back centuries. Each religious group's appeals to definitive past events and to ongoing political conflicts abroad helped to reinforce and sustain their collective political and social interests based on religion. For example, evangelical Dissenters in Canada drew inspiration from the great revivals and missionary efforts in the United States, Europe, and Asia.[22] International ties with the British Isles were further strengthened by the successful laying of telegraph cable from Ireland to Newfoundland in 1866, whose achievement many Canadians ascribed to the "Providence of God."[23] In Toronto in 1865, the Congregationalist Rev. T.M. Reikie remarked, "May Heaven smile on the effort, and link in closer bonds Britain and America!"[24]

The most notorious example of international religious identities affecting Canadian politics in the 1860s was the Fenian crisis. Although the Fenian Brotherhood sought primarily Irish independence, and was condemned by many Roman Catholic officials, it emerged within and was shaped by Roman Catholic grievance under Protestant British rule in Ireland. Indeed, both Catholics and Protestants in Canada often viewed the Fenian crisis through this lens. For example, the *Irish Canadian*, a Toronto-based weekly clearly sympathetic to the Fenians, asserted that they "hold their religion first, their country next. It is idle to say that a sincere and zealous Catholic *cannot* be a Fenian, in the face of existing facts."[25] Protestant Dissenters underlined the link even more vehemently, and blamed Catholicism for inspiring Fenian disloyalty. As the Congregationalist *Canadian Independent* asked in an 1866 article, "Who rebel [in Ireland]? … Only Roman Catholics, whom the priests call their subjects; not one Protestant." The author went on to blame state–church grants to the Catholic church for enabling the radical independence movement: the British government "pays the priests in their colleges. She pays the priests in their schools … What does England get? … The fruits; the last ripe fruit, FENIANISM."[26]

Some liberal politicians in Canada tried very hard to diminish the power of these divisive religious identities so as to encourage tolerance, accommodation, and pluralism. For example, Thomas D'Arcy McGee, a former Irish nationalist and a Conservative MP (Montreal West), spoke out against Fenianism in a speech of August 1867. Less than a year later he was murdered in Ottawa, shot in the back of the head at close range, apparently by members of a Fenian conspiracy. Patrick James Whelan, who was convicted for his murder and sentenced to death, claimed to his dying breath that he did not pull the trigger. Whelan maintained he had been falsely identified: "I knew that they were prejudiced against me; and men of opulence, too, and why? Because I am a Roman Catholic."[27]

Despite Canada's potential for a fresh start in 1867 and the best efforts of its liberal visionaries such as McGee, the new dominion would be shaped as ever by enduring conflicts forged in another land and in another age. This chapter examines the divisive religious context of the Confederation era from the aftermath of the Reform Convention of 1859 to the hanging of McGee's accused killer Patrick James Whelan in 1869. In particular, it focuses on controversies surrounding religion and immigration, the Catholic push for more separate schools, and the religious dimensions of the Fenian crisis. Building on discussions in chapter 3 and the work of Silver and Romney, it analyses Confederation as not only a movement of national unification but also a separation of the United Province of Canada. Most important, it highlights the seemingly irreconcilable religious differences that made this separation necessary.

"The Protestant Part of Canada": Cultural Reassertions in the Confederation Era

The Irish Catholic Thomas D'Arcy McGee, a rising star in Canadian liberal politics and newcomer to the united province, observed in 1859 the prevalence of Protestant Dissenters, particularly Scotch Presbyterians, in the Upper Canada reform party. "They have been born and bred in hostility to Popery," he observed. "Their religious antipathy, lies in the interior of the man – it stands in no need of daily exercise to keep it alive." Nevertheless he joined the party and made it his mission to change it from within, to try to make it more attractive to Irish Catholics. Reformers should stop "making the Protestant view … a party test," he argued, because it prevented "the Catholics of Upper Canada, from acting with them in perfect cordiality and confidence."[28] His attempts would be short-lived. In 1863, the party's re-commitment to opposing separate schools led him to abandon the Liberals to join John A. Macdonald's Conservatives.[29] He never lost faith in the notion that Canada could overcome "all the politico-religious issues possible between us and our Protestant fellow subjects,"[30] but the rest of his life offered little validation for this faith. In defiance of such optimistic words, the divisions that had defined the union period only seemed to crescendo in the Confederation era.

At the start of the 1860s, Upper Canada's Protestant culture continued to be assertive and successful in retaining affiliates. Upper Canada had a substantial Catholic minority (18.5 per cent in 1861), but the Protestants still dominated at about 80 per cent. Dissenting denominations made up just over half of the total population throughout the 1860s, compared to Anglicans, who decreased from 22.3 per cent in 1861 to 20.4 per cent in 1871, and the Catholics, who fell to 16.9 per cent. Each major Dissenting denomination expanded: Baptists from 4.4 per cent to 5.3 per cent, Methodists from 25.1 per cent to 28.5 per cent, and Presbyterians from 21.7 per cent to 22 per cent.[31]

Contemporary anecdotal evidence also reveals the liveliness of Protestant public expression. In *Canada in 1864: A Settler's Handbook,* Henry T. Newton Chesshyre recalled travelling through the colony and making the mistake of lodging at a tavern on 5 November. Local Protestants were celebrating Guy Fawkes Day, or Bonfire

Night, commemorating the capture of the Catholic terrorist who had attempted to blow up Westminster Palace (Parliament) in 1605: "About seven o'clock three fiddles struck up, the dance commenced, and ended not until seven the next morning; the shoutings and yellings exceeded anything I have ever heard." To reassure the reader of the locals' courtesies, he added, "No charge, however, was made to me for that night's unrest."[32] The Glorious Twelfth of July similarly offered an annual public expression of Protestant pride throughout the colony, marking the British Protestant victory over the forces of the ousted Catholic King James II in the Battle of the Boyne in 1690. One witness described a celebration in Ottawa in 1865 in which an estimated three thousand Protestants marched together in the pouring rain. Although their banners, Union Jacks, and orange regalia became soaked, they resolutely followed drum and fife through the city before gathering in a field to drink cold ale and hear speeches. An Irish-Catholic observer compared the procession to "a caravan of Fanaticals on a pilgrimage."[33]

The evangelical movement represented another bold expression of Protestantism in Upper Canada. Henry Chesshyre's bewildered description of a revival camp meeting captures this element:

> In the midst of the forest … with some small shanties … [and] large fireplaces … the minister jumps to his feet, and opens with a prayer in a soft and gentle tone, in the course of which a few groans are audible from the kneeling assembly; these become gradually louder and louder; then the women begin to scream, and soon the scene resembles Bedlam – or rather ten Bedlams – broken loose; the males beat their heads, the females shriek and faint, and this exhibition may continue for an hour or more, till all are quiet from sheer exhaustion. After a while rises another minister and the whole programme is repeated over and over again, with only an interval of rest at night, for a week and upwards.[34]

Despite Chesshyre's little sympathy for the event, evangelical Dissenters believed such emotional displays indicated the vitality of their faith and God's work in the colony. As the *Canadian Independent* explained in 1860, "God's people in Canada" needed the revivalist camp meeting and similar evangelical efforts to effect genuine salvation: "There is room for the deepest feeling. The fountain of tears may well break up, in view of dying men. Break, hearts of stone." What the province needed, the author declared, was "an outpouring of the Spirit of God … A deep, burning, all-consuming love of souls will recognise the need of revival."[35] In addition to local efforts from Dissenting churches, during the 1860s the colony also became increasingly integrated into the international revival circuit, with star evangelists such as American Phoebe Palmer visiting several centres and claiming thousands of enthusiastic attendees at her revival meetings.[36]

The 1860s began with a series of interdenominational revival meetings around the province during January 1860. The Second Congregational Church played host to the meetings in Toronto, and pastor Francis Henry Marling noted with astonishment that the gatherings had attracted Christians from all denominations *every night* for four weeks of January: "During the seventeen years acquaintance with the city, we have never witnessed such a feeling as prevails." Marling believed that the events heralded a great spiritual renaissance: "What does all this betoken? … Is not God about to visit our land? … Is not 'the time to favour' Canada, 'yea, the set time, come?' *We believe it has, if we 'quench not the Spirit.'*"[37] Reformer James Lesslie attended some evenings with great interest and noted in his diary their millennialist significance: "These meetings seem to indicate with the other 'signs of the times', that the Lord will ere long, 'make bare His arm' in the defense of His church, and in the overthrowing of its enemies."[38]

Across the ocean in England, the former commissioner of crown lands James Hervey Price expressed a similar optimism about Canada's spiritual future. Price had returned to his native land a few years after failing of re-election in 1851. Though now settling into a quiet life after Canadian politics, he was following events in his former home. In the autumn of 1860, he reflected on his time in the reform party fighting for "the great principles of human liberty" and captured the evangelical zeal of the day: "We live on the eve of some great event that is to bring about some great change in the moral and religious condition of this fallen world."[39]

Likewise, many Canadians looked back at England, to some of the religious and political movements whose influence seemed to be growing. The Liberation Society, for example, previously the Anti-State-Church Association, advocated for the disestablishment and disendowment of the Church of England.[40] Though never achieving its main goal, it helped to rally Dissenters behind Britain's new Liberal party and pushed many of its key issues into the House of Commons. In 1861, it promoted a bill to abolish church rates – mandatory taxes to support the Church of England. Despite the bill's eventual failure, the society proved its organizational capabilities by launching a massive campaign to generate public sympathy for the idea, including about one hundred public meetings and lectures.[41] In Canada, the *Globe* wrote glowingly about the society, stating that it "fairly represents the real Nonconformists of the country," and applauded its efforts to influence the political process.[42]

A notable anniversary in 1862 allowed Protestant Dissenters on both sides of the Atlantic to celebrate a shared religious heritage. The occasion was the bicentenary of England's Act of Uniformity of 1662, just after the end of Puritan rule and the restoration of Charles II, and the subsequent ejection of two thousand ministers from the established church. The law had required swearing adherence to the *Book of Common Prayer* to promote unity within the Church of England, but it ended up provoking and entrenching resistance.[43] Two hundred years later, several Dissenting denominations in England commemorated the ministers' ejection as a victory of conscience over conformity.[44] Although they acknowledged that they differed politically and doctrinally from the principled reverends of 1662, they still asserted a common bond as "Nonconformists" and took inspiration from their willingness to stand up to the established church.[45] In Canada, the Congregationalist minister William Fletcher Clarke celebrated the ejectees as the "spiritual ancestors" of Canadian nonconformity.[46] And Francis Marling used the occasion to reinforce contemporary differences between his own faith and the Church of England: "Our fathers did right, in coming out, for the like reasons, in 1662, and we, in staying out, are thankful to be able to join such a goodly company."[47]

It is no surprise that all of this Protestant cultural assertiveness found powerful political expression in Upper Canada. As Dissenting ministers and reform politicians had done for decades, the Congregationalist pastor J. Wood of Brantford in 1864 encouraged his members to take their faith to political matters, such as temperance and education: "When will Christian men learn that this is *God's* world, and not the *Devil's,* and is to be ruled, as far as possible, by them for Him! In my judgment, Christians ought to be the most earnest politicians in the country."[48] As usual, the threat of Catholic ascendancy provided endless political motivation: speaking of the "encroachments of Popery" embodied in the 1863 separate-schools bill (Scott Act), the *Canadian Independent* exhorted, "Let Protestants unite vigorously to oppose the inroads of what history proves to be a determined foe to liberty."[49] To ensure the colony's liberty and the favour of God, it was supposed, Protestants should take their evangelical zeal to the hustings and make their power known.

Since religious affiliation remained a reliable predictor of voting patterns,[50] some politicians took a keen interest in the colony's religious demographics. In early 1860, the *Globe* reprinted an English translation of a letter attributed to a French Jesuit observer: "In a State half Protestant and half Catholic, two principles of legislation are constantly struggling the one against the other." Faced with such a struggle, the writer concluded that immigration was necessary to tip the scales in favour of his side: "We [Catholics] only desire an emigration of the religious, the moral, the intelligent … By such an emigration our ranks would be doubled, and we could then contend in numbers and in influence with the Anglo-Saxon race, which, every year, received immense reinforcements from the mother-country."[51] Thomas D'Arcy McGee made a similar argument, proposing that Lower Canada remember "the only remedy we know for representation by population – to encourage emigration [*sic*]."[52]

What followed turned immigration into a contest to bolster each side's religious demographics and, presumably, its political chances. One 1861 editorial in the *Globe* spoke out against sending emigration agents to France and argued that the Macdonald government was attempting "to use the machinery of emigration as a political weapon, as a means of strengthening classes or creeds" at the expense of Upper Canadian Protestants. Its alleged efforts "to strengthen the French Catholic element" would allow it to deny Upper Canada's claims for more representation and, if many of the newcomers went there, would further divide the population. Upper Canadian cabinet ministers who supported such actions, the editorial said, were "swamping their countrymen with their hereditary enemies."[53] Years later, Henry Chesshyre recalled the Macdonald–Cartier government's response to his immigration guide of 1864 and accused the Conservatives of using immigration as a political tool. He believed that they were actively encouraging immigration to Lower Canada to bolster its claims to more seats. The Conservatives in government, he wrote, had withheld support for his immigration guide "because it was in favour of Canada West – the Protestant part of Canada."[54]

Throughout these assessments, the underlying assumption was that religious homogeneity, at least within the parameters of Protestantism, was the ideal for Upper Canada. To promote more non-Protestants, said the *Globe* in December 1861, was to provoke increased inter-religious conflict: "Dare any one say that it is wise of us to add to the numbers of people who differ with the majority of the inhabitants of the province on so many points, and whose selfish prejudices and fears have created gigantic evils?"[55] One month later, another commentator suggested that the Canadian government's effort "to secure a Popish tide of Emigration to Canada," by sending emigration agents to France and southern Ireland, would ultimately "injure the prospective integrity of the British empire."[56] According to these observers, changing religious demographics threatened not only the Liberals' political prospects but also the very harmony of Protestant society.

Upper Canadian liberals in the 1860s often took for granted the desirability of a large degree of religious and cultural homogeneity. In reference to a proposed Scottish emigration scheme in 1863, the *Globe* wrote, "The emigrants will find themselves among a people, of their own race, nation, and religion, cherishing the same recollections, sharing the same feelings, and animated by the same hopes."[57] While race and nationality were often in the background, the centrality of religious divisions in Canadian politics meant that religious demographics frequently took precedence over other considerations. For example, in 1869, the *Globe* condemned John A. Macdonald's government's idea to send emigration agents to Belgium, as most Belgians were "strict Catholics"; instead, the liberal paper suggested stationing more in several cities in Britain and among "the Protestant populations of Holland and North Germany."[58] The fact that the religion of prospective immigrants was considered more important than their national origin or even language attests to the importance of religion to Upper Canadian society.

Although clergymen were often open about their desire for religion to influence politics and for Upper Canada to be a Protestant colony, Liberal politicians in 1861 appeared to avoid direct denominational appeals – likely in an effort not to sabotage the outreach to Catholic voters pursued by reformers such as Thomas D'Arcy McGee.[59] Thus the Liberal platform during the election campaign in summer 1861 was relatively devoid of religious rhetoric and instead used sectional terms. For example, in a campaign speech in Toronto's St Lawrence Hall, George Brown declared that he would not allow Upper Canada "to be ruled by Lower Canada, to be taxed by Lower Canada, to be kept in a position of degradation by Lower Canada."[60] His decision to ease up on the explicitly religious rhetoric, however, was not matched by everyone. Conservatives reportedly campaigned to Catholics in the Norfolk riding by depicting the local reform candidate as too Protestant, as "riding on Mr. Brown's 'high Protestant horse,' and voting for the Orange Incorporation."[61]

The 1861 election was generally a disappointment for reformers. Party leaders George Brown and A.A. Dorion were both defeated, leaving Sandfield Macdonald to lead the Liberals and the Macdonald–Cartier ministerialists to continue to rule with a narrow majority.[62] Despite McGee's recent efforts to sway the Catholic vote to the reform party, there is little evidence that he was successful. George Emery's study of election data in Oxford County indicates that Catholics and Anglicans there were most likely to vote conservative in the 1861 election, and the most likely reform voters were still Protestant Dissenters (data included for Baptists, Methodists, and Presbyterians) of Scottish, Canadian, or American origin.[63]

After the campaign's minimal religion-based mudslinging, more explicit references to religious division surfaced again. In celebration of local Tory victory, a gathering of Catholics in Trenton assembled to honour their local priest for "uniting the Catholics under his watchful guidance at the late elections." The *Globe* remarked indignantly that these "are men not only led by the nose by their priests, but who rejoice in their degradation and blazon it to the world!" Most troubling, these Catholics had "sold their country to please their priests!"[64] Another editorial blamed the "potent influence" of "clerical authority," which allegedly promised to support the Macdonald–Cartier ministerialists in exchange for a new separate-schools bill.[65] Months later, in November 1861, the *Globe* again reflected on the late election by questioning the disproportionate power of Catholic leaders: "At the direction of the Roman Catholic Hierarchy, they assailed the school system of Upper

Canada … The people of the West are tired of all this, and they will have an end to it." To neutralize the apparently outsized influence of the hierarchy and of Lower Canada in general, the editorial insisted again on either representation by population or dissolution of the union.[66]

The threat to break apart the union escalated as ruling coalitions repeatedly failed to sustain cross-sectional support. Within a year of the 1861 election, the Macdonald–Cartier government was defeated on a conscription bill that had proved particularly controversial in Lower Canada. Consequently, Governor General Lord Monck chose two liberal Catholics, John Sandfield Macdonald of Upper Canada and L.V. Sicotte of Lower Canada, to form government.[67] Within a year, they again faced turmoil after the legislature passed the Scott Act regarding separate schools in March 1863, by seventy-four to thirty, with the Brownites voting against Sandfield Macdonald, their own party leader. After his by-election victory in mid-April 1863, George Brown himself was back in the legislature after a brief hiatus and joined the charge against separate schools. The Liberal caucus again thoroughly divided along sectional and religious lines, which emboldened the conservative Macdonald–Cartier opposition to move non-confidence in early May. Brown accused the Conservatives of ignoring the real issue of sectionalism and reiterated his desire for constitutional reforms, including the separation of the Canadas, but, despite his support, the government was narrowly defeated, sixty-four to fifty-nine. Monck dissolved the legislature and called a new election.[68]

How could this separate-schools bill have split the Liberal party and brought down the government? The new legislation was a bold departure, giving the Catholic church full control over the separate schools' curriculum, rules, and holidays, sidelining the provincial superintendent, and it exempted Catholic church property from education taxes.[69] Richard W. Scott, a Conservative (later a Liberal) Catholic MLA from the city of Ottawa, had been working towards such changes since 1860. Scott's letters include extensive correspondence with high-ranking clergymen keen to craft the new legislation. Beginning in April 1860, Bishop Edward John Horan of Kingston wrote to Scott expressing his approval of an early draft.[70] In April 1862, Horan advised him that the political situation had improved (i.e., with Catholic co-premiers, and George Brown out of the legislature) and that therefore they should "aim at something more and endeavor to obtain a larger measure of justice." The bishop forwarded his own draft of "the amendments which I think ought to be comprised in any Bill to be proposed this Session." Horan did not expect that more extensive changes to the separate schools would face "anything like the opposition with which it would have been received some years since."[71]

Thus the Scott bill was drafted in close consultation with high-ranking Catholic clerics and carefully timed to be introduced during the government of liberal Catholic John Sandfield Macdonald. The bill's proponents, such as Thomas D'Arcy McGee, pitched it as a "final" adjustment that would settle the matter for good, a claim of which Upper Canadian reformers were understandably skeptical. Indeed, Upper Canadians had previously been promised that changes to the separate schools would be the "final" compromises on the subject, only for the issue to come up time and time again.[72] Some proponents also assured the legislature (falsely) that Egerton Ryerson, the chief superintendent of schools for Canada West, approved of the bill's contents. Due to illness, Ryerson could not repudiate that claim and express his severe disapproval for it until after it had passed.[73]

A public forum at St Lawrence Hall in Toronto on 7 April 1863 revealed how divisive the bill proved to be in Upper Canada. According to the Toronto *Leader*, Catholics showed up in droves and formed the majority of attendees. Standing before a mixed panel of Catholic and Protestant speakers, and a mixed crowd, the mayor reportedly claimed neutrality and urged the audience "not to carry on any violence." The first panel speaker was the conservative Orangeman Ogle Gowan, who argued that the bill would add to the Catholic hierarchy's power, drain the common schools of resources, and ultimately "indirectly … establish Roman Catholicism in Upper Canada." As he continued, however, many in the Catholic-majority crowd reportedly made a "great uproar and rush[ed] towards the entrance to the Hall." The mayor cried for order, and a "noisy man" was removed before Gowan was allowed to continue. After he decried the bill as being dictated by the hierarchy rather than demanded by "the people," however, the crowd yet again became hostile. As the *Leader* reported, "The greatest confusion again took place in the hall," and the meeting was ultimately shut down for lack of order.[74]

The following week an open-air meeting was held at Queen's Park (future site of the Ontario legislature), where an estimated three or four thousand attendees (this time "a purely Protestant assembly" of "all Protestant denominations") gathered to hear speakers on the separate-schools issue. This conclave was reportedly flanked by police bearing arms in anticipation of potential conflict, which did not occur. Before addressing the bill itself, the first speakers each acknowledged the disaster of the earlier meeting at St Lawrence Hall and emphasized the importance of free speech. When Ogle Gowan took the stage again, he said the crowd at St Lawrence Hall had offered "but a continuation of the same spirit of increasing boldness and exclusion, manifested within the last few years by our Roman Catholic fellow subjects in various parts of the Empire." Several more speakers, representing a variety of denominations, urged that MLAS vote against the bill and advised the crowd to continue to be "fully aroused to a sense of their danger" and "put their shoulders to their work and do what should have been done long ago – a determined opposition to the separate school bill." After cheers for the Queen, for the mayor, and for "the memory of King William III [the Protestant king also known as William of Orange]," the crowd followed a musical band and marched in a procession from Queen's Park over to St Lawrence Hall, where it disbanded.[75]

The Scott Act of 1863 again illustrates very different Catholic and Protestant understandings of religious freedom. Dissenting Protestants had generally framed religious liberty in terms of voluntarism. If the state would simply refrain from offering support to any church and instead allow free competition and a free exchange of ideas about religion, "Popery" would cease to be an immediate threat in Canada. As one Congregationalist remarked on separate schools in 1863, "To Popery we yield a fair field and no favour, to meet on the lists of controversy its antagonists, and to spread itself by fair and moral influences; but that is widely different from special grants and exclusive legislation."[76] A Liberal from West Elgin named Scoble told a party meeting: "Let him [a Catholic] have his conscience, provided it is honest. If he will have Separate Schools, let him pay for it. When he tries to make Protestants pay for it, he touches their conscience."[77] For voluntarists in the 1860s, as in previous decades, freedom of religion was best guaranteed by keeping the state separate from church institutions and allowing multiple denominations to compete for the voluntary contributions of their supporters in a free market of religion.

The problem in 1863, however, as earlier, was that the majority of Catholic clerics, Catholic voters, and politicians who relied on Catholic votes did not accept this voluntarist version of religious freedom. Instead of *voluntarism*, most Catholics expected their religious liberties to be guaranteed by *state accommodation* in the form of grants, separate institutions, and even restrictions on speech that criticized their faith. Thomas D'Arcy McGee, for example, argued in 1863 that it would be a violation of religious freedom to deprive Catholics of state-funded separate schools: "You are bound, if you be friends of religious freedom, to respect their plea of conscientious conviction, and to exempt them from the imposition of your opinions, as opposed to theirs, on the subject of education."[78] McGee ultimately left the Liberal party over his disagreement with the Brownites on separate schools, saying that the Conservative party better protected Catholic rights.[79]

The Scott bill passed easily, but with only a minority of Upper Canadian votes. The fact that it affected Upper Canada exclusively, but that most Upper Canadian MLAs voted against it, yet again raised questions about the union's fairness. Even the conservative-leaning Toronto *Leader*, which had defended separate schools, stated that it seemed unfair that the bill would pass without Upper Canada's approval: "There will be no possibility of its obtaining the assent of a majority of the members for the section of the Province which it exclusively affects … The complaint that a measure has been forced upon Upper Canada, by Lower Canada votes, will possess a reality which has never been attached to it before."[80] After the government fell in the wake of the bill's enactment, the province prepared for yet another summer election. After a disappointing electoral showing two years earlier, the Brownite Liberals were reinvigorated by the public reaction against the Scott Act. They ran on the assertion of sectional interests, emphasizing representation by population.[81] One *Globe* editorial depicted stark and competing sectional interests: "The contest to-day is between the representatives of Upper and the representatives of Lower Canadian interests … Lower Canada, aided by renegades in our midst, has of late years … acted so selfishly that our existence has been ignored." The Conservative party, the article added, had only "trampled Upper Canadian rights under foot," and its representatives in Upper Canada were merely "champions of the Lower Canadian cause."[82]

As during the 1861 election campaign, Liberals in 1863 spoke in sectional rather than explicitly religious terms. However, Catholic schools were the main cause of the recent flare-up in sectional tension, and the competing positions corresponded closely to religious affiliation. Just as the Catholic Liberals Thomas D'Arcy McGee and John Sandfield Macdonald broke with the majority of Upper Canadian Liberals on this issue and sided with most of their own co-religionists, Conservative politicians knew they could count on Catholic leaders to solicit their adherents' votes. In May and June 1863, Richard W. Scott reported to John A. Macdonald that he had written letters to Catholic leaders in various ridings to secure the Catholic vote for several Conservative candidates: "I generally send off a batch every day to different parts of Upper Canada. All I fear is that the Catholic Vote going En Masse one way may raise the No Popery Cry."[83] Scott was so confident that at times his comments appear as though he was single-handedly deciding who won wherever there lived a substantial Catholic population. In one letter to Macdonald, Scott wrote, "The County of Ottawa [across the river from Ottawa in Lower Canada] is still open, I can elect either [Alonzo] Wright [who won] or [William McDonell] Dawson [the incumbent]. There are from 400 to 500 votes kept open for me to use as suits my interests."[84]

Although the Liberal press was not privy to Scott's claims of influence, it was very suspicious of Catholic priests instructing their parishioners how to vote. One contributor to the *Globe* wrote that Catholic voters were "under the yoke of the Roman Catholic clergy" and that the "Protestant and liberty-loving spirit of this free country will not brook any priestly dictation in such a sacred matter as the exercise of the elective franchise."[85] Whether or not the politicians themselves were willing to make explicit appeals to religious affiliation, religious divisions remained the touchstone of the 1863 campaign.

Voters responded well to the Liberal campaign to put Upper Canada first, granting the party forty-one of its sixty-five seats.[86] Yet despite its victory there based on demands for sectional fairness, the Macdonald–Cartier Conservatives' results in Lower Canada matched it more or less equally. Although John Sandfield Macdonald and A.A. Dorion (L.V. Sicotte's replacement) were allowed to remain as co-premiers, their mere two- or three-seat lead numbered their days as government.[87] In a party meeting in Brantford that August, MLA Dr J.Y. Bown laid out the dilemma: "Owing to sectional, religious, and national distinctions, Canada had been cursed for years by a weak Government; and … weak Governments were always necessarily corrupt." A Mr Notman warned that Conservatives had "sold themselves to the Lower Canadian priests" and that "dissolution will have to be resorted to, if we are to be governed by rascally recreants from Upper Canada."[88] Even after their recent victory, the Liberals were still in a bind, due primarily to perpetual religious division in the legislature. In the coming year, they would take decisive action to end the cycle of weak coalition governments and to escape the rule of the "Lower Canadian priests" once and for all.

"The Founding of a Christian State": The Religious Context of Confederation

Gazing out at the waters of Cape Canso, Nova Scotia, the Congregationalist Rev. S. Snider contemplated the significance of the British Empire for liberty and for religion in North America. He composed the following lines that were printed in the Toronto-based *Canadian Independent* in May 1864:

> Tho' modern despots round thee rave,
> Whose counsels fiendish arts employ,
> Seeking thy free born sons to enslave,
> Thy well earned glory to destroy –
> Almighty Power will intervene;
> God is thy help; – God save the Queen.
> …
> Britannia! rule for God alone,
> And on the fallen nations call!
> May Truth, which long in thee has shone,
> Make Islam, Pope and Buddha fall!
> Earth's Jubilee shall then begin,
> While Britain shouts 'God save the Queen.'[89]

For this Protestant writer, the empire had an explicitly spiritual purpose and destiny: to take capital-T "Truth" to the "fallen nations" through the intervention of "Almighty Power." Although the poem anticipated its ultimate victory, that would not occur without the fall of despotic powers that had conspired to "enslave" freeborn Britons. The speaker's Protestant worldview is made clear by his listing of the papacy among a list of religious competitors ("Islam, Pope, and Buddha"), which he believed would fall before the inauguration of "Earth's Jubilee," or millennial peace. In the years after this poem appeared, Protestants of various denominations would make similar statements about the political entity that would come to be known as the "Dominion of Canada," expressing their hope that it would claim that same sense of divine destiny that they had assigned to the British Empire.

In order to understand what Upper Canadian liberals envisioned for Confederation, it is necessary to grasp how this Protestant sense of destiny fuelled their desire for provincial autonomy. As we saw in chapter 3, the 1850s' religion-based sectional tension had convinced Upper Canadian Dissenters that to avoid domination by the Catholic-majority Lower Canadians, they needed representation by population and / or a dissolution of the united legislature. Political deadlock following the elections of 1861 and 1863 only seemed to reaffirm this necessity. Although some historians have understood these political tensions in sectional terms,[90] one must not underestimate the centrality of religious differences to their predicament. As George Brown's *Globe* explained in the summer of 1864, "If we, in Canada, were a homogeneous people; if we spoke the same language, believed in the same creed ... then there would be no reason for effecting a change."[91] It is precisely because of the persistence of cultural, linguistic, and, above all, *religious* differences that the Upper Canadian liberals believed Confederation to be necessary in the first place.

Recent histories have done much to elucidate various aspects of modern Canada's founding. E.A. Heaman's recent *Tax, Order, and Good Government* (2017) emphasized financial concerns, arguing that Liberal politicians sought primarily "fiscal federalism" to obtain tax fairness for their respective provinces. The author addressed mid-century sectional tensions in the same way: "Pre-Confederation debates about how to free Upper Canada from French-Canadian influence were debates about how to protect Upper Canadian wealth from supposedly poor and tax-evading French Canadians."[92] She looked at George Brown's worries about Catholic dominance but related such rhetoric to concerns about fiscal transfers to Lower Canada, which Brown believed stunted Upper Canada's economic viability in competition with the United States.[93]

Although this study agrees with Heaman's assessment that Brown valued fiscal fairness, it finds such concerns secondary and argues that they came late for Brown and for his reformers. For three decades, Protestant Dissenters like him had mobilized over non-fiscal issues related to cultural dominance: for example, the effects of immigration on religious demographics, the "sectarian" status of King's College, the use of the Bible in public schools, and the freedom to criticize Catholicism in public. One editorial in the *Globe* in 1863 emphasized that issues such as tax fairness were perceived to be derivative of clergy-sponsored Lower Canadian dominance. Sectionalism "took its rise when at the bidding of the Roman Catholic Bishops the first assault was made on the Common School system of Upper Canada. It has grown since to larger proportions from the injustice inflicted on the Western Province by the heavy taxation which it bears."[94] The following month, the *Globe* again downplayed financial issues: "The struggle ... includes the control of the finances ... but that is far from being all." Rather, a substantial Liberal victory was necessary to shut out "the Ultramontane French."[95] Thus Brown's concerns about tax fairness reflected rather than motivated longstanding Protestant–Catholic competition.

Heaman's assessment is consistent with a handful of recent works that advanced a "neutral-materialist" interpretation of Confederation. This perspective typically suggests that the founders wanted the new nation to be neutral towards religion and culture and to base national unity on common material interests. As Heaman put it, they "envisioned a new civic nationality based on economic self-interest" so designed a government to manage "wealth, not identity."[96] Political scientist Janet Ajzenstat offered another variant in *The Canadian Founding* (2007), arguing that the new nationality was based on common adherence to law rather than on common identity. She said the founders "rejected the idea that a nation would require a describable social character. Insofar as the new nation was to have an 'identity,' it would be procedural and neutral – civic, not cultural."[97] This interpretation gave religion and culture little to no role in founding or defining the new nation.

This viewpoint finds little disagreement from the British North America Act, which lacks explicit cultural vision. As Ian McKay has said, students often become disappointed when they read the legislation expecting grand declarations of principles and find instead "the lackluster language of a tedious text ... [and] an endless succession of details. Who should administer the poor asylums? What about the lighthouses? Who gets Sable Island?"[98] There is no doubt that the monumental task of organizing a federal union of existing colonies required a large degree of sorting through the minutiae of various practical matters. The founders had to work across denominational, cultural, and sectional lines and therefore had to find common ground in other areas. For these practical reasons, religious and cultural issues simply could not take priority during the actual crafting of the constitution.

However, religious considerations helped launch the Confederation talks, and there are several indications that the founders and their contemporaries took great interest in the cultural and religious future of their new dominion. In contrast to the viewpoint of materialism and cultural neutrality, this section reconsiders the work of William Westfall and A.I. Silver, who took the religious context seriously. Westfall observed that, for Ontario's Protestants, the new dispensation included a spiritual component in addition to representation, railways, and tariffs: "Beneath this materialistic ethos rests a deeply spiritual vision … a new type of society on the earth when the wilderness of sin and injustice will become the dominion of the Lord."[99] A.I. Silver similarly argued that French Canadians pursued the project to achieve provincial autonomy and thereby protect the "sacred heritage" and majority rights of Catholics in Quebec.[100] This study builds on these conclusions to propose that the colonies' religious context affected what emerged in two major ways. 1) *Religious differences demanded provincial autonomy*: with both sides treating Confederation as a divorce of the United Province of Canada, Upper Canada's liberals pursued it to protect Protestant culture, just as Lower Canada's leaders sought to protect Catholic culture. In this sense, religion was the primary reason for the introduction of the federal system. 2) *Protestant conceptions informed the broader English-Canadian nationality*: building on their notions of Protestant liberty, and looking abroad to the non-Christian lands of the northwest, Upper Canada's liberals imbued the new dominion with a sense of spiritual purpose.

The first impetus for talks came in the chaotic aftermath of the Canadian election of 1863. Outrage in Upper Canada over yet more concessions to the separate schools had helped to propel the Brownite wing of the Liberal party to electoral success. Although the party had tried to focus on sectional rather than religious differences, the Protestant–Catholic division remained central to it. For example, one

Globe editorial from September 1863 answered ex-Liberal Thomas D'Arcy McGee's accusations of anti-Catholicism by summarizing religious divisions in Canadian politics: "If the Hierarchy will abandon its attempt to destroy the Common School system, and cease its efforts to subject Upper to Lower Canada, there will be no longer a necessity to deal with it as a political power. But so long as Bishops are politicians, so long may we expect to see Protestant and Catholic opposed, for the simple reason that a large majority of the Catholic body vote in accordance with the commands of their clergy."[101]

Despite their victory in the 1863 election, however, Upper Canadian Liberals saw no immediate end in sight for the attempt "to subject Upper to Lower Canada." The liberal press mused that Liberal electoral success should have reproved the conservatives' old strategy of achieving power through coalition with Lower Canadians, despite having only a minority of seats in Upper Canada.[102] However, the Liberals' narrow majority under Sandfield Macdonald barely hung on to power until March 1864, when the embattled premier attempted to form a new coalition with conservatives rather than deal with his own perpetually infighting caucus. He resigned after Étienne Taché rejected his offer, producing yet another conservative coalition, led by John A. Macdonald and Taché.[103] There, liberal Upper Canadians found their ideas and interests vastly underrepresented, with only three out of twelve ministers supporting representation by population, for example.[104] The new ministry appeared to one observer a repeat of the MacNab–Hincks–Morin team of 1854.[105] As the previous chapter revealed, the 1854 election had similarly produced groundbreaking victories for the Brownites, but ultimately a conservative coalition emerged based on the strength of conservatives in Lower Canada. Unless some major constitutional change took place, Upper Canadian Liberals could expect more of the same difficulties: namely, politics that they perceived to be at the mercy of special interests and "Lower Canadian priests."[106]

It is in this context, with all of its religious implications, that George Brown proposed the Great Coalition of 1864. Conceived as a temporary alliance of Upper Canadian Liberals with the Macdonald–Taché Conservatives in pursuit of a federal solution, the Great Coalition emerged from George Brown's initiative to secure the provincial autonomy that his Protestant Dissenting base had dreamed of in 1859.[107] As we saw in chapter 3, the Upper Canadian Liberals' decision in 1859 to seek a federal system came after years of frustration with perceived Catholic dominance. Indeed, Brown and supporters had originally proposed a confederation to assert Upper Canada's autonomy from the "alliance of Roman Catholic bishops who command the votes of three-fourths of the people of Lower Canada."[108] Now, in the spring of 1864, Brown had some political leverage in the weak new government, which had only a narrow majority. Rather than forcing another general election, which would likely have produced more of the same, in June 1864 Brown opted to support the ministry in exchange for promises of constitutional change that would "lay the axe at the root of the whole sectional evil."[109] Brown spoke before the caucus of Upper Canadian Liberals in Quebec later that month and proposed that representation by population was the best way out of political deadlock and pushed for federal union of the Canadas and ultimately of the other British North American colonies and the northwest. The resolution to accept Brown's plan to pursue the Great Coalition passed in the Liberal caucus by thirty-four to five.[110]

On 22 June 1864, the plan to federate British North America was announced in the legislature to break the deadlock. When asked whether it included representation by population, John A. Macdonald replied, "Yes," which evoked cheers. When George Brown rose to address the House, he emphasized the cultural and religious differences that had forced them to this point of political crisis: "We have two races, two languages, two systems of religious belief, two sets of laws, two systems of everything – so that it has been almost impossible that, without sacrificing their principles, the public men of both sections could come together in the same Government. The difficulty has gone on increasing every year." He stressed the towering significance of these cultural differences over other matters such as finances: "Social questions after all affect the mind of a people much more deeply than those which are merely pecuniary."[111] While Brown certainly emphasized financial fairness in other contexts, he clearly believed the main impetus was to solve the political problem that had emerged due to "social" differences, based largely on religion, between the two Canadas.

George Brown's decision to pursue the Great Coalition for the sake of federalism was consistent with his long career as an advocate for Upper Canada's political autonomy, and – crucially – his religious and cultural motivations remained the same. An earlier generation of historians, represented by Donald Creighton and J.M.S. Careless, interpreted the Great Coalition as a major departure from his previous track record as a fiery opposition leader. These historians emphasized that Brown had in 1862 married for the first time, and their works showcased his private love letters in order to suggest that his focus had begun to gravitate away from politics and towards home life.[112] Ultimately, they suggested that his willingness to enter a coalition, and to initiate Confederation, represented a softening of his personality that resulted from his marriage.

Even some more recent works have retained aspects of this interpretation; Richard Gwyn, for example, described Brown's political actions of 1864 as possessing "an out-of-character generosity for which Anne Brown surely deserves a share of credit."[113] More recently, however, historian Carmen Nielson suggested that it is an incomplete reading to interpret his letters solely as a pivot away from public life. Although it may have been well-meaning to credit Anne Nelson Brown as a kind of "Mother of Confederation," Nielson explains that Brown's letters sought to justify his continued dedication to his political ambitions and to reconcile that demanding public life with his new role as a husband.[114] For example, whereas Careless quotes part of one letter expressing his distaste for legislative work, Nielson points out that the missive also expresses his resolve to fulfil his "public duty" despite the personal cost.[115] Just as Brown did not seriously detach himself from politics, he also did not change policy by joining the Great Coalition. As Paul Romney has recently reiterated, his positions during the Confederation debates were consistent with those of the Reform Convention of 1859 and with the long-term struggle for Upper Canadian autonomy.[116] Thus his post-marital "metamorphosis," as Creighton put it, has been somewhat exaggerated.

By focusing on Brown the swooning sweetheart, some historians lost track of Brown the shrewd politician, persistent advocate for Upper Canadian interests, and Protestant crusader – all of which he remained in the summer of 1864. For Creighton, his "metamorphosis" made him more willing to yield to the influence of John A. Macdonald and George-Étienne Cartier, whom Creighton depicted as the main architects of Confederation.[117] However, Brown's own words during the coalition talks suggest that his purposes had not changed. Just as he and the reformers had resolved at the Reform Convention back in

1859, their idea in 1864 was to overcome sectional turmoil by achieving greater autonomy for Upper Canada within the new framework.[118] Importantly, he continued to blame "social" clashes based on religious and cultural differences between the two Canadas for this turmoil.[119] His decision to join in coalition with his antagonists may have been a new strategy, but he employed it to achieve a very old goal: self-rule for a Protestant Upper Canada.

In the weeks that followed the announcement of the Great Coalition, liberal commentators continued to reiterate the hope that this new federal arrangement would eliminate political problems arising from cultural differences in the united province. They did not anticipate that the new federation would be culturally neutral so as to accommodate pluralism but typically believed that the 1841 union's forced integration of competing cultures had created the political crisis in the first place. The new framework would solve their political problem by *separating* the two major cultures into two provincial jurisdictions. According to one commentator, "Hitherto, Canada, instead of being a united, has been a divided country … The two nationalities of the Province were brought into direct antagonism one with the other. The most distinct and opposite characteristics of the descendants of Britain and of France were compelled to strive for the mastery … But let us hope that the time has now come when the causes which created the strife will be removed."[120] The same month, an editorial in the *Globe* noted, "The existing union between Upper and Lower Canada [was] based on no real foundation, and the result only of expediency." The proposed federal union, hoped the writer, might enable more cultural unity: "The Colonies of British North America … actually have resolved to become one people … an amalgamation of British interests promises strength and greater harmony to our race" while keeping divisive differences (i.e., issues that affected Protestant–Catholic sensibilities) for the provincial legislatures.[121]

Provincial powers were intended to safeguard the "social" rights of the majority in each region. Representatives of both sections of the United Province of Canada (later Ontario and Quebec) insisted on provincial autonomy to safeguard their respective religions and cultures. At the Charlottetown Conference in September 1864, the Lower Canadians were particularly careful to ensure that Britain would guarantee provincial powers, so they would not be subject to revision by a majority in the federal parliament.[122] As Arthur Silver has explained, the provinces were intended to be "political manifestations of distinct nationalities." Indeed, the *bleus* of Lower Canada even pitched Confederation as a move for "separation" and "independence" for Quebec to protect its particular religious and cultural character.[123] According to Hector-Louis Langevin, for example, "Under Confederation there will no longer be domination of one race over another" because the provinces would safeguard the interests of their respective "race" (i.e., French or English).[124] This perspective is perfectly consistent with the rhetoric of the Upper Canadian Liberals, who – as illustrated throughout this chapter – advocated a strong set of clearly defined provincial powers for the exact same reasons.

While religious matters would be relegated to provincial jurisdiction, Protestant Dissenters anticipated that Confederation would also enable the cultivation of a national Christian culture and the spread of Protestantism throughout the northwest. As historian Doug Owram has demonstrated, English Protestants wanted the northwest not only for its commercial potential, but to establish their cultural influence there.[125] The Congregationalist *Canadian Independent* emphasized the profound sense of mission that the new dispensation now opened up for Canadian Protestants: "It is … a noble work which the Providence that 'sets the bounds of our habitations' has assigned us, – the founding of a Christian State in this northern part of North America." Canadians could rise to the task, the author proposed, by keeping the Sabbath day holy, by helping parents teach their children Christianity, by upholding Christian morality, and by ensuring that churches were present in every community "to plant in every part of the land a living witness for Christ." It was not just any form of Christianity, of course, that he had hoped for, but the Protestant or "reformed Christian faith, for which our fathers paid so great a price." Canada would be "on a probation not unlike Adam and Eve in Paradise, when the destiny of the race hung upon their obedience." Posterity depended on the living generation to lay the foundation for the perpetual "Christianisation" of Canada.[126]

Methodists conveyed similar hopes. In October 1866, many of them gathered in Toronto to mark the centenary of Methodism in North America, and several speakers reflected on the role of religion in the new nation. Rev. Dr. Corson of Brampton sketched "the bright future which he anticipated for Canada," in which "the Protestant churches should be successful in christianizing this land" and instill a sense of duty to God and country through the Bible. Rev. Samuel D. Rice of Hamilton combined this Protestant mission with racialist concepts to suggest that North America was guided by Providence and that "God had apportioned that it should belong to the Christian Anglo Saxon race."[127] Two months later, the Congregationalists held their annual meeting in Toronto, during which Rev. Dr Burns of St Catharines spoke about "the grand future promised our own land by the character of our people" and predicted that "they would still advance until righteousness would pervade the entire earth."[128]

The expectation that Canada would be dedicated to Christian faith was a natural outgrowth of the British Protestant tradition of attributing a nation's success to the piety of its citizens. In a study on public days of thanksgiving to God throughout nineteenth-century Canada, historian Joseph Hardwick called this concept "national providentialism." He noted a total of at least eighty-seven public days of worship, wherein Christians of multiple denominations met together to publicly offer gratitude to God for a successful harvest or after a period of crisis, and he emphasized how these events reinforced a sense of "Canada's providential mission."[129] On Thanksgiving Day in October 1865, for example, the Presbyterian Rev. Topp's Knox Church in Toronto participated along with several other churches in publicly thanking God for an abundant harvest. In his sermon, Rev. Topp called for men in political office to advance the Christian righteousness of the nation: "Let those invested with civil power ever act out to their functions, as indicated by the Apostle when he calls them the messengers of God for good. Let them do what they can … to further the interests of truth and righteousness."[130]

One British Congregationalist clergyman, whose sermon was republished in Toronto in 1863, illustrated the concept of national providentialism using the biblical example of Jesus cursing the fig tree in Matthew 21 and Mark 11. In the story, Jesus examined a fig tree for its fruits, but after finding none he cursed it so that it withered up. In Matthew's version, Jesus goes on to offer another parable before explaining that the tree represented a nation: "The kingdom of God shall be taken from you, and given to a nation bringing forth the fruits thereof."[131] Although the original context referred to ancient Israel,[132] the British author in 1863 related it to his own nation, as an example of what could happen if it ever abandoned its national piety. By extension, the fact that this sermon was published by a Canadian newspaper suggests that Canadian Dissenters applied similar lessons to their own colonies. Indeed, God would have greater expectations for the righteousness of Christian lands than for a non-Christian country, said the author, because they had the full benefit of Christian civilization: "In summing up the history of nations, God deals with them differently ... 'It shall be more tolerable for Tyre and Sidon in the day of judgment' than for those who trifled with a fuller civilization or shut their eyes to the noon-blaze of Gospel light."[133]

The Dissenters' belief that judgment accompanied a nation's turn from righteousness meant that they were often careful to scrutinize the actions of Canadian political leaders. When John A. Macdonald was accused of public drunkenness in 1866, the Liberal press suggested that he was not "fit to be the ruler of a free, enlightened, and Christian people."[134] Another editorial was more explicit: "We aspire to the character of a Christian country, let us deserve it by putting our feet upon the cause of most of the sin and misery with which the world is afflicted, and teaching even those in high station that they cannot commit crime with impunity."[135] As previous chapters in this study have argued, the Dissenters' expectation that the state would be separate from church institutions did *not* entail its neutrality towards Christian culture. The fact that they attributed national success to national Protestant piety indicates just how much they took for granted that Canada would be a Christian nation.

Underlying all these grand prescriptions for a "Christian state" was the idea that a well-designed constitution was not in itself sufficient for success. For the outspoken Protestant Dissenting clerics, *culture* mattered eminently more than laws and institutions, which some commentators anticipated would reflect changes in culture. As the Congregationalist *Canadian Independent* declared in March 1867, "Paper constitutions depend for their efficiency upon the temper of rulers and people. Laws are unavailing if public opinion does not sustain them ... It may be said of nations, 'The People are the Constitution.'" Thus, the new Confederation's laws and institutions were important, but ultimately secondary to "the most essential element in national life, that is – THE CHARACTER OF THE PEOPLE." In this case, that depended on the population's adherence to the Protestant faith.[136] The idea that culture was the starting point in determining a nation's success was captured in the old phrase, quoted in a Canadian magazine in 1863, "Let me write the ballads of a nation, and I don't care who makes the laws."[137] For Protestant Dissenters at the time of Confederation, it was not merely the *form* of the new nation that mattered (i.e., laws and institutions), but its *content* (i.e., culture and religion).

The false premise that the founders envisioned a nation based on common material interests rather than on culture has arisen in part because some historians have neglected the scope of provincial jurisdiction. Proponents of the neutral-materialist perspective have emphasized that there was no consensus on religious matters at the federal level.[138] However, this point sidesteps the provincial dimension. So that the federal government could govern in a way that would not constantly pit Protestants and Catholics against one another, the constitution relegated issues historically pertaining to religion (e.g., education and immigration) to the provinces.[139] In George Brown's speech before the legislature in February 1865, he argued that the "questions that used to excite the most hostile feelings among us have been taken away from the general legislature, and placed under the control of the local bodies." The federal government would no longer be concerned with "local prejudices," he said, and "all these subjects of discord are swept from the discussion of our [federal] legislature."[140] Rendering that level of governance neutral to Protestant–Catholic controversies, however, did not reflect indifference towards cultural and religious affairs. This chapter reveals that many founders and their contemporaries clearly intended a "Christian state." Indeed, in the very same speech that Brown advocated keeping religious issues out of federal hands, he anticipated that the new dispensation would enable the spread of "Christianity throughout the land."[141] Many of the founders wanted it to advance Christian culture, but relegated that role to the provinces to ensure that Catholics and Protestants would not have to constantly contend for cultural dominance at the federal level.

Understanding this religious and cultural context, with a clear distinction between provincial and federal powers, challenges the now-prominent neutral-materialist interpretation of Confederation. While the founders could not productively express distinctive religious conviction in their negotiations, they took for granted a Christian nation. The neutral-materialist interpretation suggests their indifference to the long-term future of Protestantism and Catholicism in Canada and their expectation of expanding cultural pluralism. Nothing could be further from the truth. Janet Ajzenstat's argument that "Canada's founders did not build on a cultural foundation"[142] appears to be more reflective of early-twenty-first-century post-national thought than nineteenth-century liberal thought, which was often rooted in particularly British and Protestant understandings. Canada's founders absolutely *did* build on a cultural foundation – or more precisely, two cultural foundations: Protestant British for the English-speaking colonies and Catholic French for Quebec. They intended the "neutrality" of the federal authority not to enable the pluralization of religion or the secularization of Canadian culture, but to ensure that it would not interfere with the provinces' safeguarding of their respective religious and cultural characteristics.

Confederation inaugurated a new phase in the development of Canadian liberalism, but religion and culture helped shape this emergent liberal order. This study agrees with Janet Ajzenstat that a form of liberalism provided *the* underlying ideological basis to the new country.[143] However, the tendency to summarize liberalism as only a set of neutral institutions and procedures based on "non-discrimination"[144] is to offer an abstract theoretical version of liberalism removed from its nineteenth-century cultural context. A properly historicized understanding of nineteenth-century liberalism, or what Ian McKay called "actually existing liberalisms,"[145] reveals the extent to which Confederation-era liberal thought coexisted with assertions of Christian cultural identities. In short, the founders imagined both a tolerant liberal nation *and* a Christian nation. The two were not only mutually compatible, but inseparable – especially for nineteenth-century Canadian liberals who believed that adherence to the Protestant faith was the only real guarantor of liberty.[146]

"The war has already begun": Unity and Division in the New Dominion

During the Confederation debates in 1865, anglophone Lower Canadian MLA Christopher Dunkin (Brome) predicted that older identities rooted in a particular religion, ethnicity, or region would continue to take precedence over any proposed new national identity. "In the times to come," he said, "when men shall begin to feel strongly on those questions that appeal to national preferences, prejudices, and passions, all talk of your new nationality will sound but strangely. Some other older nationality will then be found to hold the first place in most people's hearts."[147] Although Confederation succeeded in relegating most divisive religion-related issues to the provincial level, the underlying Protestant–Catholic tensions remained long after 1867. Liberal politicians such as George Brown had imagined that such tensions could be "swept away forever" through constitutional reform.[148] If the events of the following few years are any indication, however, Brown's optimism was misplaced.

The most obvious signs of strain were the Fenian crisis and the murder of Thomas D'Arcy McGee, both of which contemporaries often understood within a Protestant–Catholic dichotomy. This section not only addresses the persistence of Protestant–Catholic animosity in Ontario politics, but highlights the ways in which some officials attempted to diminish these disputes through appeals to liberal concepts of individualism and blindness of the law towards historic group differences. Although this study has argued that nineteenth-century liberalism was rooted in Protestant conceptions, it has also noted the emergence of a competing expression of liberalism (i.e., the "neutral liberty" of Robert Baldwin and Francis Hincks), which downplayed the Protestant roots of its ideas in order to appeal to non-Protestant voters. By examining key events in the years right after Confederation, this section spotlights the growing disjuncture between an emergent "neutral liberty" narrative, which emphasized the universalism of liberal thought, and the traditional narrative identities of Protestants and Catholics in Ontario.

George Brown's expectation of a reset in Protestant–Catholic relations was very soon challenged in the lead-up to the first federal election of 1867. First, the matter of separate Catholic schools, supposedly settled in 1863, reappeared in 1866. MLA Robert Bell (North Lanark) drafted a bill that would have, for Upper Canada's Catholics, established a normal school (to teach teachers), created a deputy superintendent of education, and allocated more funds to their schools.[149] Bell pitched the bill as simply placing Upper Canada's Catholic schools on a par with Lower Canada's "Protestant" schools, although the latter were non-denominational, state-run, and attended by many Catholics.[150]

The bill was ultimately withdrawn following widespread Protestant outrage and the resignation of the Protestant Conservative cabinet minister Alexander Galt (Sherbrooke).[151]

Despite conciliatory words expressed in the preceding years, Protestant–Catholic divisions resounded again during the campaign for the 1867 federal election. When Conservative MLA Thomas D'Arcy McGee (Montreal West) issued a public statement condemning the Liberal party for its lack of Catholic candidates, Brown's *Globe* decried him for raising religious discord when Confederation was supposed to set those differences aside. Accusing McGee of being a self-serving "political trickster," the editorial argued that his comments only served to "rake up the embers of old sectarian feuds!" To justify the absence of Liberal Catholic candidates, the author explained that Canadian politics had historically been divided along religious lines, with the implication that this division was the reality in 1867 as well: "What right had the Catholics to expect special favour at the hands of the Reform party? … How many of them vote for Reform candidates? Not one in twenty of them, and D'Arcy McGee knows it … The Roman Catholic vote for many years has been cast almost unanimously for the Tory candidates."[152]

Aside from some idealistic politicians, few Canadians seemed to expect the old religious animosities to wither after Confederation. Many Irish Catholics in Ontario, for example, held firmly to their historic grievances against Anglo-Saxon Protestants as an act of solidarity with fellow Irishmen who still challenged British rule (or at least sought to reform it) in their homeland. One poem written in Ireland and republished in Toronto's *Irish Canadian* in 1866 said that "our sneering Saxon tyrant" had long urged the Irish to abandon their religion, language, and history. "He mocks our simple patriot love; he'd steal with ruffian hand / Our Faith, our Name – as he has stol'n our Language and our Land." But the poet said the Irish were wise to the Saxon's schemes, spoke of their "memories that will not die, but burn the fiercer still," and emphasized that, wherever they went, they were "Irish everywhere."[153] Holding on to their historic grievances, even the anti-Saxon animosity of their fathers, was to this poet an act of defiance towards a group that they perceived to represent past and present oppression. For readers of the *Irish Canadian* and others like them, politicians' optimistic words about Confederation offering a fresh start meant little in the larger context of this historic and transatlantic contest.

While Irish Catholics had political reasons for animosity towards the English, the religious element of their struggle was never far from the forefront. At a St Patrick's Day celebration at St Michael's Cathedral in Toronto in 1865, for example, one speaker romanticized the time when "Catholic Ireland … employed her resources for the propagation of the Gospel, for the education of youth, for the sanctification of the people." But, he added, that was all before a plan was "concocted by Satan" and enacted by Protestants who "denied the faith of their fathers and seized with sacrilegious hands the property of the church of God and pursued with direct vengeance any one who refused to conform to the new opinions and false doctrines of the so-called reformation." The speaker offered a Roman Catholic version of the "persecution narrative" long employed by the Protestant Dissenters, emphasizing the righteousness of the Catholic cause because of historic persecution: "The life of a christian is a life of suffering" and "No country has suffered for its faith like Ireland." In the end, this narrative was intended to reinforce a sense of solidarity with Irish Catholics across the Atlantic. Though far removed from their homeland, Irish Catholics in Canada retold stories of past persecutions to remind themselves of their common cause with the "millions of our countrymen who yet writhe under the lash."[154]

Protestants similarly recalled past persecutions for contemporary political purposes. In the South Lanark election of 1869, for example, the memory of past religious conflicts appears to have helped secure Conservative victory. The Liberal candidate was a Mr Doran, an Irish Catholic. The two conservative-leaning candidates should have split the conservative vote, but the Catholic Doran lost. An anonymous contributor to the *Globe* suggested that Liberals there chose religion over party. He or she reported pamphlets distributed throughout the riding suggesting that if voters elected Catholics, "the Catholics were going to have full sway in the land; Popery was again going to Triumph; and the days of the Inquisition and Martyrdom were to be renewed." The day after the election, large posters reportedly went up around the village of Glen Tay saying, "Down with Doran and the POPE."[155] However distant the actual events recalled, past persecutions, inquisitions, and martyrdoms continued to reverberate in Canadian politics.

For Protestants in Canada, the habitual retelling of past conflicts with Catholics also helped to reinforce a sense of patriotism. During the 12 July celebrations in St Catharines in 1869, the Conservative Alderman Medcalf reminded the crowd about the events of the Battle of the Boyne 180 years earlier and said that "the memory of that day remained as fresh as ever." Although Medcalf acknowledged that critics denounced them as "bloodthirsty bigots," he believed the annual event passed on a strong sense of British loyalty and Protestant identity to the next generation. For him, taking time to remember the conflicts of the past also reminded Protestants of the dangers that still faced them: "We have enemies," he insisted, "but they can do us no harm. We watch them too closely." Still, he insisted, Protestants had to continue to "put our trust in the Lord and keep our powder dry."[156] Military concepts such as keeping one's (gun)powder dry were occasionally invoked when Protestants discussed their ongoing conflicts with Catholics. A few years earlier, for example, at a speech for Congregationalist college students in Montreal in October 1865, Rev. E.J. Sherril invoked rhetoric about warfare. He emphasized Canadian Protestants' unique challenge because of the strong presence of the Roman Catholic church – "a foreign and false religion of unknown power … For years, that power has here been increasing and culminating. The battle between truth and error will be fought in Canada. The war has already begun."[157]

Rhetoric about inter-religious warfare was mostly metaphorical in Canada, but there were several moments in the Confederation era when such animosity escalated to violence. Historian William J. Smyth has noted four religious riots in Toronto during the 1860s: in response to the visit of the Prince of Wales in 1860, the Separate Schools Bill in 1863, the Catholic Corpus Christi parade in 1864, and Guy Fawkes Day that same year.[158] On 26 May 1864, after Orangemen attacked the Catholic procession for Corpus Christi – a movable feast, on the Thursday after Trinity Sunday – there was potential for a broader armed conflict in the city. On 5 November that year, in response to Protestant celebrations of Guy Fawkes Night, approximately four hundred members of the Irish-Catholic Hibernian Society met at Queen's Park at midnight and marched through the city with guns and pikes, firing their weapons at various locations as a show of force. In the coming months, some Protestants began to spread rumours that Catholics were stockpiling weapons in their churches and cemeteries, planning to massacre the Protestants of Upper Canada. In December 1864, an Orange Hall in Toronto was attacked, its furniture and banners and even Bibles destroyed.[159] Again, Protestants believed it was a targeted, religion-motivated attack by Catholics.

All the while, the covert presence of the Fenian Brotherhood in Canada continued to haunt Protestant–Catholic relations. Irish-Catholic politicians such as Thomas D'Arcy McGee downplayed the threat, saying that there were only a dozen or so bad eggs in the city.[160] The Fenian-sympathizing Toronto newspaper the *Irish Canadian* gave a different impression, however. For example, in its coverage of a St Patrick's Day event in Toronto, the paper reported that the local audience cheered when Mr McDermott of New York announced that "there are Fenians in Canada, too," and applauded when he added that they had his "warmest sympathy and prayers."[161] The following year, an actual Fenian invasion confirmed Protestants' worst fears. In March and April 1866, James Lesslie recorded in his diary that there were reports of Fenians organizing to raid the province, and the militia and the U.S. army had sent lookouts near the Canadian border.[162] In June, however, Fenians entered the country and attempted to take Fort Erie.[163] Lesslie recorded that Canadian troops and volunteers had thwarted their attempt and lost about five men in the battle. "The excitement arising from the invasion of the Fenians and the sad results following the armed collision – is very great," he wrote. "Lord avert from us the horrors of war."[164]

Only two years later, Fenianism again attracted nationwide attention with the murder of Thomas D'Arcy McGee. McGee had been a consistent advocate for Irish-Catholic minority rights, pushing for separate schools, representing his people in the first federal cabinet,[165] and working to prevent backlash against Irish Catholics after the Fenian invasion.[166] At the same time, he was also an outspoken critic of the Fenian Brotherhood. Active for Irish independence when he was younger, McGee was keen to redirect those radical passions towards moderate liberal-conservatism in Canada. As historian David Wilson put it, McGee was so passionate about fighting Fenianism because he "was trying to exorcise the Fenian within himself."[167] He gave his first major public speech against it in Wexford, Ireland, in May 1865, calling adherents a "pack of fools" and praising how Canada's concern for minority rights had given Irish Catholics a satisfactory position under British rule in North America.[168]

From that moment McGee became a target of radical Irish separatists in Ireland and Canada alike. He endured several violent confrontations during the first federal election in summer 1867, including at one public meeting in Montreal where a group of men threw stones at him when he called out Fenianism. His opponent in Montreal West, a fellow Irish Catholic named Bernard Devlin, actually confronted him in the streets, spat in his face, and called him a traitor to his people. McGee won Montreal West, but only by about two hundred votes. Support for the Irish plight was strong enough in his riding that his condemnation of Fenianism had alienated quite a few Irish-Catholic voters.[169]

In the early hours of the morning of 7 April 1868, Thomas D'Arcy McGee was shot through the back of the head on Sparks Street in downtown Ottawa. An Irish-Catholic tailor named Patrick James Whelan was arrested and charged with the murder, although he claimed innocence. The main evidence against him: Whelan had been in the area at the time of the shooting without a clear alibi, possessed a revolver that had recently been used, and had reportedly made threats against McGee at other times, and a witness near his cell claimed he heard the accused bragging about killing McGee.[170] A jury heard his case and deemed him guilty in September 1868. On 11 February 1869, before an estimated crowd of six thousand people, Patrick James Whelan climbed the scaffold and uttered his last words, "God save Ireland, and God save my soul," before dropping to his death at the end of the noose.[171]

Although the murder of a high-profile political figure was rare in nineteenth-century Canada, several details of the case reveal more general elements of Protestant–Catholic relations in the mid-to-late 1860s. The main thrust of Whelan's defence was to claim that he had been targeted due to his religion: "This is my impression," said Whelan, "that we Roman Catholics are looked on as traitors … I am accused of being a Fenian. Every Irish Roman Catholic has to stand just the same imputation."[172] During his trial, an Irish-Catholic witness named William Mitchell testified that Catholics had been treated differently at his place of work (for the Northern Railway) after the Fenian disturbance. According to Mitchell, several Protestant employees had demanded that the Catholics be dismissed. Alternatively, the employer decided to make all the employees swear an oath of allegiance, which some of the Catholics reportedly refused to do. According to the witness, this whole episode had been a "slight so unjustly cast upon his co-religionists."[173] McGee himself, despite praising Canada's general treatment of Catholics, had made similar claims about their occasionally being targeted with false accusations of disloyalty.[174]

Whereas Whelan and Mitchell offered a narrative of British-Canadian injustice towards Irish Catholics, Whelan's trial judge offered an alternative, liberal narrative. When Whelan claimed to have been targeted for his religion, Judge William Richards (later first chief justice of Ontario and later of Canada) reportedly interrupted him to remind him of the impartiality of his trial. In response to Whelan's claims that the English received favourable treatment in England, Richards snapped, "We are not in England!" He went on to give an eloquent defence of Ontario's liberalism and the equality of all individuals before the law regardless of religion or ethnicity: "Every man in this country is equal in the eye of the law, and … is no man especially disregarded on account of his religion or country. Your countrymen are on the same level as others … In this Province, your sect is equal to any other, and only across the river [in Quebec], you will find it actually superior, as the priests there have rights by law established which they enjoy in no other country on the northern part of this continent."[175] In other words, perceived injustices in the past were not supposed to exist today (except perhaps in Quebec). Just as George Brown had worked to relegate religious issues to the provinces, Judge Richards sought to relegate them to the old world and to the past. Canada was resolutely *not* England, after all, and thus should have no part in its inter-religious conflicts.

Richards was certainly not alone in his belief that Canada ought to be an even playing field wherein the animosities of the past were irrelevant. However, even in 1869, this expression of the "neutral liberty" perspective still had a long way to go before it would convince the rest of the population. For others, including most Liberal voters in Ontario, this emergent liberal narrative competed with the specific Protestant or Catholic narratives that emphasized historic mistreatment at the hands of the other group. Despite their fierce suspicions of one another, the devout of both groups shared the belief that the old feuds could never die. "Liberty" for Protestants meant freedom from the popish "Inquisition" that had long haunted the shadows of their imaginations.[176] By the same token, "liberty" for Irish Catholics meant freedom from the "sneering Saxon tyrant" who had sought to extinguish their language and faith. Whatever their differences, both sides agreed that they could never be free if the other group regained the upper hand. In that sense, for both sets of adherents, it was not a setting aside of the memory of the past that made them free. Rather, it was precisely *because* they remembered past conflicts, and fought against their recurrence in Canada, that they could now hope to be free.

Conclusion

Canadian Confederation was a major diplomatic achievement not only because it brought together people of different religious and cultural backgrounds to form a new political union, but because it secured the amicable divorce of Protestant Upper Canada from Catholic Lower Canada. Contrary to the twenty-first-century celebrations of Canada's founding moment as a harbinger of modern pluralism, political and religious leaders in the Confederation era explicitly expressed preference for societies with a high degree of religious and cultural homogeneity and had little interest in the further pluralization of their respective provinces. After being bound for twenty-seven years in a legislative union wherein each side tussled for its own interests, Protestants and Catholics alike had recognized the need for separate jurisdictions and had become deeply pessimistic about the feasibility of their bicultural united province. Even after Confederation, all sides jealously guarded the representation of their own people at all levels of government, sought to encourage people abroad from their own group to immigrate to the new dominion, exercised extreme caution regarding the intentions and actions of rival groups, and were occasionally willing to take up arms against the other side. With the exception of allowances for each province's respective Protestant or Catholic minority, provincial autonomy was based on the idea that Ontario was a "Protestant part of Canada" and Quebec was the Catholic part.

Liberalism in Confederation-era Canada thus occupied a position that would appear paradoxical to some observers today. In a land in which everyone was theoretically treated as an individual without regard to religion, it was still perfectly normal to make appeals to past religious conflicts during election campaigns, politicize immigration based on concerns about religious demographic change, and to speak about Canada as a Christian nation. The reality was that, despite liberal insistence on an even playing field in which the past was not supposed to matter, all sides were incapable of fully separating their public life from their historic collective identities. For Protestant Dissenters, it was not a contradiction to say that Canada would be a tolerant liberal nation and a Christian nation. Indeed, many believed that the only way that Canada could be the former was if it upheld the principles of Protestant Christianity and kept in check the "tyrannical" impulses of illiberal non-Protestant faiths. The narrative of "Protestant liberty" had not yet given way to its counterpart, "neutral liberty."

Returning a strong sense of this religious context allows us to reconsider the relationship between the new dominion and culture. Whereas some recent studies have argued that the founders purposefully designed a country neutral to cultural identity with a loose form of national unity based on common material interests (the neutral-materialist interpretation), placing Confederation within the forty-year trajectory of the Upper Canadian reform movement brings a startling gestalt shift. First, the Confederation talks would not likely have taken place when they did (or at all) if it had been left to the proponents of neutral liberty, who were often content with working across sectional lines and continuously seeking out concessions between Protestants and Catholics. Rather, it was the Protestant liberty of George Brown and his supporters that demanded an end to the status quo of the united province: they refused to offer further concessions to Catholicism and saw a wider federal union as the way to secure their own provincial autonomy. Second, it is clear that Protestants and Catholics alike took for granted that Canada would be a Christian nation, and many politicians and clergymen expressed the expectation that their particular version of Christianity would thrive and set the tone for future generations. In the words of the *Canadian Independent*, Providence had assigned them a monumental task: "the founding of a Christian State in this northern part of North America."[177]

5

Truckling to Rome

The Early National Period, 1870–1878

After Confederation, George Brown's leadership in the Liberal party had come to an end. Brown had failed to win his seat in the 1867 election, and subsequently played a more secondary role in Canadian politics, later serving as a diplomat to the United States and as a member of the Canadian Senate. Still, at the start of the 1870s, Brown looked back on the previous two decades with a strong sense of accomplishment. Reflecting in 1871 on his time as Liberal leader, he emphasized the significance of federalism for Protestant autonomy in Ontario: "French Canadian interference in our affairs has been brought to an end … The protestant majority is completely dominant in our province, and the catholics placed by their scattered position at disadvantage."[1] Now that the Liberals had helped secure provincial autonomy for Ontario's Protestant majority, however, Brown had passed the baton on to a handful of men with different priorities and strategies. At Ontario's provincial level, the Liberal opposition to new provincial premier John Sandfield Macdonald's coalition first revolved around longtime Brownite Archibald McKellar. By 1870, however, the provincial leadership fell to the young lawyer Edward Blake, who served briefly as premier before joining federal politics. The provincial mantle then fell to Oliver Mowat, who went on to govern as premier from 1872 to 1896. At the federal level, longtime Brownite Alexander Mackenzie emerged as George Brown's successor and ultimately served as Canada's first Liberal prime minister from 1873 to 1878. These years of relative success for the Liberal party from 1870 to 1878 also moved it away significantly from Brown's legacy, as it tried to solidify its political position by courting the Catholic vote and downplaying the more divisive aspects of its Dissenting Protestant heritage.

This next generation of leaders began to modify the relationship between the party and Protestant Dissent. Although both Alexander Mackenzie and Oliver Mowat came from a background of Protestant Dissent and from the party's Brownite wing, their new way of handling religion-based controversies indicated the growing strength of the "neutral liberty" ethos. If Brown's two decades in politics marked the pinnacle of Protestant expression within the Liberal party, the 1870s represents a transition wherein electoral strategy nudged it away from its Protestant roots. The shift is most visible in party rhetoric, which increasingly omitted and / or condemned Protestant assertiveness, provoking discontent from longtime liberal reformers. For example, the liberal Quebec Protestant Robert Sellar was at first a strong supporter of Alexander Mackenzie, but quickly became disillusioned by what he perceived to be the new leader's abandonment of liberal principles in order to appeal to Catholic voters. After Mackenzie publicly expressed support for New Brunswick's separate Catholic schools, allowed separate schools into the North West Territories Act of 1875, and granted amnesty to participants in the Red River Rebellion of 1869–70, Sellar issued "a warning to Mackenzie that his truckling to Rome is alienating from his Ministry the support of all true Liberals."[2]

This "truckling to Rome" represents a major step in the making of Canada's emergent liberal order. Ian McKay has emphasized Quebec's changes in the last quarter of the century to conform to liberal perspectives, particularly its gradual abandonment of the Catholic communitarian critique of capitalism.[3] However, this attempt to integrate Catholics into the liberal order also altered how politicians expressed their principles, and perhaps even the principles themselves. Thus, Mackenzie and Mowat's leadership in the 1870s became a transitional period, as Canadian liberalism sidelined direct appeals to Protestant liberty. Electoral strategy motivated this sea change: facing pressure from Catholic leaders and the realities of voter demographics, particularly the large Catholic population in Quebec and in several Ontario ridings, liberal politicians chose to broaden their message to bring in more votes. This conclusion is inspired in part by historian Margaret Evans, whose biography of Oliver Mowat explained how Catholic voting shaped his electoral strategy.[4] As this chapter demonstrates, Mowat's strategy coincided with the federal Liberals' approach under Mackenzie, and this demographic reality prompted a transformation in the way party leaders expressed liberalism.

On a deeper level, the shift correlates to the post-1870 reorientation in the role of religion in Canadian public life. Some historians have characterized this change as secularization, arguing that the influence of religious authority in public life began to wane and the Protestant churches in particular began to downplay the supernatural elements of their faith.[5] For proponents of the secularization thesis, this societal change was a direct consequence of Canadian liberalism and pluralism. According to David B. Marshall, "In a modern liberal society such as Canada the key to understanding the process of secularization rests in the fact that religion and the churches are part of a pluralistic society and are thrust into a market-place of competing ideas, values, activities, and institutions."[6] Faced with increasing pluralization, competitors in the religious marketplace often tailored their ideas to appeal to wider audiences, downplaying any supernatural sentiments that might have been alienating to new audiences and instead underlining more accessible ideas.[7] Other historians have disagreed, postulating that religion remained central in Canadian public life until after the Second World War and that Protestant churches held on to their essential beliefs.[8] Some critics still acknowledge significant changes for religion, such as emergence of traditionalist and progressive camps within Protestant denominations, but see "reorganization" and "metamorphosis" rather than secularization.[9] As this chapter illustrates, the Liberal party's declining public relationship with Protestant Dissent appears to fit the pattern of secularization described by Marshall and others, wherein some institutions silenced seemingly divisive religious expression in favour of more widely accessible neutral alternatives. The Liberal party's rejection of "Protestant liberty" appears to correspond to a broader pattern in which increased competition between Christian subcultures encouraged the neutralization of Christian expression in Canadian society.

These major changes in the Liberal party's relationship to Protestantism were highly contested, and it is unclear whether this new direction was inevitable or even necessary. As this chapter highlights, Liberal leaders such as Lucius Seth Huntington (MP for Shefford, near Sherbrooke) resisted Alexander Mackenzie's attempt to make the party neutral towards religion. In December 1875, Huntington proposed to continue the tradition of Protestant liberty by inviting Protestants of all political stripes to join forces with liberal Catholics to combat ultramontanism.[10] As we saw above, ultramontanism was a Catholic movement based on the assertion of papal supremacy in civil affairs. Its ideas were on the rise throughout the 1870s, in part due to Rome's declaration of papal infallibility during the Vatican Council of 1869–70, after which supporters in Canada issued a call for Catholic political action, which became known as "The Programme."[11] Although Mackenzie privately supported Huntington's views on ultramontanism, he publicly denounced the plan and insisted that religion be kept out of politics.[12]

Still, as this chapter reveals, Huntington found support from several prominent public figures such as former Conservative cabinet minister Alexander Galt and longtime reformer Charles Lindsey, who insisted that the fight for the separation of church and state was far from over.[13] The existence of such robust opposition serves as a reminder that the decline of the Dissent–liberal relationship required conscious choices by political leaders, and was not simply inevitable. The fact that Mackenzie's conciliatory approach did not save his party in the 1878 election also suggests that conciliation did not achieve what it was designed for, at least in the short term.

This transformation of Canadian liberalism from Protestant liberty to neutral liberty has been ignored by most political historians. Dale C. Thomson's *Alexander Mackenzie: Clear Grit* (1960) covers the religious controversies during the first Liberal ministry, including Huntington's controversial speech in 1875, but offers no interpretation of these events beyond illustrating the diplomatic difficulties Mackenzie faced as a statesman.[14] Peter Waite's *Arduous Destiny* (1971) includes a chapter on the religious controversies of the 1870s, noting Quebec's pressure on Mackenzie's approach to the Red River amnesty.[15] Rather than identifying Mackenzie's policies as the start of a significant conceptual shift for the party, however, these writers use such controversies mainly to set the stage for Wilfrid Laurier, whose new conciliatory approach would eventually win over Quebec to liberalism.[16] Ben Forster's entry on Alexander Mackenzie in the *Dictionary of Canadian Biography* highlights a legacy of electoral reform (i.e., secret ballot), economic liberalism, and fighting perceived corruption in government contracts, but does not detect a change in his approach to church–state issues or in the relationship between liberalism and Protestant Dissent.[17] More recent studies of Canadian liberalism generally downplay religion, sometimes treating it as a means of colonization, imposing aspects of liberalism on unwilling subjects.[18] Reducing religion to the handmaid of imperial expansion masks the subtleties of the changing relationship between religion and liberal thought, an oversight that this chapter (and indeed this entire study) hopes to correct. As we saw above, however, some historians have recently rediscovered the need to address religion as a factor in nineteenth-century Canadian liberalism,[19] a call to which this chapter responds.

This chapter examines the Liberal party's approach to religion at the federal level and at Ontario's provincial level, from the religious rhetoric surrounding the Red River Rebellion in 1870 to the end of Mackenzie's government in 1878. It explores the pressures on the party after George Brown's leadership and explains the transition from advocacy of "Protestant Liberty" to support for free trade, fiscal responsibility, and other policies that were neutral towards cultural differences. Although Dissenting culture had shaped the formative generations of Canadian liberalism, the 1870s represent a turning point in which, when pressed, most liberal leaders muted the religious origins of their ideas and invoked secular and culturally inoffensive explanations. By the end of this decade, the stage was set for a new generation of liberals, epitomized by the Quebec Catholic Wilfrid Laurier, who, like LaFontaine and Baldwin, would attempt to reconcile Protestant and Catholic Canadians. Thus, despite the disapproval of several vocal Protestant liberals, the era of Alexander Mackenzie and the early Oliver Mowat wound down the five-decade Dissent–liberal relationship that had characterized, even defined, early Victorian Canada.

"The Banishment of Religious Jealousy": Liberals Seek the Catholic Vote

After leaving the Great Coalition of 1864, the Liberal party had yet again been relegated to the opposition in both post-Confederation Ontario and the new federal Parliament in Ottawa. However, after two very close calls in elections in 1871 in Ontario and for federal Parliament in 1872, they began to realize that governance was within reach. Beginning in Ontario in 1871, the party began to solicit the

Catholic vote directly as a centrepiece in its electoral strategy.[20] Still, many Liberal voters were devoted to the concept of Protestant liberty: they watched with caution as the Catholic hierarchy mobilized voters under the ultramontane *programme* in Quebec, as the Catholic bishop of St-Boniface, Alexandre-Antonin Taché, negotiated a deal between the Métis at Red River and the Canadian government, and as Catholic clerics continued to exercise political influence in a number of ridings in Ontario. Liberal leaders, however, began to believe they needed a new strategy lest they become the perpetual opposition. This section follows the Liberal party in Ontario from the aftermath of the Riel Rebellion in 1870 to Alexander Mackenzie's seizing of power in Ottawa in 1873 to explain how party leaders shifted their strategy to become more inclusive vis-à-vis Catholics and Protestants alike, just as the Conservatives had been for several decades. Despite a few public instances of Protestant outrage, the party tended to suppress inter-religious animosity and redirect its message to accommodation in the hopes of achieving and maintaining power.

The last major flashpoint of Protestant angst the party exploited was the fallout from the Red River Rebellion. By the summer of 1870, Ontarians had read for months about the crisis at Red River. The conflict had begun as a dispute over land and sovereignty following the recent sale of Hudson's Bay Company land claims to the government of Canada. The young Catholic Métis leader Louis Riel and his supporters had resisted the efforts of the land surveyors and established their own provisional government before ultimately negotiating for Manitoba to join Confederation with demands for Catholic schools, land guarantees for the Métis, and a bilingual legislature.[21]

By the early spring of 1870, news had reached Ontarians that one of their own had been killed in the conflict, a Protestant named Thomas Scott, and several more had been imprisoned for defying Louis Riel and his provisional government.[22] In an attempt to end the conflict peacefully, John A. Macdonald's Conservative government had enlisted Bishop Taché to mediate between Ottawa and the Catholic-majority rebels. Protestant Ontarians were concerned, however, that Taché sympathized too much with the rebellion, and that his promises of amnesty had left justice unserved. Worse still, some members of the Ontario press speculated that the rebellion had been incited by the Catholic clergy, which, one writer reported, had even threatened to excommunicate the faithful who refused to support Riel. In the words of the *Globe:* "The whole disturbance was instigated, fomented and maintained by the French clergy … Others had been excommunicated who declined prompt obedience to the revolution."[23]

The role of Catholic clerics was only one of many Protestant Canadian objections about the Red River conflict and its eventual settlement. Carl Berger argued that the conflict posed the question of which culture would define the region and "what institutions were to be permanently stamped upon the garden in the west."[24] As Doug Owram explained, the majority of Canadians favouring expansion were Protestants who had "an almost instinctive suspicion of the Roman Catholic church" and tended to see the Métis as acting under priestly direction rather than out of their own volition and interests.[25] Thus, when the Red River delegates communicated their Bill of Rights in April 1870, Protestant Canadians examined the sections that demanded recognition of a vast expanse of land for the Métis, French-language provisions, amnesty for rebels (implying no justice for the death of Thomas Scott), and Catholic schools.[26] For Protestant Ontarians, such concessions meant that the ruling Conservatives in Ottawa had essentially created "a New Quebec" and had thus given the French-Catholic Canadians an upper hand in an ongoing culture war.[27]

When worried citizens met in Toronto's St Lawrence Hall in July 1870 to condemn the Conservative federal cabinet's proposed amnesty for the rebels, Catholic–Protestant divisions in the crisis led their concerns. Captain James Bennett declared the conflict and later negotiations "a trial of strength between Protestant Ontario and Catholic Quebec." Holding aloft the very rope reportedly used to bind Thomas Scott before his execution, Bennett asserted that the recent negotiations had been "part of Bishop Taché's scheme to keep the North-West for the French Catholics." Bennett ended with a direct call for political action, saying that, in defiance of Taché's supposed scheme, "the people of Ontario would unite to elect Protestants to represent them." Kenneth Mackenzie expressed concern that the settlement was "under ecclesiastical rule" and argued that it was "wrong that Red River should be possessed entirely by Roman Catholics." William McDougall, appointed lieutenant-governor of the North-West Territory before being turned away by Riel's supporters, equated Riel with the Fenians and urged the dominion government to send men to Red River who would "not permit the Fenian flag to float any longer over Fort Garry."[28] According to these speakers, the very same religious controversies that had shaped Upper Canadian politics – Catholic versus Protestant, Fenian disloyalty versus Protestant loyalty, Catholic ecclesiastical rule versus Protestant separation of church and state – now appeared to apply to the northwest.[29]

The Liberal party in Ontario was at the forefront of this public outcry and fully expected to use the controversy to redirect votes away from Macdonald's Conservatives. The strategy at first appeared to be working. Three ex-members of Macdonald's cabinet had denounced the government's actions and either sat as independents or sided with the Liberal opposition: Richard Cartwright, Alexander Galt, and William McDougall.[30] At the July meeting, a Mr Fleming announced that, although he had never voted for the Liberals before, he would do so in the future as long as they would "sustain the integrity of the British empire."[31] Even after Riel received recognition and praise from Lieutenant-Governor McDougall for helping to put down a Fenian threat in 1871, the Liberals of Ontario continued to demand justice for the death of Thomas Scott. When Alexander Mackenzie served briefly as the treasurer of Ontario in 1872, he offered on behalf of the province a $5,000 reward for the capture of Louis Riel.[32]

Examined in hindsight, however, the Liberals' anti-Riel campaign appears to be their last unabashed appeal to Protestant identity. Despite their willingness to lobby for the Protestant vote right after the 1869 rebellion, over the next four years several Liberal leaders realized that they must stop their Protestant appeals so they could expand beyond that historic voting base. In March 1871, George Brown wrote a public letter to Roman Catholics in response to a Catholic group in Ontario that had inquired about the party's position on their religion.[33] Brown indicated his desire to bury the hatchet and invited Catholics to consider voting Liberal again. He painted a rosy picture of interfaith relations: "We have banished sectarian discord from our legislative and executive chambers," and both sides now "have a degree of consideration for the religious views and feelings of each other, that no living man ever witnessed in Canada till now."[34] Such statements pair awkwardly with that of Captain James Bennett, who only seven months earlier had anticipated "war was to be declared between Catholics and Protestants" in the wake of the Riel Rebellion.[35] Thus when Brown declared the "banishment of religious jealousy and discord" from Canadian politics,[36] it was more a gesture of diplomacy than a statement of reality.

George Brown issued his public letter to Roman Catholics as a campaign manoeuvre just weeks before the Ontario election of March 1871. For Liberals, the campaign began with a strong sense that if they could capture the province they would soon be able to win federally as well. As one *Globe* editorial put it, "Much depends upon the Local [provincial] election. Mr. Sandfield Macdonald is the bulwark of the Ottawa Government. If one falls, the other must also go. The fate of the whole Dominion will be decided in many important particulars by the exertions of Reformers now."[37]

Seizing their opportunity, the Liberals under Edward Blake followed Brown's lead to carefully avoid alienating Catholic voters. Early on, Blake's formal campaign statement made no mention of religion or culture and instead condemned a few key policies of Sandfield Macdonald's government. Most of Blake's criticisms emphasized fiscal restraint, attacking too much money spent on a new College of Technology, a "palace" for the lieutenant-governor in Toronto, and grants for railway companies. He promised that if elected he would work with "earnestness and sincere desire for the advancement of your material interests."[38] When Alexander Mackenzie addressed two thousand people in Hamilton, he accused the premier of being in Sir John A.'s pocket and urged voters to support Liberals, who, he promised, "would pass such enactments as would bring wealth, contentment, and happiness to all the sections of the country."[39] Two weeks later, Blake himself also spoke at a rally in Hamilton. He referenced religion twice. First, he mentioned Roman Catholicism in the context of separate schools, only to explain that he believed the matter to have been settled at Confederation – thus reassuring Catholics that he would leave the existing system in place. Second, he suggested that the province must rely on God, and "to appeal to Him in this crisis of our national existence, and to call upon Him, as I ask you to join with me in doing, in the prayer that 'God may defend the right.'"[40] Surely such a vague statement would have been acceptable to both Protestants and Catholics. During the 1871 campaign, party leaders chose rather to emphasize material progress, fiscal restraint, and independence from coalitions.

Still, some voters clearly believed that the Liberals were the best representatives of Protestant interests. For example, some commentators continued to raise the question of justice for Thomas Scott to remind Protestants of the Conservatives and coalitionists' apparent softness. The Orangemen in particular appeared willing to abandon their traditional Conservative vote to support the Liberals. "A Protestant Orangemen" wrote to the *Globe*'s editor that, despite much of the Orange Order remaining Conservative, he believed its "best thanks are due to Mr. Blake for having taken action in the matter of Scott's murder. They [Orangemen] will unite with their fellow-Protestants in hurling Sandfield Macdonald and his colleagues from power."[41] Another called on his fellow Orangemen to abandon the Conservatives, whom he described as selling out Protestants on the Red River issue: "Those office-seekers; they would sell us for a mess of pottage. They *have* sold us."[42] At the same time that Liberals reached out to Conservative-voting Catholics, it looked as if they might have some appeal to similarly leaning Protestants.

When the results came in, Liberals had gained seats but not a majority. Still, with the ruling coalition seriously weakened, now reliant on independent members, Blake's Liberals could wait for a non-confidence motion and perhaps form government. That summer Liberals held several celebratory dinners and rallies throughout the province, trying to convey that they were ready to govern. Their message focused on the economy and trade. Since the election, details of the Washington Treaty (a U.S.–British agreement that directly affected Canada) had begun to emerge, and the Liberals were ready to criticize perceived concessions such as increased American access to Canadian waterways and fisheries.[43] They also continued reaching out to Catholics, even using Brown's wording in his March letter. For example, at a dinner in North Wellington, Oxford South MP Ebenezer Vining Bodwell was "glad to observe that the Reform Catholics of Ontario were throughout the whole Province returning to the ranks of the party … all those vexed questions which separated them in the past, having long ago been settled."[44] Brown's March letter had stated, "All the vexed questions that caused the separation have been settled and swept away, and now all are free to act together for the advancement and prosperity of our country, and to treat all men alike, without regard to their religious opinions."[45] Brown's signal from the top had apparently resonated through the ranks.

The premier's tenuous grasp on power quickly slipped away in the autumn of 1871. Edward Blake's Liberals had launched court challenges in a handful of close ridings. Due to the recent Controverted Elections Act, seats had to remain vacant during a court challenge, and several MLAS who would have supported the government were ineligible to vote. Blake called and won non-confidence motions, but the premier contested them because of the ongoing court cases. Still, a few in his inner circle began to notice the writing on the wall, and expressed interest in crossing the floor to Blake's Liberals. On 19 December 1871, the cabinet admitted it had lost the confidence of the House, and the premier resigned.[46]

Premier-designate Blake immediately sought to reach out to Catholic voters. He invited into cabinet Catholic Liberal MLA and Speaker Richard W. Scott (city of Ottawa) – a longstanding advocate for separate schools, which had been entrenched in the Scott Act of 1863, which the Brownites had strongly opposed.[47] Scott reported privately to John A. Macdonald on 20 December 1871 that Blake was so "anxious" to recruit him that he had offered him "any portfolio I chose to name."[48] Before accepting, Scott wrote to several Conservative colleagues to ask their advice and to assure them that such position "will not affect my allegiance to old political friends but rather help them."[49] John A. wrote back the next day saying he would "not offer you advice against taking office" but counselled him that any agreement with Blake should "be secured by writing."[50]

Clearly Blake gave Scott a prominent position (commissioner of crown lands) to send a signal to Roman Catholics about the Liberal party's openness to their religion. Only the previous month, the Conservative John Carling had offered Scott the Speakership for the same reason, noting that Scott's prominence in Conservative circles would "render his position useful hereafter with his co-religionists at the Dominion Elections."[51] Although John A. publicly accused Scott of "having turned turtle,"[52] their correspondence indicates otherwise. With Scott agreeing to join Blake's cabinet, the Conservatives effectively had a mole in the cabinet – if Scott's own words are any indication. The Liberals seemed willing to accept his questionable allegiance to present a Catholic-friendly face to the province.

Some of the push to include Catholics appears to have come from local pressures from substantially Catholic ridings. In private correspondence with leaders, some Liberal organizers conveyed the urgency of placing Catholics in the new cabinet to appease local voters. In December 1871, a Mr Jarnot wrote to Alexander Mackenzie about a by-election in Simcoe North. Jarnot reported that local Liberals had contacted the archbishop of Toronto, John Joseph Lynch, in hopes that "he would urge the Catholics to go as one man" for their preferred candidate, Mr Ramsay. However, in the end the archbishop favoured the Conservative incumbent, William Davis Ardagh, to which Jarnot remarked, "Politics is a muddy sea to fish in."[53] The riding ultimately went to the prelate's pick.[54]

In December, a Mr McCauley wrote to Alexander Mackenzie that "in this riding [unnamed] no man need attempt to run unless the R.C. vote can be minded." McCauley suggested the Liberals were indebted to the Catholic clergy for their local success and should reciprocate: "I would not for the moment entertain the idea of a Cabinet without R.C. support."[55] Catholics made up only 16.9 per cent of Ontarians in 1871, down from their record high of 18.5 per cent in 1861.[56] Still, their concentration in a handful of eastern ridings, such as Ottawa, Glengarry, Prescott, and Russell,[57] offered the Liberals an edge in forming government. As the Liberals realized it was possible to seize provincial power for the first time since before Confederation, the temptation was difficult to resist.

If Catholics had become influential in Ontario's politics with only 16.9 per cent of the population, they were absolutely essential at the federal level, with 43 per cent of the national total.[58] As they dreamt of controlling Parliament, Liberals such as George Brown and Alexander Mackenzie realized that they simply could not afford to risk alienating that community. In the lead-up to the 1872 federal election, the Liberals made several direct overtures to Catholic voters while claiming to run a religion- and ethnicity-blind campaign. At a rally in Toronto's St Lawrence Hall in July 1872, Alexander Mackenzie and other Liberal leaders publicly offered their support for the Catholic candidate for East Toronto, John O'Donohoe. In the opening speech, Mr K. McKenzie emphasized: "Questions of religion or class should not be considered in the election of a candidate. With Reformers all men were equal in the eye of the law." Mr Merrick celebrated the "generous action of the Protestant Reformers of East Toronto" and hoped that O'Donohoe's nomination "signalizes the union between the great Reform party and the Catholic body." If Liberals supported Catholic candidates, Merrick promised, "the great Catholic heart of Ontario would return it a hundred fold."[59]

Later that summer, the *Globe* republished George Brown's letter of the previous year, urging Catholics to vote Liberal.[60] And in perhaps one of the most delicious ironies in Canadian newsprint history, the *Globe* even accused a rival newspaper of stoking "shameful" anti-Catholicism for political purposes![61] One can only speculate about the temperature in hell that day. In any case, the *Globe*'s newfound sensitivity to Catholic feelings was merely one in a series of indications that the Liberals of Ontario had by the summer of 1872 wholeheartedly forsaken their "No popery" image of days gone by.

The 1872 federal election raised the issue of the Conservative government's handling of several issues, both economic and social, which ultimately weakened John A. Macdonald's party. On the economic front, rural Ontarians found nothing in the Washington Treaty to support their exports to the United States and interpreted the deal as serving the large railway interests, and Quebeckers began to question an economic policy that left so many of their people to migrate to New England for jobs.[62] On the social front, hardline Protestants could still not forgive Macdonald for the perceived lack of justice for Thomas Scott at Red River, and Catholics in New Brunswick found him unresponsive to their province's defunding of separate schools the previous year.[63] Thus the Liberal strategy to focus on the economy and to reach out to Catholics (without yet alienating Protestants) ultimately earned them many more seats, leaving the Conservatives with a very narrow majority.[64] George Brown looked on in optimistic approval, saying, "The elections have gone splendidly, and the final result does not now seem doubtful … To-morrow is our grand day!"[65]

The most surprising details of the 1872 election campaign were yet to be made public, however. As Liberals would later expose, Macdonald's Conservatives had apparently accepted a large campaign donation from American railway investors who expected in return to receive the lucrative government contracts to build the Canadian Pacific Railway. In April 1873, Liberal MP Lucius Huntington (Shefford) stood before the House and revealed this secret deal, which later came to be known as the "Pacific Scandal."[66] A parliamentary committee was formed the next day to investigate the matter, and the government managed to hold off on any fallout until the autumn session of 1873. Then the Liberals pressed the issue in the House for two weeks before calling and winning a vote of non-confidence in Macdonald. In November 1873, Alexander Mackenzie met with Governor-General Lord Dufferin to discuss forming government.[67]

The following January, the Liberals sought to secure their ascendancy by asking for a popular mandate in a new election. Party leaders were anxious not to lose their Protestant base in areas with a Catholic Liberal candidate, such as John O'Donohoe for Toronto East. Some Protestant Liberals openly complained about this Catholic nominee, but the party moved quickly to silence the objection. At the public nominations for Toronto East, one Mr Bain, who called himself a reformer, argued that "the reason that Mr. Donohoe was brought out was that it was felt by the friends of the Government [Mackenzie government] that this must be done to conciliate the Roman Catholics throughout the country." But "no Protestant would allow himself to vote for Mr. O'Donohoe" or "put it into the power of Roman Catholics to make laws for him." Bain was met by a "storm of hisses and groans" from the audience and took his seat. When O'Donohoe spoke next, he accused Bain of "religious fanaticism and extreme bigotry" and proposed: "The time for such ideas as these had passed." In order for the country to continue "progressing in the future," he insisted, such sentiments would have to disappear.[68]

On election eve, an all-star cast of Liberal leaders stumped for O'Donohoe at a massive rally in Toronto East, showing party solidarity above religious differences. The new prime minister, Alexander Mackenzie, spoke in support of O'Donohoe, and also on his government's plans for the next few years if re-elected. He promised that Macdonald's alleged corruption would be replaced by honesty and that he would also seek to meet government commitments to build the transcontinental railway while keeping construction costs low. He added that he was disappointed in some people's objections to Chinese labour on the railway and asked "why [they] were not prepared to welcome to our shores men of all creeds and colours." In hindsight, this statement was the perfect expression of the liberal ethos that would come to characterize Mackenzie's government: a seamless blend of cost effectiveness *and* benevolent tolerance. When George Brown spoke next, he denied the rumour that O'Donohoe had been chosen "because he was a Roman Catholic" and reiterated that "the time had now arrived when all religious and sectional feeling should be laid aside."[69]

With critics like Bain thoroughly shouted down and rebuked by the party leadership, the Liberals had a clear path to victory. When votes were counted, Mackenzie secured a formidable majority, with 138 out of 206 seats. His party claimed strong representation in every province except British Columbia, and even captured a majority of Quebec's federal seats, with thirty-five out of sixty-five there.[70] Party leaders had learned a powerful lesson, it seemed: if they were willing to deny their "No popery" roots and silence the element that still clung to them, they could win over a large portion of Quebec and enough Catholic voters to make gains in Ontario. Yet the question remained: how long could they continue on such a path before more longtime Protestant devotees would come to share Mr Bain's perspective? How long before they began to wonder whether their own interests and concerns had been sacrificed for electoral gain? Such questions had no doubt crossed Mackenzie's mind. He knew the strength of conviction in the "No popery" cry. He was a Protestant who had lived through mid-century Upper Canada, and such convictions had once stirred his own soul. Bain's objections had been silenced for now, but they were not so alien to many in the party, least of all Mackenzie himself. Now holding power through a delicate balance of factions and interests, he no doubt wondered when the ghosts of Protestants past would come to call.

"Mr. Huntington prefers to strike back": The Turning Point for Protestant Liberty

The old reformer James Lesslie was an elderly man now, retired from the public eye and managing his farm in Eglinton, Ontario (now fairly central in Toronto). His diaries reveal that his evangelical faith had only strengthened with time, with frequent notes about assisting with Bible classes, distributing tracts about the Word of God, and regularly noting exceptional current events such as earthquakes and wars as "signs of the times" pertaining to Jesus' return.[71] On his seventieth birthday, Lesslie wrote in his diary about his gratitude to God for leading him through so much in his life, and he resolved, "May my remaining days be more consecrated to the service of Him who loved us & gave himself for us."[72] In the true spirit of evangelical conversionism, he also shared his faith directly with anyone who would listen. For example, in 1872 he described sharing a carriage ride with an old friend on their way back from a funeral in Toronto. The occasion apparently raised the subject of life after death, as Lesslie mentioned he had "a conversation with him on the mighty theme of 'life and immortality' only through the Lord Jesus."[73]

Lesslie's faith in the Liberal party, however, had waned. The party that had seemed to align so well with his faith in earlier years now appeared unrecognizable. When he had served as editor of the *Examiner* back in 1851, he had proudly defended George Brown's use of the phrase "high Protestant ground" and had even encouraged reformers in their "application of moral and religious principles to political duty."[74] Two decades later he described his incredulity at seeing placards "from two professed 'Reformers'" supporting an unnamed individual who had apparently "been convicted of a degrading crime." Sharing a carriage ride on his way to vote in the civic elections in 1872, Lesslie had a conversation with an old acquaintance who "had ceased to vote on such occasions" because he only saw "each party seeking to subserve their own interests while ostensibly acting for the good of the whole." Lesslie himself said he was "almost led to form a similar determination." Although he continued to vote, he appeared to see little redeemable in the earthly politics of his golden years and could only cling to the old hope that governance would be different in the Millennium. As he concluded, "There will come, ere long, *under Jesus*, a reign of righteousness."[75]

The Liberal party that Lesslie had helped to build would, over the next few years, secure its transition away from the "Protestant liberty" that Lesslie had championed. Instead it would move towards a neutral expression of liberal principles that was more useful in an ostensibly bicultural society. This shift was marked by a series of religion-based controversies the Liberal party faced as it ruled in Ontario at both the federal and provincial levels. Premier Oliver Mowat began his first government with attempts to appeal to both Protestants and Catholics, with dubious results. Early in 1873, a private member's bill proposed incorporating the Orange Order, which would have allowed it to hold property. At first, Mowat reasoned that the bill was simply a matter of tolerance and fairness to an old organization and voted with a majority of MLAs to pass the bill. However, the backlash from Catholic leaders was swift. Archbishop Lynch warned Mowat that Catholics would not only riot but also cease voting Liberal. The pressure forced the premier to walk back his support. His first strategy was to ask the lieutenant-governor to reserve the bill for Parliament to overturn, but John A., still prime minster, refused to take the fall for his enemy's mess. In the end, Mowat argued that the bill was ineligible for royal assent because previous attempts to incorporate the Orange Order in British jurisdiction had been denied (namely, in Prince Edward Island in 1863). Thus, the bill stopped dead at the viceroy's desk, and Mowat redeemed himself in the eyes of the Catholic hierarchy.[76]

The premier's decision to walk back the incorporation reveals not only the rising influence of Catholic leaders, but also the contested nature of "tolerance" in Ontario. Whereas Mowat and some people in the liberal press had referred to the bill as a matter of toleration, Catholic leaders disagreed. In a private letter dated March 1873, John Walsh, Catholic bishop of London (Ontario), thanked Catholic, Liberal MLA Richard W. Scott (Ottawa) for opposing the measure. The prelate argued that it would have been "more than toleration, it is positive approval." Central to the bishop's concerns was the perennial liberal question: to what extent can a tolerant society tolerate the intolerant? He emphasized the Orange Order's history of "hate and bigotry" and rebuked it at length as "the embodiment of intolerance and hatred." To grant it legal recognition, he said, would be "the greatest outrage that could probably be offered to the Catholic body in Ontario."[77] Mowat's original instinct to tolerate the supposedly intolerant was ultimately overridden. For a premier dependent on Catholic voters, any philosophical debates about the nature of tolerance gave way to electoral concerns. In this sense, the feelings of one sizable portion of the population held a strong veto over philosophical consistency.

One of Prime Minister Alexander Mackenzie's first challenges in balancing Catholic and Protestant perspectives was to determine Louis Riel's fate. Technically still a fugitive in Ontario for the alleged murder of Thomas Scott, the Métis leader had actually been elected MP for Provencher, in Manitoba, in the 1874 federal election. Although in opposition the Liberals had adamantly condemned Macdonald's talks of amnesty, by the time they were ruling in 1874 they knew their position was untenable outside Ontario. The French-Canadian press generally expressed sympathy for the Métis and accused Mackenzie's government of leading with only Ontario's interests in mind.[78] The prime minister certainly had to shake this reputation if he wanted to maintain sufficient support in Quebec. With some of his Quebec MPs expressing support for Riel, he had to reconsider his hardline position to preserve party unity and possibly even his new government.

One of the most eloquent proponents of amnesty was the young Quebec Liberal MP Wilfrid Laurier (Drummond-Arthabaska). Elected for the first time in 1874, Laurier rose in the House during his first session to offer support. He appealed primarily to "the guarantees of British liberty," saying it was wrong to "deprive another man of his liberty, his property, his honour and all that makes life dear."[79] Aside from references to British law dating back to Magna Carta, the rookie MP was explicitly neutral towards culture. He claimed that he had "no bond of sympathy" with the Métis leader and was "as impartial as if I was in the jury box."[80] He downplayed his own French identity, and Riel's, and emphasized the fact that all Canadians regardless of culture were British subjects entitled to the familiar Lockean rights to life, liberty, and property: "I am of French origin and my education has been French, but I have this of the Briton in me: an ardent love of fair play and of justice … I shall never consent, in this instance or any other, to deprive a man of the smallest particle of his rights or property without first having given him the benefit of all the legal forms to defend himself."[81] Indeed, all of the Métis actions at Red River, he said, stemmed from the fact that "they wanted to be treated like British subjects and not to be bartered away like common cattle."[82] His rhetoric mirrors the way Riel's opponents appealed to "British liberty" to support the opposite position, calling for vengeance for Thomas Scott's death. For example, one commentator in the Toronto *Globe* back in March 1870 had written that Scott's execution meant that "the sacred nature of a Briton's life and liberty have been cast to the winds by Mr. Riel." It was the Britons who stood up to him, said the writer, whose "rights are denied."[83] Four years later, Laurier had turned the sentiment on its head by casting the rebel leader as a British subject merely standing up for his British rights and liberties.

Early in the new year 1875, Mackenzie's cabinet decided to address the issue once and for all. The pressure again came from the Quebec side of the caucus, with MP Luther Holton (Châteauguay) writing in late

January that "the Gov't *must agree on a policy* before Parliament meets or very serious embarrassments will arise for the House ... A complete or conditional amnesty (I should hope the former) will be found to be the only practicable mode of [dispensing] with the matter."[84] In February 1875, Mackenzie announced amnesty for Riel provided that he exile himself from the country for five years and a general amnesty without conditions for the other participants in the uprising.[85] The resolution's preamble effectively blamed the previous government for creating the problem and for making public announcements of amnesty that tied the hands of subsequent governments and judiciaries.[86] Mackenzie added that although Scott's execution was a crime, the proposed compromise "tempered justice with mercy" and would allow the country to move past the difficulties caused, he again stressed, by the previous government.[87] While Mackenzie wished to indicate that his decision came from a place of mercy, close observers knew he had to placate his Quebec members who sympathized with Riel.

Only one month later, the familiar Protestant–Catholic disagreement surrounding education re-emerged, this time in Parliament. On 12 March 1875, the cabinet proposed a bill to consolidate the laws governing the North-West Territory – roughly the remainder of Rupert's Land outside of Manitoba (including present-day Alberta and Saskatchewan). The initial bill did not refer to education, a point that Mackenzie admitted "did not in the first place attract [my] attention." It was MP Edward Blake (Bruce South), former Ontario premier, who raised the matter, stating that it was "essential under the circumstances of the country" to include a clause on separate schools so as not to "introduce into that territory the heartburnings and difficulties with which certain other portions of the Dominion and other countries have been afflicted." Mackenzie consented to revisions to include separate Catholic or Protestant schools where either faith was the minority. The revised bill passed the House with ease, but received some serious objections in the Senate, before becoming law. George Brown, recently appointed a senator by Mackenzie, argued to exclude the education clause because such matters were provincial. Brown also noted, "There would be no end of confusion if each class had to have its own peculiar school system." Nearly half of the senators agreed with him, but their amendment lost by twenty-two to twenty-four, and the original bill passed with separate schools intact.[88]

Although to preserve his government Mackenzie had remained neutral towards religious differences, new religion-based controversies continued to emerge in 1875 and forced Liberals to take sides. In March an MP from New Brunswick proposed restoring Catholic separate schools there, which the province disbanded a few years after Confederation. Mackenzie insisted that the matter was provincial, but surprised his Protestant supporters by expressing the hope for the schools' reinstatement.[89] In September 1875, a violent encounter between Protestants and Catholics on Toronto's streets was named the Jubilee Riot for Pope Pius IX's declaration of a Year of Jubilee for Catholics to make pilgrimages to receive a special remission of sins. Protestants confronted eight thousand Catholics marching peacefully between several local churches and holding aloft crucifixes and banners, and several injuries and arrests followed.[90] Several Protestant denominational papers and some Protestant clergymen advocated banning Catholic processions, calling them idolatrous and violations of the Sabbath. Most liberal politicians, however, including George Brown, again signalled good wishes to Catholics by insisting that they be allowed to march. The Presbyterian Rev. James Gardner Robb publicly condemned Brown's "spurious liberality," which he said represented a failure to stand up for Christian truth.[91]

By the end of 1875, enthusiasm for Alexander Mackenzie had clearly faded among some Protestant Liberals, chiefly because of his neutral approach to Protestant–Catholic controversies. The Huntingdon *Gleaner*, for instance, a Quebec newspaper run by the Liberal Protestant Robert Sellar, had praised him at the beginning but since grown mutinous. Soon after he was sworn in, the *Gleaner* had celebrated his rise from stonemason to prime minister through "perseverance and untiring energy, united with integrity."[92] However, on discovering his support for separate Catholic schools in New Brunswick and the North-West, and his amnesty for Louis Riel, the *Gleaner* concluded that he was in the pocket of Catholic leaders. When the Liberals lost a Toronto by-election in November 1875, the newspaper called it "a warning to Mackenzie that his truckling to Rome is alienating from his Ministry the support of all true Liberals."[93] The following month, reporting on an alleged Catholic arson attack on a Protestant church on the Oka First Nation reserve near Montreal, the *Gleaner* condemned his inaction: "If he does not desire that he should be looked upon as a tool of the Hierarchy, as one who sells his convictions for support, he must at once interfere on their behalf."[94] For those who shared Sellar's perspective, Mackenzie did nothing to correct this impression.

The prime minister's rough year of politicking across Protestant–Catholic lines would end with perhaps the biggest bombshell of them all: Lucius Huntington's controversial speech at Argenteuil, Quebec. The address came before a by-election, at a candidates' forum in Grenville on 30 December 1875, which showcased the local Liberal, Dr Christie, and the Conservative, Mr White. Lucius Huntington (Shefford) was postmaster general (a cabinet position) and attended the forum in support of Dr. Christie. According to the earliest news report, White raised the issue of religion first, claiming to have been mistreated for being a Protestant. In response, Huntington accused him of hypocrisy because White's Conservative party had courted the support of ultramontanists in Quebec, whom Huntington believed intended to suppress the free practice of Protestantism in the province. He warned about the danger they posed to the liberal principles of free speech and religious tolerance, "fighting in Lower Canada to make the State subservient to the Church, and to declare that the only duties of the former were the domination of the latter." Such a course of action, he feared, would "plunge Lower Canada back into the darkness of the middle ages." As a solution, he proposed that Protestants of all political stripes ally with Liberal Catholics to defend "the British idea of free thought and free speech" from the ultramontanist threat. Finally, he asserted that the entire Liberal cabinet supported his perspectives and that he "would be at once prepared to resign his position if he believed the party with whom he acted was not equal to their maintenance."[95]

For Alexander Mackenzie, who was trying as prime minister to patch over Protestant-Catholic tension, these comments were extremely unwelcome. Although he privately agreed with Huntington's views, he knew that such statements presented what we might call a public-relations crisis with the Roman Catholic voters who perceived the speech as an attack on their faith. Early in the new year he wrote to George Brown, "I fear Huntington's speech has done us harm with the Priests … The speech was correct in principle but I fear we are not strong enough with the English in Quebec hostile to us to carry that principle into effect."[96] Joseph Cauchon, president of the Privy Council, who had close ties to Catholic clergy, sought to smooth tension by communicating with Quebec's Archbishop Alexandre-Antonin Taché. The prelate had written to Cauchon about this "anti-Catholic" speech, which, he charged, sought to incite "a war of races and religions."[97] He later called the remarks a "serious and unjustifiable attack on Catholicism."[98] In a series of letters, Cauchon replied that the minister was stating his own individual views, which the cabinet did not share: "M. Huntington being a Protestant, spoke as a Protestant; and not as a Minister giving expression to the views of the Government as a whole."[99] Taché insisted that the government formally disavow the speech, or he would assume its tacit "approval at least by their silence."[100]

One minister from Quebec also demanded an apology. Luther Holton (Châteauguay), an anglophone Protestant but an outspoken proponent of conciliation with Catholics, condemned Huntington in the strongest terms and asked Mackenzie to rebuke him immediately. Holton explained that he had been a Protestant MP in a Catholic jurisdiction for several years and had never experienced such animosity, and warned that his colleague's comments threatened to undo every bit of progress they had made in Protestant–Catholic relations.[101] A few days later he called the address "the deadliest blow at the Liberal party of Lower Canada delivered these twenty years."[102] Mackenzie himself realized the stakes for his party's electoral prospects in the province, writing to George Brown: "That speech of Huntington's has given me such difficulty and has unfortunately lost us Lower Canada without any other gain being made … We cannot govern without a large following from Quebec and any aggressive act is seen to lose it for us."[103]

Pressure came from the other side too, with several Protestant Liberals celebrating Huntington's comments and demanding that the party stand up for him. An editorial in the Toronto *Nation,* which had emerged as a voice for the Canada First movement, labelled the address "the most remarkable utterance that has ever been made by a Minister of the Crown in Canada." It emphasized the ultramontanists' ongoing attempts to influence elections and argued that a Protestant alliance against them would be effective: "In the midst of active enemies, it would be poor strategy to pretend not to see them; to receive their blows with submission and without any that the attempt at self-defence. Mr. Huntington prefers to strike back."[104] The *Gleaner* similarly pronounced the MP was simply telling the truth about the ultramontanist danger and suggested that the government stand with him because the entire purpose of the Liberal party was "to denounce all manner of oppression and never cease to agitate until it is reformed." No apology or disavowal was necessary, and the party should support the remarks: "He has no reason to be shamefaced or apologetical; let him stick to what he said at Argenteuil and beard Mr. Holton and the Ultramontane hirelings to their face."[105]

Mackenzie avoided issuing a public response to Huntington for over a month, but finally Luther Holton forced his hand. During the debate on the throne speech in February 1876, Holton changed the subject to "a matter of very grave importance which had stirred the public mind of the Province of Quebec to its very depths," referring to the "unfortunate speech" at Argenteuil. After describing its contents, he asked the prime minister whether he directed Huntington to make those comments, and whether he "now approved of the substance of these remarks." Rising before the House, Alexander Mackenzie declared that he had nothing to do with the speech and that he did not approve of "anything that had a tendency to bring religion into public discussion in the politics of this country." A few others expressed support for the Catholics who, the House was reminded, had been so offended by the MP's words. Eventually, Lucius Huntington rose and was reportedly "loudly cheered on taking the floor." He simply stated that he made the comments as an individual, not as a minister, and did so "in reply to the attacks being made upon him and his party by those he assailed." He offered no apology, no disavowal. The last word went to Luther Holton, who made an impassioned plea for his party not to take a "new departure," which he said would inevitably convert "the society of the Province of Quebec, composed of mixed elements, into a pandemonium." He offered himself as an example, as an English Protestant who had served in Quebec "without referring to or dealing with the burning questions of race or creed."[106]

Despite Mackenzie's private agreement with Huntington about the ultramontanist threat to civil liberties, the party's precarious position in Quebec meant that such concerns had to remain unspoken. The stated purpose of Huntington's vision was to cooperate with liberal Catholics against ultramontanism; however, the Catholic leadership, the Catholic press, and some high-profile politicians all interpreted his remarks as an attack on the Catholic faith. Caught between the pressure of both Protestants and Catholics, Mackenzie tried to govern as neutral, which satisfied few and made several suspicious that he secretly supported the opposing side. In the end, it was Huntington's assertions of Protestant liberty that were placed on the defensive against accusations of bigotry and intolerance, and Holton's assertions of neutral liberty claimed the moral high ground. Facing the "mixed elements" of his electorate, Holton had made a virtue of neutralizing his own identity as an English Protestant. For Huntington and his supporters, however, this religion-blind approach prevented even open discussion of ultramontanists' influence, let alone organizing opposition to their designs. Neutral liberty may have helped maintain loose coalitions of diverse groups, but it came at the cost of prohibiting any substantive discussion about the future of religion in Canadian society, politics, and culture.

Huntington's speech at Argenteuil represented a turning point for the Liberal party in matters of religion because it forced the leaders to pick a side in a debate they had been avoiding. Huntington offered the party a clear alternative to its ongoing policy: rather than ceding ground to the Catholic hierarchy on issue after issue in the name of neutrality and accommodation, it could reawaken the cultural assertiveness of Canadian Protestants and their liberal Catholic allies. Together they could openly challenge the ultramontanists, whose express purposes were to subject civil law to church control (e.g., marriage, education, and acceptable speech about Catholicism). Protestant liberals might have also drawn strength from across the Atlantic, where Britain's former Liberal prime minister William Gladstone had the previous year issued a strong critique of ultramontane concepts like papal infallibility.[107] Canada's Liberal prime minister faced a different political reality, and felt he could not speak so openly on the subject. However, after years of scrubbing religion from his public life, Mackenzie could not ignore his minister's remarks.

Of course, by publicly distancing himself from the speech, Mackenzie killed any possible Protestant alliance with liberal Catholics under the Liberal banner. Although there was clearly some interest, as expressed by former Conservative minister Alexander Galt, who publicly wrote in support of Huntington's speech in early 1876,[108] Liberal leaders had already decided that their coalition would contain a strong contingent of Catholics. Appealing to Protestants as Protestants, therefore, was out of the question. As historian Robert Hill put it, Huntington's vision failed because "the spineless Liberal party that Conservatives were being asked to support was hardly a vehicle through which the separation of church and state could be achieved."[109] The Argenteuil speech had forced Mackenzie's hand: he could either revisit the tradition of Protestant liberty and insist on the strict separation of church and state, or remain silent to avoid offending his Catholic MPs. Rising in the Commons in February 1876 to express disapproval for Huntington's speech, Mackenzie had sealed his decision. In doing so, he placed the final nail in the coffin of the old alliance between the Liberal party and Protestant Dissent.

"To Harmonize all Those Interests": Liberals Seek a New Foundation

If the Liberal party had rejected Protestant Dissent as its primary cultural basis, what other foundation could it propose to offer the country a sense of purpose, unity, and direction? Over the two years that passed between the Argenteuil speech and the next election, prominent liberal politicians and writers experimented with a variety of rhetorical strategies for imbuing meaning into the nation, including appeals to British imperialism, Anglo-Saxonism, "Common Christianity," and Canada First. However, the overriding theme of the 1878 federal election would be the economy, not culture. With the country facing a decline in economic growth since 1874,[110] both major parties shifted their focus towards economic policy. Mackenzie's speeches abandoned the discomfort of Protestant–Catholic tensions and instead advocated for free trade. Meanwhile, the Conservatives promised to alleviate the recession through protectionist tariffs and the completion of the transcontinental railway. With John A. Macdonald leading his campaign with the "National Policy," the Conservative party secured the political comeback of the century following its collapse during the Pacific Scandal of 1873. If the election results are any indication, the Canadian voters had forgiven Macdonald's trespasses and responded warmly to his proposal to unite the country on the basis of economic nationalism. This section analyses Mackenzie's last two years as prime minister to explain how politicians within and outside the Liberal party explored various ways to redefine Canadian liberalism and national identity in lieu of their Protestant Dissenting roots.

One attempt to redefine liberalism came from the Canada First movement. Composed mostly of younger liberals, it briefly threatened Mackenzie's agenda by attracting Liberal leaders such as Edward Blake and liberal intellectuals such as Goldwin Smith to its ranks. The movement began with a small circle of supporters led by the Toronto lawyer William A. Foster, who published a pamphlet – "Canada First, or, Our New Nationality" (1871) – calling on his compatriots to begin developing their own national sentiment to rival that of the United States and Britain.[111] Although they advocated greater national self-governance, Canada Firsters were generally ardent imperialists who believed that the British Empire would one day mature into a great federation of nations.[112] In January 1874, Canada Firsters organized the Canada National Association and called for increased autonomy within the empire, more representation for minorities in Parliament, and democratic reforms such as an elected Senate and compulsory voting.[113] Mere months later, supporters bolstered MP Edward Blake's ego enough that he even privately offered to take over Mackenzie's job as prime minister. On receiving the incumbent's stern rejection, Blake resigned from the Liberal caucus to sit as an independent. In an October 1874 speech in Aurora, Ontario, he escalated his Canada First rhetoric by calling for autonomy from British foreign policy and for the emergence of a "national spirit."[114] Besides rocking the boat, however, Blake's patriotic odyssey produced little political capital, and by May 1875 he had agreed to rejoin the Liberal caucus and become minister of justice.[115]

While short-lived, Canada First indicated a desire among some citizens to explore alternatives to the version of liberalism upheld by the two major parties. Its central mission was to inject a sense of nationalism into politics that would, it hoped, inspire people of all backgrounds to develop a shared national identity and culture. This call included a direct critique of the perceived emptiness and materialism of the nation's contemporary liberalism. In the words of William Foster in 1871, "We need some cement more binding than geographical contact; some bond more uniting than a shiftless expediency; some lodestar more potent than a mere community of profit."[116] In addition to identifying the challenge of materialism, Canada First was starkly aware of the sustained hostility between religious and ethnic groups. Summarizing well the task that lay ahead, Foster wrote, "The difficulty is not in the multitude of differences, real or fancied, that exists, but rather in finding some common basis of agreement strong enough to counteract disintegrating tendencies. Where are we to look for such a basis?"[117]

Canada First's answer to that all-consuming question was not immediately apparent beyond a few assertions of abstract commonalities. Foster-type appeals to a shared identity were expressed largely through romantic descriptions of the natural environment, accounts of overcoming adversity, and optimism about the country's future. Reflecting years later on the movement's legacy, Goldwin Smith admitted that outsiders had difficulty understanding exactly what members envisioned: "The aim of Canada First was never very clearly defined ... To some probably Canada First was rather a vague sentiment than a distinct opinion or idea."[118] Historian Carl Berger emphasized the racial undertones of its descriptions of a northern nation for a "northern race," some underlining a specifically Anglo-Saxon identity but much of it envisioning a broadly northern European heritage.[119] Such appeals appear to have been part of a strategy to bridge Canada's historic French–English divide. Indeed, Foster's writings explicitly drew on both French and British examples of Canadian history, claiming them equally as objects of pride. For example, in a list of historic war heroes who demonstrated "skill and valour," Foster included men who had served on opposing sides of their respective conflicts, synthesizing them all retroactively as Canadians rather than distinctly French or British.[120] Enduring hardships together, he wrote, also united citizens regardless of background: "The sense of a loss shared in by each, of a danger encountered by all, brings before us with startling vividness how much we have in common." To support this point, Foster raised the examples of Canadians fending off invasion (possibly a reference to the War of 1812 or the Fenian invasions of 1866), surviving harsh storms together, and collectively hearing the tragic news of the deaths of Thomas D'Arcy McGee and Thomas Scott.[121] It was through recognition of these shared tragedies, shared histories, and shared accomplishments, Foster proposed, that Canadians would be able to overcome their many differences.

In some limited and superficial ways, Canada Firsters may have appeared to share the language and concerns of Protestant liberty. For example, they shared some of the Protestant Liberals' outrage over the death of Thomas Scott, even granting him a larger-than-life martyr status. Speaking of Scott in 1871, Foster said, "He was a Canadian; his mental gifts may have been few – yet he died for us."[122] Foster also criticized recent Catholic political influence on the Liberal party, lamenting what he described as "the late alliance between the Catholics and the Clear Grits."[123] Some of the movement's enemies even attempted to depict it as anti-Catholic, with scant evidence. For example, when member Sidney Smith reportedly expressed reservations about voting for a Liberal candidate who was Catholic, the *Globe* – true to its new-found pro-Catholic attitude – rushed to condemn the hesitation as based on intolerance, and even compared it to religious persecution. Anyone who "votes against a candidate or refrains from voting for him because of his religious opinions," the journal thundered, "is guided by a spirit of persecution, and violates the tacit covenant existing between citizen and citizen."[124]

Despite these loose similarities with Protestant liberty, Canada First made several overtures to patriotism that was inclusive towards Catholics and had nothing to do with Protestant tradition. Foster's proposed solution to Catholic prelates' political influence, for example, did not denounce their supposedly tyrannical impulses, as some Protestants like Lucius Huntington and Charles Lindsey were inclined to do. Instead, he expressed interest in experimental models of democratic representation that would, for example, ensure seats for religious minorities.[125] Indeed, like the adherents of neutral liberty, Foster and other Canada Firsters expected that the volatility of religious differences would eventually fade away before the shared national sentiment. In an undated address by members of the Canadian National Association, the authors lamented that a "serious impediment to our progress towards unity has been, and, unfortunately, still is, the hostility of *creed towards creed*," in addition to class and ethnic divisions.[126] Distinctive and exclusive Protestant or Catholic religious convictions, then, were counterproductive to the aims of Canada First. At least in the interim, while such divisions remained prevalent, the kind of national sentiment that the movement envisioned would require a large degree of neutrality towards religion and culture.

Canada First's departure from the Protestant-liberty perspective may be understood best through its veneration of Thomas D'Arcy McGee, whose reputation as a Catholic-rights activist was inextricable from his legacy as a "Father of Confederation."[127] William Foster heaped praise on his memory in his pamphlet "Canada First" (1871): he "breathed into our New Dominion the spirit of a proud self-reliance, and first taught Canadians to respect themselves." Rather than remembering the politician as an advocate of Catholic rights, he called him "impartially liberal in the teeth of sectarian strife." With biblical echoes, Foster further wrote of his ability "to convert the stagnant pool of politics into a stream of living water."[128] Years later, he continued to treat the man as a national martyr: "Were Thomas D'Arcy McGee alive to-day he would find that the seeds which he scattered broadcast through the land and watered with his blood, have yielded a rich harvest."[129] This kind of fervent praise for the man was not common among Protestants of that generation. As we saw in the previous chapter, his defection to the Conservatives and his support for separate Catholic schools had failed to endear him to many Ontario Liberals, who usually resented having to pay the bills for such a scheme. But in a departure from the earlier Protestant-liberty ethos, Canada First celebrated the contributions of patriotic Catholics like McGee.[130] Thus, in matters of religion and culture, it actually shared the underlying hope of neutral liberty – and of the Mackenzie government – that the continued pacification of minority interests would allow for the gradual evolution of a unified Canadian polity in which religious differences would ultimately become irrelevant.

In hindsight, Canada First may have been more effective at pointing out the absence of a cohesive Canadian identity than at creating one. Its flagship newspaper, the Toronto *Nation*, offered regular complaints about Canadians' continuing to identify strongly with particular French, English, Scottish, or Irish interests, but beyond expressing the hope for a unified Canadian identity, it offered no substantive proposal. For example, in its inaugural issue, the *Nation* wished that "the fragments of a number of nationalities" would "one day [be] welded into the compact mass of a distinct Canadian nationality," but presented no blueprint or short list of common interests.[131] The bulk of what the movement proposed was institutional tinkering, as though compulsory voting and a domestic Supreme Court would inspire the Irish Catholic and the Orangeman to set down their banners, tear off their sashes, and lock arms in a tearful embrace of brotherly love. Although the movement illustrates an emerging dissatisfaction with the parties' expressions of liberalism, it fizzled out before it could deliver a substantive alternative.

Prime Minister Mackenzie had his own ideas about what could ground Canadian society and nationality, but he was often cautious about sharing them in Canada. In the summer of 1875, he travelled to Scotland, his homeland, where he made several public appearances to promote emigration to Canada.[132] In his domestic speeches, he typically characterized liberal values in terms of tolerance, free trade, and government transparency,[133] but in Scotland he also spoke about Canada's sense of mission, rooted in Christianity, British imperialism, and the Anglo-Saxon people. The *Dundee Advertiser* reported that he believed "the Dominion of Canada is to share the glory of carrying our Anglo-Saxon civilization over the globe – which Mr. Mackenzie considers to be the mission of the British people."[134] The empire's mission also for him involved spreading the Christian faith. Referring to the Union Jack, comprised of "the Red Cross of England and the Cross of St. Andrew," Mackenzie said, "our flag represents a still greater work … We present upon our flag the greatest of all God's works – the Cross, as the emblem of the redemption of man."[135] While he also described Canada as "a mixed population," which prevented "the cropping up of any feeling which would present national origin or religious belief as a bar to political preferment,"[136] Mackenzie presented these statements as compatible with an overall mission to spread Anglo-Saxon Christian civilization. His speaking thus in Scotland and not in Canada, however, underlines the contrast between the two countries' political climates.

Of course, it was one matter to speak of Christianity as a unifying feature of Canadian culture, but quite another to apply the concept to Canada's rival denominations. Some writers attempted to bridge these gulfs by emphasizing doctrines shared by most groups. The Methodist Egerton Ryerson, for example, had back in the 1840s designed Upper Canada's public-school system around the concept of "Common Christianity." In an 1875 letter, he explained the application of that principle and argued for its continuation. Since the system was "acting for a Christian Country," schools must "provide facilities to aid Trustees and Parents to give such Religious Instruction in the Schools." Although this mandate did not "compel the use of any book," books that taught the doctrine of the Trinity and the evidences of Christianity seemed widely accepted and should be included. Such principles, he said, "are common to all Christian Denominations, and are, I believe, essential to the well-being and highest civilization of this Country."[137] Despite the effort at inclusivity, this concept had been controversial from the start, as many critics demanded a less centralized approach and more parents' input.[138] Even Mackenzie had criticized Ryerson's approach two decades earlier.[139] However, as prime minister, he had generally accepted the idea of Common Christianity. In one of his Scottish speeches in 1875, he even mentioned the concept as a reason that emigrant Scots would be happy about Canadian public schools: they were, he boasted, "free also from any denominational bias, though the Bible was read and all the schools opened and closed with prayer."[140]

While some Protestant denominations in the early national period seemed willing to work together for common aims – sometimes called the "Protestant consensus"[141] – the persistence of rivalry with Catholics certainly precluded any wider Christian consensus in Canada. Just as Protestant liberals had long considered Catholicism antithetical to their political values, so the few but influential ultramontane Catholics perceived liberalism as anathema to their faith. As Blair Neatby explains, many Catholic priests saw liberalism in terms of mid-century radicals in continental Europe, so that "even the name 'Liberal' was identified with French radicalism and the revolutions of 1848."[142] To counteract this perceived radicalism, Pope Pius IX's *Syllabus Errorum* (1864) had condemned liberal notions such as the separation of church and state and insisted on the church's control over marriage and education.[143] The Vatican Council of 1869–70 (also known as Vatican I) reaffirmed these positions and infamously also affirmed the doctrine of papal infallibility.[144] Emboldened by such pronouncements from Rome, in the early 1870s a group of Canadian Catholic journalists and clergymen rallied around "The Programme." This document – *Programme catholique* (Trois-Rivières, April 1871) – called for Catholics to vote for candidates who promised to implement the ultramontane vision in Canada, which historian Yvan Lamonde called "a plan for a Catholic theocracy."[145] As historian J.R. Miller has explained, the movement's growth in the decade following Confederation was also assisted by the fact that French Canadians were increasingly defensive about their position in the predominantly English-Protestant dominion.[146] Thus, in both national and international contexts, neither Protestants nor Catholics were keen to set aside their three centuries of separation to embrace "Common Christianity."

In response to the ultramontanists' blatant mobilization of Catholic identity politics (as we would call it today), Protestants such as Lucius Huntington and Alexander Galt continued to raise the "No popery" cry as like-minded people had done over the previous fifty years. In 1876, the Toronto-based *Grip* captured the Protestants' apprehension of Catholic political power:

> Quebec obeys the Pope, and rules the House
> What will come of it? Should great Pius choose
> To make us all turn Catholic, what lacks,
> But that they move for it in Parliament
> And move us straight to Rome?[147]

The most extensive Protestant critique of ultramontanism in Canada came from longtime Ontario reformer Charles Lindsey, whose *Rome in Canada* (1877) was a lengthy exposé of the movement. Back in the 1850s, Lindsey had worked for James Lesslie's *Examiner* and had avidly supported the Clear Grit cause. He was also both a son-in-law and an early biographer of the late William Lyon Mackenzie. Just as Lindsey's generation of liberals had fought the establishment pretensions of the Church of England and the Roman Catholic church, the now fifty-seven-year-old Lindsey was convinced that the battle was far from over.

His new book minced no words on the ongoing threat from Rome, warning about "a contest between medieval ecclesiasticism and the civilization of the nineteenth century."[148] The volume documented the writings of several clergymen, journalists, university instructors, and even playwrights who condemned liberal values such as freedom of speech and freedom of the press, and even some who said that Protestantism was illegitimate and should not be tolerated in Catholic societies.[149] Faced with such evidence, Lindsey asked his readers to consider seriously what would happen if such people actually seized power: "If those who make loud profession of these dogmas could grasp in their hands the whole political power of the country, what guarantee would remain for the maintenance of the rights and liberties of the rest of the population?"[150] The implication was clear, and in other pages explicitly spelled out: such a path could end only in inquisitions, heresy trials, and the worst "blood-stained crimes" imaginable.[151] Lindsey was sure to distinguish between reasonable liberal Catholics and their ultramontane counterparts,[152] but his general depiction of the Catholic hierarchy as scheming for power over civil society suggests that he still held strongly to the main premise of Protestant liberty: that a nation's enjoyment of civil liberties depended on keeping in check the tyrannical impulses of non-Protestant faiths.

The minority of Catholic liberals had an even more delicate task: to advocate liberalism in a way that did not bring church sanction. The *Annuaire* for 1868 of Montreal's Institut canadien had been placed on the Catholic *Index* of forbidden works and attracted the scrutiny of the local bishop. In 1869, Catholics in Montreal had been forbidden to read the publication and could even be denied the church's sacraments if they were caught.[153] As Blair Neatby explains, the clergy often did not take seriously the liberals' claims to be sincere Catholics, and during elections they even spoke from the pulpit about the dangers of the Liberal party.[154] It is in this context of Quebec's religiously charged political tension that the young Catholic Liberal MP Wilfrid Laurier emerged with a new pitch for liberalism.

At a speech in Quebec City in 1877, Laurier spoke out against the recent ultramontanist revival in Quebec's Conservative party and sought to reconcile Canadian liberalism with the Catholic faith. His stated goal was to challenge two prevailing ideas in Quebec society: first, that "Liberalism is a new form of error, a heresy already virtually condemned by the head of the Church," and second, that "A Catholic cannot be a Liberal."[155] His first task was to redefine liberalism in a way that would not offend his Catholic-majority electors, many of whom had associated it with heresy, debauchery, and anarchy. His definition was necessarily abstract, drawing on the British historian Thomas Macaulay to describe the liberal sentiment as a combination of optimism, open-mindedness, and a desire to improve one's society.[156] He was also quick to distance Canadian liberalism from its continental European counterpart, which he said was understandably associated with the blood-stained excesses of revolution and disorder.[157] By contrast, he argued that the gradual reforms of English liberalism had actually prevented the horrors of revolution experienced in continental Europe: "How many reforms has it not brought about, how many abuses corrected, without shock, disturbance and violence!"[158] Canadian liberalism was part of this broader English tradition of reform, said Laurier, which he credited for the freedoms that Catholics enjoyed under British rule in Canada.[159]

Although Laurier's "Political Liberalism" speech has rightly been recognized as a defining moment for liberalism in Quebec, it was also indicative of the broader transformation of Canadian liberalism that was well under way in Ontario. Yvan Lamonde wrote that in this speech Laurier in effect adopted the English liberal tradition of gradual reform and began to market it anew to French Canadians.[160] The current study further suggests that it was a particular kind of English liberalism that was only beginning to take precedence among the leaders of the Liberal party. Like many Protestant Liberals, Laurier had embraced a version whose primary virtue was its supposed neutrality towards culture. In his speech defending Louis Riel a few years earlier, he had praised the cross-cultural transferability of "British liberty" and had stressed keeping the liberal state impartial towards religion and culture.[161]

Now in 1877, Laurier similarly urged keeping religion out of party politics. Speaking of the Conservatives, but hinting at the ultramontane movement for which their Quebec members had become a vehicle, he warned that if they succeeded in setting up "a Catholic Party" the Protestants would organize as well, and the results would be catastrophic. When religion drives politics, he said, "you throw open the door to war, a religious war, the most terrible of all wars."[162] It was this neutralization of religion and culture in politics that gave Laurier's liberalism the claim to be so well suited to Canada. Instead of having roots in a particular culture, it claimed a universal origin as "an attribute of human nature" itself.[163] Thus Laurier's speech was an attempt not only to "secure the [political] neutrality of the clergy," in the words of Blair Neatby,[164] but also to confirm the cultural neutrality of politics.

With political expediency curtailing Protestant liberty, the expression of liberalism that came to dominate political discourse after the 1870s was ultimately an economic doctrine that professed neutrality towards culture. In addition to Laurier's speeches, Alexander Mackenzie's Canadian speeches may be the best representatives of the ideology's new developments. When speaking in Canada, Mackenzie adhered strictly to neutral liberty, which emphasized economic progress and free trade. For example, in an 1877 address in Kingston, Ontario, he praised his party's legacy as the one that "first gave perfect civil and religious rights to the people of Canada."[165] However, when elaborating on "what is the difference between the parties at the present moment," he focused on the size and efficiency of the federal government: fiscal responsibility, low taxation, and transparency with government contracts.[166] Anytime he referred to church–state relations, he brought out old chestnuts such as the clergy reserves and laws about weddings: "Who does not remember our early struggles, forty years ago, when we strove to wrest the public domain from the hands of one denomination? Who does not recollect when Presbyterian and Methodist clergymen were sent to gaol because they dared to perform the ceremony of marriage? … I spent my earliest days in the political agitation incident to these struggles; my first political meetings were held in behalf of that cause."[167] Mackenzie invoked past religious controversies in order to reinforce his own reputation as an old-generation Upper Canadian reformer, but he was strictly silent on contemporary church–state controversies such as the ultramontane *Programme*. Separation of church and state may have been a staple of liberalism in Canada's past, but Mackenzie would do everything in his power to keep it there, safely tucked away in the past, where it could not disrupt party unity or his electoral chances in Quebec.

As the country drew closer to the federal election in autumn 1878, Mackenzie's expression of liberalism became increasingly synonymous with free trade and the free market. In May, he addressed a "Workingmen's Demonstration" in Toronto, reportedly a three-hour effort.[168] He started by crediting workingmen for the country's prosperity and development, and emphasized that labourers had a higher standard of living in Canada than in many other parts of the world. Specifically, he contrasted their status in Canada and in England, emphasizing that the Canadians were more likely to own property. For this discrepancy, he blamed England's "laws which have a tendency to prevent the free exchange of labour … which make the employee a mere serf to the employer … laws which unnecessarily interfere with contracts between man and man."[169] He pivoted to the wider principle of free markets in both domestic and international trade. He spoke highly of Britain's repeal of the Corn Laws (protectionist tariffs) in the 1840s and claimed that those measures had led to starvation: "It is well known that starving thousands were patrolling the streets, cursed – cursed I say – by the demon of protection."[170] He warned that his Conservative opponents desired to go back to protection and force Canadians to pay more for basic commodities. Emphasizing the effects of protection on the working class, he summarized Macdonald's economic strategy as a plan, in effect, "to tax the very bread which the poor man eats, the coal he burns, and the oil he consumes."[171]

Framing the 1878 election as a contest over economic principles, Mackenzie marketed the Liberal party as championing the class interests of the "workingman" rather than interests based on religion, region, or culture. Even his references to earlier religious struggles became subsumed within the language of class. Consider the secularization of King's College, Toronto,[172] which Mackenzie raised to challenge the notion that the Conservatives were "friends of the workingman": "Sir, who does not remember the day when these same friends of the workingman shut the doors of our University against him? No one could go to that University unless he became a subscriber to the Thirty-Nine Articles and became a member of the Church of England … The University was opened to every man and upon such terms that the humblest son of the humblest workingman may find his way to the position that I now occupy."[173] Here he invoked a classic episode of the liberal plight in Canada, which had pitted Dissenters against the Anglican proponents of church establishment. But he subtly transformed it into a struggle of workingmen against the elite. This reorientation illustrates the stark transformation in Ontario's political context from the early colonial days to the Mackenzie government, wherein politicians had generally come to prioritize economic policy over the religiously charged concerns of previous generations. In conjunction with this political sea change, Canadian liberalism had essentially metamorphosed from a vehicle for the Dissenters' intercultural competition into a culturally neutral economic doctrine.

The main reason for this transformation was that political leaders who wanted to govern were understandably very responsive to voter demographics. Mackenzie himself emphasized the pressures he faced as a politician with a pluralistic electorate. Speaking in Kingston in 1877, he said that Canada was "vast in respect to its sectional views, and in its diversity of creed and race; and it is a task which any statesman may feel great difficulty in accomplishing, to harmonize all those interests, and bring a genuine feeling of union to bear upon the prosperity of the country which he has to govern."[174] In the face of such diversity, iterations of liberal principles that had long appealed to English Protestants, for example, might have been alien or even offensive to other groups. To adapt, Mackenzie typically defined liberalism either by its economic dimensions or in terms of tolerance and mutual accommodation. For example, in Rimouski, Quebec, in November 1875, he assured the audience that "in every portion of the Dominion, all reasonable concessions will be made, so as to enable both the Catholics and the Protestants to unite cordially and to act harmoniously with each other." He praised Quebec for granting property rights and suffrage to Jews long before the rest of the British Empire, a fact that he described as an example of French-Canadian "liberality." Further, he expressed the hope that "this feeling of liberality will continue to expand and extend, so that the narrow prejudices of class and creed may be made to fall back before the liberal views."[175] Thus, in addition to promising free markets and low taxes, Mackenzie's liberalism had evolved to include as well the "reasonable concessions" that he had come to believe were necessary to ensure inter-religious coexistence in Canada.

In the weeks before the 1878 election, the Liberals maintained their strategy of celebrating free trade and reiterating their friendliness to Catholics. At a town hall in Niagara, for example, the Liberal candidate, Patrick Hughes, announced that he was Catholic and accused his opponent, the Conservative incumbent, Josiah Plumb, of being anti-Catholic. After Plumb denied the charge, Hughes declared that he would never go "between any man and his God" and expressed his hope that Canada "had heard the last of this religious cry." Plumb countered by reminding Catholic voters of "the abuse heaped by The Globe for years and years upon their co-religionists, their bishops, priests, and holy sisters."[176] At a rally in Glengarry, Mackenzie avoided religion altogether. Instead, he reiterated that protection benefitted the manufacturing companies at the expense of the workingmen, who would have to pay more for basic consumer goods.[177] At a Liberal rally in Toronto Centre, the speakers took turns invoking Adam Smith and John Stuart Mill to underline the benefits of the "unrestricted and untrammeled negotiation and interchange of commodities between nations."[178]

On the Sunday before the polls opened, Protestant clergymen throughout Toronto urged their congregations to vote with their Christian principles in mind. While Liberal politicians were more likely to quote Smith and Mill to support a platform based on economic concerns, these clergymen emphasized other priorities. Although their sermons did not mention any politician by name, the fact that the Liberal *Globe* reprinted them suggests that contemporaries may have perceived the comments as subtle condemnations of John A. Macdonald for his role in the Pacific Scandal of 1873. The Congregationalist Rev. Warriner, for example, reminded his listeners that it was their duty "to secure the return of conscientious Christian men to rule over us ... Immoral men should be kept out of power." The Presbyterian Rev. Macdonnell likewise suggested that voters must "condemn any winking at dishonesty" and hold politicians to account for any unscrupulous actions. Further, he advised his congregation to seek "the spirit of Christ ... in their political work" so that their "political lives would be consecrated" to God. If the voters did this most spiritual duty, then Canada "would prosper in that which constituted the true wealth of a nation."[179] In an election fought primarily over the surest path to prosperity, a few quiet voices continued to suggest that Canada should be more than the sum of its gross domestic product.

The Liberal party's devastating election loss came as a major surprise to most members. On reporting early results, the *Globe* stated, "Contrary to the anticipations of most persons, the verdict of the electors at the ballot-boxes yesterday was unfavourable to Mr. Mackenzie's Administration."[180] When all was said and done, the Conservatives had claimed 164 seats and left the Liberals only sixty-four. The Liberals lost most heavily in Ontario, dropping from sixty-six seats to twenty-six (out of eighty-eight), and in Quebec, from thirty-five to eighteen (out of sixty-five).[181] It is widely accepted that the main election question was protection versus free trade to address the recession,[182] and this study does not challenge that general assessment. However, for at least a vocal portion of Protestant Dissenters, it was Mackenzie's handling of religious controversies rather than his trade policy that disillusioned them with his party. The writings of Robert Sellar, for example, reveal that he did not see his fall as something to be mourned. His *Gleaner* eulogized a party that had failed to represent his interests: "Events of late years have taught earnest-minded Protestants ... the futility of giving their adhesion to any existing political party, so that to them the names of Conservative or Reform are of slight import. It signifies nothing to us what a politician may call himself, if he is not disposed to aid in rescuing this Province [Quebec] from the domination of the priesthood. Mackenzie was weighed in this balance, and ... found deplorably wanting."[183] In response to reform journals that had reportedly blamed Catholic voters for turning against Mackenzie, the *Globe* warned Liberals to avoid that lest they make Catholics feel "in any danger of being ostracized by the Protestant majority."[184] Whatever the next few years would bring, the paper reassured its readers, Canadian Liberals would continue to "stand by their time-honoured principles more firmly and vigorously than ever."[185] However, as the party's various disagreements, disavowals, and compromises over the preceding decade had proven, the so-called "time-honoured principles" of Canadian liberalism were still very much in flux.

Conclusion

The early national period transformed the role of religion in Canadian politics and the way politicians conceptualized their liberal principles. Although the alternatives offered by Lucius Huntington and Charles Lindsey included strong reverberations of Protestant liberty, such notions no longer had the official sanction of the Liberal leadership. In stark contrast with the party's earlier days, the political class now prohibited religious criticism and expected politics to be blind towards religion. One Mr Turner, who spoke at a Liberal rally in West Toronto in 1875, captured this sentiment perfectly, declaring that he "did not know a man by his religion" and that he fully condemned anyone "who endeavoured to raise an issue between persons and classes of the community who held different religious convictions."[186] Political expediency had demanded a stripping of specific cultural appeals from the Liberal platform, lest the party risk the charge of anti-Catholicism or bigotry. Instead, liberal politicians focused their rhetoric on free trade, mutual accommodation of various interests, and ill-defined notions of progress.

Two years after losing the 1878 election, Alexander Mackenzie resigned as leader of the Liberal party of Canada, and Edward Blake took his place.[187] Blake had long supported accommodations for Catholics, but he had also expressed a desire to replace the old Protestant sentiment with some other form of "national spirit." There is some indication that Blake at one time expected some form of "Common Christianity" to form the basis of a national identity. For example, in an 1877 speech in Teeswater, Ontario, he observed, "We are, fortunately, all united in this country in the theoretical recognition … of Christian morality which are handed down to us in the Gospels; and I believe it is on the basis of these doctrines that the politics of the country should be carried on."[188] But what could Christian unity possibly mean in the divisive sectarian climate of late-nineteenth-century Canada?

Blake's answer may be gleaned from an 1879 speech referring vaguely to Jesus' teachings: "After nearly nineteen hundred years since the message came to earth of peace and good will to men … the cause of freedom of transactions between man and man … is one which we may vindicate on these higher grounds. I believe that the laws of morality, the real interest of the world in its highest sense, are and will be served by the cause of Free Trade."[189] Thus, in the aftermath of the Mackenzie government, little remained of the old Protestant sensibility in the Liberal party of Canada. By the time the great Liberal statesman George Brown had passed away in 1880,[190] his successors at the head of the party had ruthlessly abandoned his mid-century vision for the party. In the place of Brown's "high Protestant ground," the new leader offered an abstraction of Christian morality designed to justify "the cause of Free Trade" and to offend as few voters as possible.

Although the Dissenters' convictions regarding Protestant self-rule for Upper Canada, national providentialism, and opposition to church establishment had formed the basis of the early reform movement, such beliefs would not define the next generation of the Liberal party in any substantial way. Party leaders of the early national period had worked hard to scrub these origins from living memory, repackaging and marketing a more culturally neutral version of reform history to reflect the sensitivities of a new electorate. By the late 1870s, Wilfrid Laurier had already demonstrated his commitment to keeping religion out of politics in order to maintain "the peace and harmony now prevailing between the different elements of the Canadian population."[191]

After Blake's leadership failed to secure federal governance, Laurier would carry the baton into the twentieth century. Even as a young MP, his passionate political speeches epitomized the ethos of neutral liberty, in which his version of liberalism rested on the ethereal qualities of optimism and institutional reform, and claimed a universal origin in human nature rather than in a particular culture or creed.[192] Although it might be accused of lacking in substance, and of ignoring issues that risked upsetting one portion of the electorate or another, the party's new expression of liberalism was well suited to a generation of Canadian statesmen whose central challenge had become, in the words of Alexander Mackenzie, "to harmonize all those interests" of class, ethnicity, and religion.[193]

Conclusion

A Mere Community of Profit

By the last quarter of the nineteenth century, Canadian liberalism had fundamentally changed from the earlier days of the Upper Canada reform movement. Early Canadian liberals who had heralded liberty as synonymous with the Protestant tradition – from William Lyon Mackenzie and Marshall Spring Bidwell, through James Lesslie and David Willson, to Charles Lindsey and George Brown – had come up against a formidable group of fellow liberals led by Robert Baldwin, Francis Hincks, and Thomas D'Arcy McGee who had come to see the Protestant tradition as a liability to reform and who had thus sought to strip their political vision of its religious roots. The mid-century contest between these two expressions of liberalism, summarized here as Protestant liberty versus neutral liberty, was ultimately decided in favour of religious neutrality as politicians responded to the pressures of the non-Protestant electorate and their advocates in the legislature and Parliament. Tempted in the early 1870s by the possibility to form government for the first time in decades, liberal politicians re-articulated their own history in a way that downplayed their Protestant origins and instead presented their ideas as universal and culturally neutral.

The significance of this transformation for the study of nineteenth-century Canadian liberalism may be summarized in two points, each explored below. 1) *The origins of Canadian liberalism:* in contrast to works that have downplayed religion's role in the rise of Canadian liberalism, this study argues that the historically specific cultural context of Protestant Dissent for about fifty years helped organize the Upper Canadian reform movement and determine many of its priorities and policies. 2) *The transformation of Canadian liberalism:* this volume argues that the primary driver of change in Canadian liberalism was the pressure of demographic change (specifically, the rise in numbers of Catholic voters in Upper Canada / Ontario from the late 1840s to the 1870s, often concentrated in a handful of ridings)[1] on the Liberal party's electoral strategy. Although Upper Canadian liberals initially resisted this change, they eventually accommodated the new electorate by modifying their message and image. The nature of this shift, as articulated here, ultimately supports Ian McKay's conclusion that Canadian liberalism came to prioritize individualistic materialism over concerns about public interest.[2] However, the Protestant vision for Canadian liberalism explicitly and frequently rejected the materialistic vision in the days of Robert Baldwin and Francis Hincks. The neutral liberty that prioritized railways and trade policy eventually triumphed in spite of Protestant objections, largely because its proponents could pitch their railway liberalism as universally applicable across cultures. Thus politicians' need to claim cultural neutrality determined what kind of liberal order could take shape in late-nineteenth-century Canada. In short, in the absence of a politically acceptable cultural vision (such as "Protestant liberty"), individualistic materialism stepped in to fill the void.

The Origins of Liberalism: Rethinking Lockean Thought in Canada, 1828–1878

This study substantially revises existing interpretations that have emphasized liberalism's perceived universality. Many of these have overlooked the contested nature of the liberal reform movement in order to focus on one or two key individuals (e.g., Robert Baldwin and Thomas D'Arcy McGee) and assert that they were representative of Canadian liberalism. For example, John Ralston Saul's *Louis-Hippolyte LaFontaine and Robert Baldwin* (2010) argued that by 1848 these two men laid the foundation for a form of Canadian exceptionalism, whereby the country's democratic ideals would be based on diversity and mutual compromises between "opposing religions, languages and races," rather than on a particular religion or culture.[3] While these co-leaders certainly believed in a more culturally neutral version of liberalism, that perspective was highly contested among Canadian liberals for fifty years. Saul takes them as representative of the liberal reform movement to the point of ignoring the severity of discontent Baldwin faced within the party. The oversight is most noticeable in his discussion of Baldwin's retirement from politics, which he describes as voluntary, and he even claims that he "did not leave office for political reasons."[4] He waits several pages before mentioning the fact that Baldwin lost his seat in the 1851 election, which he dismisses by saying he was too tired to campaign and "seemed to lose his senses" by running in the first place.[5] As we saw at length in chapter 3, Protestant Dissenters had concluded that he had sold out to Lower Canada on the issues that mattered most to them (especially the clergy reserves), and this caused his fall.[6] Thus, to overlook the collapse of Baldwin's career and to insist that he "could have stayed in power for a decade"[7] is to fundamentally misunderstand the importance of religion in mid-century Canadian politics.

By contrast, Michael Cross's biography of Robert Baldwin called *The Morning Star of Memory* (2012) takes seriously the Clear Grit surge that overthrew Baldwin's leadership in 1851. Importantly, he acknowledges the role of the Quaker sect known as the Children of Peace, under long-time reformer David Willson, in rejecting Baldwin's bid for re-election.[8] Cross grasped the fundamental disjuncture between the "moderate" politician and his rural constituents, the "rough radicals who were the shock troops of reform." Cross brilliantly lays bare the awkwardness of the relationship between the aristocratic reform leader and his largely yeoman-farmer voting base north of Toronto, an incongruity that shaped their policy ideas as well as their social habits. Despite Baldwin's reliance on their vote, he knew full well that "he would never be one of them."[9] Cross's interpretation reveals a line of continuity from the agrarian radicalism of the 1830s to the Clear Grit movement of the 1850s, which makes little sense if one takes Baldwin as wholly representative of post-1840 liberal reform. Such continuity becomes even clearer, the current study adds, when one grasps the movement's foundation of Protestant Dissent, which remained remarkably consistent from the late 1820s to the mid-1870s and explains why reformers rejected Baldwin in 1851.

Beyond Baldwin's strained relationship with Dissenters, this re-examination of religion in nineteenth-century Canadian politics demands that we reconsider the contested nature of Canadian liberalism. This section offers a more general analysis of the nature of liberalism in nineteenth-century Canada, as it pertained to religion and culture, and explains how this analysis contributes to existing Canadian historiography. In particular, the scholarly understanding of "Lockean liberalism" in the nineteenth century requires a significant adjustment based on the ideology's cultural and religious context. Indeed, the term "Lockean liberalism" has been invoked in other studies to mean an approach to government that facilitated secularization and the accommodation of pluralism through the neutrality of state institutions. For example, the philosopher of religion Russell Blackford invokes the "Lockean model" for the separation of church and state, which he interpreted to mean that the liberal state is completely indifferent to religion, confining itself only to "the order of this world."[10] Similarly, political scientist Janet Ajzenstat argues that Canada's founders were "John Locke's disciples," which meant to her that they upheld a strict adherence to the "non-discrimination" principle and deliberately offered "no social vision" for the country.[11] These interpretations capture well the version of liberalism that I have called "neutral liberty," but they do not encompass the whole of nineteenth-century Canadian liberalism.

Parsing out a more complex picture of nineteenth-century liberalism is one of the aims of some recent scholarship on the subject. For example, Jeffrey McNairn suggests that historians should look at the disagreements among early liberals in order to articulate a more "pluralized view of liberalism." In so doing, they would avoid oversimplifying the history of Canada's liberal order based on a dichotomy of hegemony and resistance, of dominant and subaltern.[12] Michel Ducharme's *The Idea of Liberty in Canada* also offers a more pluralized view, distinguishing between two ideas of liberty competing before 1840. First, "republican liberty" advocated popular sovereignty, the pre-eminence of the legislative branch of government, and civic virtue. By contrast, "modern liberty" emphasized constitutional limitations on the role of government in order to best enable the flourishing of "commerce and wealth accumulation." Using this distinction, Ducharme argues that these competing ideologies underlay the political turmoil of the 1830s and ultimately produced the rebellions of 1837–38.[13] Although the current study offers a different interpretation of the events in Upper Canada (see chapter 1), Ducharme's distinction between modern and republican liberty is exemplary in the effort to map out competing strains within nineteenth-century Canadian liberalism.

Just as "liberty" had a plurality of meanings and applications that defined Canadian politics before 1840, a similar ideological battle played out between Protestant and neutral liberty. The explicitly Protestant idea of liberty originally nurtured the liberal reform movement in Upper Canada beginning in the 1820s, subsequently competed for dominance with its neutral counterpart throughout the mid-century decades, and ultimately lost the battle in the 1870s after George Brown stepped down as party leader and told his followers that Confederation had solved the country's religious divisions. For Ducharme, 1840 was a watershed moment in Canadian liberalism: the suppression of the rebellions represented a decisive break, in which the proponents of constitutional or modern liberty had defeated their ideological rivals and established themselves as the definitive arbiters of liberalism in Canada.[14] As chapter 5 of the current study explains in further detail, the year 1875–76 may be seen as a similar turning point in the contest between competing ideas of liberty, when the leadership of the Liberal party refused to support Protestant liberty when called out to do so. Until that time, Canadian liberal thought was practically inseparable from the culture of Protestant Dissent that first gave it life.

This conclusion adds to a small but growing body of scholarship that has challenged the extent to which "Lockean liberalism" anticipated cultural neutrality and indeed was applicable outside its original cultural context. For example, the political scientists Jakob De Roover and S.N. Balagangadhara argue that Locke's version of toleration presupposed a Protestant worldview in which religious practice could be largely confined to the private sphere.[15] Some historians of early modern Europe, likewise, emphasize the religious context of Locke's writings. James T. Kloppenberg, for example, writes that Locke's opposition to intolerance "was surpassed only by his anxiety concerning the even greater threat represented by 'papists' and atheists." By holding firmly to the "persistent anti-atheism, anti-Semitism, and anti-Catholicism of English culture," Kloppenberg concludes, Locke offered only "a distinctly modest contribution to religious pluralism."[16] When the historian J.C.D. Clark proposes that the American Revolution was a "Lockean moment," he means that it took on the characteristics of Protestant Dissent's opposition to establishment theological orthodoxy.[17] Such conclusions are consistent with the questions that this study poses about the relationship between religion and Lockean thought in nineteenth-century Canada.

For nearly five decades, the advocates of Protestant liberty grappled for dominance of liberal reform. In the late 1820s, the reform movement first took shape by rallying around leaders such as William Lyon Mackenzie and Marshall Spring Bidwell who opposed church–state measures like the clergy reserves and promised to legislate according to "the free spirit of Christianity."[18] During the Upper Canada rebellion of 1837, Mackenzie attracted radical reformers to his attempted coup d'état in Toronto by promising "a government founded upon the eternal heaven-born principle of the Lord Jesus Christ."[19] In the wake of the rebellion's defeat, the moderate liberal Robert Baldwin naturally rose to a position of leadership, and reformers at first tolerated his overtures to Catholic allies as a strategy to secure responsible government. However, some reformers such as Isaac Buchanan soon raised alarm bells about his apparent willingness to "sacrifice" the interests of Upper Canada to the Anglican and Catholic "High Church Oligarchy."[20] In the wake of the Irish-famine migrations of 1847, a new generation of evangelical reform leaders such as George Brown attracted public attention by expressing concern that the arrival of potentially millions of Catholics in North America was "not a scheme of emigration, but of colonization. Ireland is to be transferred to Canada, and to take possession of it."[21] The subsequent power struggle in the party soon saw the downfall of Baldwin in 1851, and the Protestant-conscious leadership of George Brown emerged to take his place.

George Brown's open insistence on Protestant liberty defined the Liberal party in Upper Canada in the later union period, and this perspective would ultimately help push the United Province of Canada towards a larger confederation. Expressing frustration with increasingly generous concessions on state funding for Catholic schools, several violent religious riots in Toronto and Montreal, and the suppression of public speech that criticized Catholicism, many Protestant liberals had come to believe that the kind of free society they envisioned was not compatible with Robert Baldwin's vision for biculturalism. As the evangelical liberal James Lesslie wrote in 1851, "Popery is seated in our land … and liberty cannot strike its roots into such an affected soil."[22] By the end of 1859, the Liberal party had officially adopted the policy of separating the two Canadas, to be replaced by a federal union with the other British North American colonies.[23] Brown first considered this idea because it would remove Upper Canada from the control of the "Roman Catholic bishops who command the votes of three-fourths of the people of Lower Canada" and instead "secure us the management of our own affairs."[24] For the Upper Canadian Liberals in 1859, the confederation project was designed to ensure Protestant self-determination for a Protestant province.

Within only a few years, George Brown had the opportunity to carry this idea into effect by offering confederation talks as a condition to prop up John A. Macdonald's government in the "Great Coalition" of 1864. As Brown made clear in the legislature, his key hope in pursuing the project was to secure greater self-determination for Upper Canada, which he believed was necessary, because the united province was unworkable with its "two races, two languages, two systems of religious belief, two sets of laws for everything … It has been almost impossible that, without sacrificing their principles, the public men of both sections could come together in the same Government."[25] Protestants of all denominations took an active interest in the idea of Confederation, seeing the change as an opportunity to renew their commitment to make Canada a Christian society, both at home in Upper Canada and abroad in the new west. Indeed, many Protestants believed that Canadians had been granted the rare opportunity to lay the foundations of a Christian state on which untold generations would continue to build to the glory of God.[26]

Most of Canada's "Fathers of Confederation" were less romantic in their language, but they were not deaf to the cultural concerns of their constituents. Beginning with the Charlottetown Conference in September 1864, representatives of both Canadas paid special attention to the division of powers, as they knew the provincial governments would have a unique responsibility to uphold their respective region's religious and cultural character.[27] While the colonies' leading statesmen set to work designing a workable constitution, leaders of the Dissenting Protestant denominations continued to remind their people that a nation's institutions alone were not sufficient to maintain liberty. Rather, Canadians had to continue to hold their leaders to account to be faithful to God and to their Protestant heritage: as one Congregationalist publication summarized in 1867, "Paper constitutions depend for their efficiency upon the temper of rulers and people … It may be said of nations, 'The People are the Constitution.'"[28] Contrary to the language of later liberals, the Confederation generation often recognized a mutual interdependence between a nation's institutions and the culture of the people who sustained them. Thus Canadian liberalism emerged out of the cultural context of Protestant Dissent and was originally conceived as a means to defend and propagate that culture as *the* necessary basis of a free and prosperous society.

The foregoing narrative demands a reconsideration of the ways that historians have typically understood the relationship of nineteenth-century liberalism and culture. While historians of political culture in nineteenth-century Upper Canada / Ontario generally acknowledge the presence of religion in early political discourse and voting patterns, most have downplayed the relationship between culture and liberalism for one of three reasons, each of which are addressed further below. 1) *There were exceptions to the Dissent–liberal relationship:* since not every Dissenter was a reformer and not every reformer was a Dissenter, some historians have suggested that emphasizing any strong correlation between the two is misleading. 2) *Denominational diversity did not lend itself to religion-based political action:* since no single denomination could claim the allegiance of the majority of colonists, the argument goes that appeals to religion were at best limited and ineffective in politics. 3) *Religious rhetoric was superficial and was isolated to only a few specific policy issues:* this approach recognizes the prevalence of religious discourse in Canadian politics but argues that it was mostly poetic in nature or limited to only a handful of political issues (e.g., the clergy reserves and church-run universities). I explore each of these arguments below, including how the conclusions of this study challenge such interpretations.

First, some historians have argued that exceptions to the Dissent–liberal affiliation negate the utility of examining religious influence in Upper Canadian politics. Carol Wilton, for example, has maintained that while religious affiliation helped to define political divisions in the colony, "religious issues were at most secondary, or even absent altogether, in many of the oppositionist campaigns," such as opposition to the Alien Bill of 1827; further, she cites exceptions to religion-based partisanship such as the Anglican Robert Baldwin who became the leader of Upper Canada's reformers in the 1840s and supported the anti-state-church organization called the Friends of Religious Liberty.[29] As this study explained in chapters 2 and 3, the Dissenters at first tolerated Baldwin's leadership because he was a formidable voice for responsible government. However, by the summer of 1850 he was thoroughly rejected by liberal Dissenters who believed that he had betrayed the voluntarist cause, and his critics specifically singled out his Anglican faith as a reason to no longer trust him.[30] Indeed, analyses of voter demographics suggest that exceptions such as Baldwin appear not to override the general pattern of the Dissent–liberal relationship.[31] Politicians like him came to their liberal conclusions via a different route, but most liberal reformers in the early-to-mid-nineteenth century reached their position through their affinity for that particular manifestation of Protestant culture.

Second, the fact that Upper Canada was denominationally diverse has led some scholars to conclude that religion-based partisanship was both limited and ineffective. Jeffrey McNairn's study of the rise of "deliberative democracy" in the colony has suggested that while some religious institutions may have encouraged lay political engagement, appeals to God's will were generally counterproductive to reasoned public deliberation in a denominationally diverse society.[32] While agreeing with McNairn's premise that religiously motivated political actors eventually "needed to translate their claims into other terms" in order to appeal to those outside their tradition,[33] this study suggests that early liberals were reluctant to do so. In the 1820s and '30s, when most voters subscribed to one of several Dissenting denominations that shared similar historic experiences outside of the established church, there was less need to tailor one's political rhetoric to audiences outside one's faith. Only later, in the 1870s, did Ontario's federal and provincial liberal leaders actively discourage the use of potentially alienating Protestant-specific rhetoric, a shift towards neutral liberty that is explored in chapter 5. Until that time, Protestant (and often specifically Dissenting) rhetoric and concepts generally defined liberalism and liberty in the colony.

Third, some historians have relegated religious concerns to one or two isolated issues, or to superficial rhetorical expressions. Though proposing that the role of religion in the pre-1840 ideology of "liberty" would be worth further inquiry, Michel Ducharme has suggested that religious questions in Upper Canada boiled down to the status of the Church of England and that these issues "did not relate to liberty or state legitimacy so much as to the relationship between church and state, between temporal power and spiritual power."[34] Similarly, Janet Ajzenstat has proposed that politicians' use of religious rhetoric was merely superficial, that quoting the Bible was equivalent to quoting Shakespeare, and that it thus did not indicate a deeper role of religion in shaping political ideology.[35] However, this study reveals that for many liberal leaders the relationship between religion and liberty was deeper than poetic language or a pet issue. As chapter 1 emphasized, William Lyon Mackenzie believed that human liberty was guaranteed only by divine sanction: "Governments are not mere social compacts, they are ordained of God," he said. Indeed, it was on this basis that he argued in 1837 that it was justifiable for devout Christians to overthrow a government of "wicked rulers" who failed to uphold their "ordained purposes" of protecting the liberty of their subjects.[36] While the revolutionary rhetoric subsided in subsequent years, Upper Canadian liberals continued to insist that the liberty of their country depended on their Protestant piety and their constant vigilance against the encroachments of what they considered to be false religions. For example, chapter 2 explained the ways in which Dissenting narratives of persecution and millennialism provided a high-stakes interpretation of what would happen if their Catholic or Anglican rivals seized power over state institutions. As the evangelical liberal James Lesslie summarized in 1848, "The whole superstructure of our liberties is, in fact, endangered by the existence of this sectarian political inequality, and that danger must be averted by wise and righteous legislation."[37] Thus the question of religion in nineteenth-century Canada went right to the heart of what it meant for the state to be legitimate and what it meant for the state to uphold "liberty."

Although the current study's conclusion about the influence of religious culture on liberalism differs from many scholars, it is not without precedent in Canadian historiography. Indeed, in 1989, William Westfall went so far as to say, "To a large extent the study of reform has become the study of religion."[38] According to Nancy Christie, early evangelicalism fostered a democratic culture in British North America in the 1800s that would go on to influence Upper Canadian politics in subsequent decades.[39] George Rawlyk's *The Canada Fire* likewise proposed that the "radical" evangelicals who emphasized the "trauma" of conversion and ecstatic spiritual experiences ultimately contributed a populist approach to politics in British North America.[40]

Although Rawlyk did maintain that evangelicalism in Upper Canada began to change once cut off from American sources in 1812, such a conclusion gives too much credit to U.S. culture as the unique preserve of democratic evangelicalism. Other scholars like the British historian David Bebbington have challenged the dichotomy of the democratic United States versus conservative Britain and proposed instead that the latter had its own legacy of democratic evangelicalism, so the successive waves of immigrants it sent to Canada (numbering nearly one million 1815–55) also "contributed some of the populism to Canadian religion."[41]

Earlier Canadian studies dating back to the mid-twentieth century often took for granted that religious concepts influenced Canadian politicians and political culture in the nineteenth century. For example, William Kilbourn's *The Firebrand* suggested not only that religion influenced William Lyon Mackenzie's style as an orator but also that his Calvinist upbringing and biblical literacy were "important sources of his later liberalism."[42] Arthur Lower's *Colony to Nation* likewise credited the early Methodists and Anglicans for shaping a particular blend of loyalism and democracy in Ontario.[43] Robert Kelley's *Transatlantic Persuasion* suggested that evangelicalism provided a common set of "motivations and models" and "archetypical world views" to the liberal-democratic mind in Canada, the United States, and Britain in the nineteenth century.[44] In most of these older works, the relationship between religious and political culture is assumed but not explored in any depth. What some of those generations took for granted about the relationship between religion and politics, however, the current study has attempted to recover with intention and with a new set of questions for contemporary scholarship.

This study also joins the company of several British and American scholars who have recognized the central influence of religion in classic liberal thought. Indeed, one of Linda Colley's central premises in *Britons* is that British national identity developed in part as a process of championing a sense of Protestant liberty, as contrasted with the perceived tyrannical Catholicism of neighbouring European nations and empires.[45] From this baseline of Protestant liberty, some British liberals redirected these critiques of Catholicism towards other Protestant denominations like the established Church of England, to the effect that Dissent developed its own rhetoric of liberty in Britain and North America. J.C.D. Clark, for example, has argued that the language of liberty in the American Revolution had all the characteristics of a war of religion, having "much to do with ancient divisions and hatreds" between establishment orthodoxy and Dissent, and only later was it rearticulated and reinterpreted in terms of natural rights.[46] In a transatlantic study on the history of democratic thought in Europe and the United States from the sixteenth to the nineteenth century, James T. Kloppenberg emphasized the "religious origins" of liberal-democratic thought on both sides of the Atlantic, which he said had been underappreciated and minimized by secular scholars.[47] Following these threads into the mid-nineteenth century makes it clear that British and Anglo-American liberalism developed a peculiarly religious (Dissenting) quality as contrasted to the secular and / or anti-Christian form of liberalism that emerged in continental Europe.[48]

One of the implications of this line of inquiry is a complete reorientation about what it meant to be a "Lockean" liberal in nineteenth-century Canada. Janet Ajzenstat has made the case that Canadian liberalism owed a lot to John Locke's ideas, particularly as they pertain to "egalitarianism and non-discrimination."[49] Her interpretation of what that meant, however, was a strict neutrality of the nation towards cultural and social differences. Consequently, she proposed that Canada's Locke-inspired founders forged for the new nation a civic identity based only on shared political objectives, an identity that was decidedly *not* based on a cultural foundation.[50] She further emphasized that Lockean liberalism in Canada was designed to be universally transferable to people "who did not share the memories, the culture, and the historical experiences of British North America's English-speaking settlers."[51]

However, there is much evidence to suggest that early Canadian liberals did not interpret Locke's ideas to be culturally neutral, and that even the philosopher himself did not envision a universal application of his ideas. First, it is necessary to understand religious liberty as Locke himself envisioned it. Although his "Letter Concerning Toleration" of 1689 was a pioneering plea for religious tolerance and one of the foundational texts of classic liberalism, scholars have rightly pointed out that his idea of tolerance was very different from today's. It did not include full political participation for Roman Catholics, for example, a position he maintained to the end of his life.[52]

The relatively recent discovery of a manuscript by Locke dated to 1667–68 sheds light on the development of his thoughts on religious toleration. In it, he suggested that he would be in favour of tolerating Catholicism if it were only a matter of having different ceremonies and "speculative" beliefs such as Purgatory and transubstantiation. However, he insisted that Catholicism was "dangerous" to England because it required loyalty to a foreign power, the papacy.[53] Like many Protestant commentators in his time, Locke was deeply concerned about the possibility of a "Popish Plot," or Catholic infiltration of the government. Such an event, he feared, would inevitably make the nation subject to Rome and begin to persecute Protestants.[54] Indeed, he wrote his famous "Letter Concerning Toleration" (1689) in the context of French-Catholic persecution of Protestants after the revocation of the Edict of Nantes in 1685.[55] Some scholars have gone so far as to say that Lockean liberalism was so rooted in Protestant conceptions that it is scarcely applicable outside that cultural context. As we saw above, Jakob De Roover and S.N. Balagangadhara have written that Locke's view of toleration "threatens to become unintelligible when it travels beyond the boundaries of the Christian West or when it has to accommodate communities from other cultures."[56] Understood within its proper historical context, Locke's idea of liberal toleration was intended for application only within decidedly Protestant societies.

Perhaps the best indication for the Protestant context of Locke's ideas is the parameters that he himself set up about which religions should be tolerated. Indeed, he was very explicit about the types of religion England should exclude. He would rule out religions subject to "foreign jurisdiction," for example: "That church can have no right to be tolerated by the magistrate, which is constituted upon such a bottom, that all those who enter into it, do thereby, ipso facto, deliver themselves up to the protection and service of another prince. For by this means the magistrate would give way to the settling of a foreign jurisdiction in his own country."[57] While refraining to call out Roman Catholicism by name in the final version of the letter, his earlier versions made it clear that he believed Catholics to be "irreconcilable enemies" who could not be trusted.[58] Indeed, even in the final published version, his quoting of historical Catholic phrases (e.g., "kings excommunicated forfeit their Crowns and Kingdoms") makes it clear that he still applied this proposed restriction to Catholicism.[59] In addition to these more cryptic references to Catholics, he singles out both Atheists and "Mahometans" as exceptions to toleration.[60] In this context, his religious tolerance really extended only to Dissenting Protestant sects that had previously been persecuted in English society. Thus he himself simply would not recognize the recent interpretation of his ideas as universally applicable outside his own Protestant culture.

Locke's sense that religious liberty was best safeguarded by Protestant culture did not disappear from liberal discourse in the century and a half from his lifetime to the Upper Canadian reformers of 1828. If anything, for Upper Canadians this concept of Lockean tolerance *narrowed* to exclude Anglicanism from what constituted the ideal conditions for Protestant liberty. When William Lyon Mackenzie, for example, wrote that he agreed with "Locke's opinion" about religious tolerance, he did so explicitly to warn that the Church of England could not be trusted to uphold those values. He wondered, does the Anglican leadership not "endeavor with all their might to promote tyranny in the commonwealth, in order that it may be established in the church? Such was Locke's opinion, and such is ours." Although adding the caveat that this warning applies to "religionists" of any denomination who desired to use state power to impose their will, Mackenzie specifically called out the Church of England and warned that to "transplant this church into our kindly soil" was to pose a unique threat to religious liberty.

Indeed, he likened the growth of the Anglican church in the colony to a man who "warmed a serpent to life in his bosom, and it stung to death its benefactor." He simply did not trust Anglican clergymen to safeguard religious liberty and believed that if they could take political power in the colony the result would be tyranny: "Give them power, let them but feel secure, and, their professed toleration will speedily resolve itself into bitter persecution. … They have all shed blood, tortured, and punished, when circumstances gave them the ascendancy; and would, if permitted, be ready to do so again."[61] For Mackenzie, to be a "Lockean" did not mean to advocate blindness towards religious and cultural differences. To the contrary, it involved safeguarding a free society by actively countering the potential threats that some religious traditions supposedly posed to freedom.

Upper Canada's Dissenting liberals usually associated the ideas of liberty with their Protestant faith to the exclusion of all others. The Quaker David Willson, for example, an active reform supporter,[62] wrote in 1834 that "the pillars of bad government" derived from "the principles of superiority" espoused by Rome and "various branches of the Christian church," whereas "good government" derived from "the established principles of the Son of God, and his ministers."[63] In the *Christian Guardian* in 1831, the Methodist minister Egerton Ryerson stated that "rational liberty" depended on whether or not a society embraces "the zeal of real Christianity."[64] As this study has attempted to demonstrate, religion did not simply wander into Canadian politics because of a few isolated issues like the clergy reserves or separate schools. Rather, Protestant liberals often asserted that government authority was legitimate when founded on truly Christian (in this case Dissenting Protestant) principles, and it could and indeed did lose its legitimacy when it strayed from that cultural centre.

Thus, in its original conception, liberalism was not designed to be indifferent to culture nor to facilitate the ongoing secularization and pluralization of Canadian society. Recognizing these culturally centred origins of Canadian liberalism helps to explain the dramatic changes the ideology later underwent during the last quarter of the nineteenth century, and thus allows for a clearer assessment of the conditions that produced such changes. Indeed, as the current study has shown, the kind of culturally specific appeal of Protestant liberty would not remain the norm throughout the nineteenth century. At various times before Confederation and even more fervently in the early national period, some Canadian liberals adapted their message to attract Anglicans and Roman Catholics, and ultimately the ideology of liberalism became something rather different in the decades that followed. However, the longstanding cultural heritage of Protestant liberty provided an incredibly resilient foundation for Canadian liberalism with which subsequent versions of liberalism would have to contend.

The Transformation of Liberalism: Religion and Materialism in the Liberal Order

This section reflects on the changing liberal order in late-nineteenth-century Canadian politics, particularly as its deep connections with Protestantism gave way to secular materialism. Focusing on Ian McKay's work about liberal hegemony, it summarizes the ways in which liberal politicians achieved success by managing cultural pluralism strategically. In his renowned article "The Liberal Order Framework" (2000), McKay proposed that historians should gather the often fragmentary and isolated works of Canadian history into a broader conversation based on how the various aspects of Canadian society interacted with the dominant ideology of liberalism.[65] Describing the origins of this liberal order, he wrote that the absorption of Quebec and Catholicism was "indispensable" to these designs and "could only be achieved through carefully articulated politics of elite accommodation and cultural compromise, which have gone on to become misleadingly mythologized as defining features of Canada itself." Rather than finding a compromise among equals, however, he suggested that the power dynamic was decidedly against the Québécois, whose victories for Catholic communitarianism were deliberately restricted to their own province and ultimately dependent on their gradual conformity to liberal hegemony.[66] This study agrees with the role of this integration in the rise of the liberal order, but argues that Canadian liberalism also changed fundamentally in the process. Or, perhaps more accurately, one of the competing strains of liberalism ("neutral liberty") decisively defeated another strain ("Protestant liberty") because of this process of absorbing Catholicism into the liberal order.

Understanding this transformation towards "neutral liberty" allows historians to reach the heart of one of the most persistent critiques of modern liberalism: the relationship between the liberal order and capitalism. According to Ian McKay, the liberal order that emerged in Canada was one in which property rights took precedence in the hierarchy of liberal principles, leaving other considerations such as "formal equality" at the bottom.[67] In his list of five "leading traits" of classic liberalism in Canada, the first two related directly to capitalism. The first was "an economic base made up of competing profit-seeking entities … all of which function in a marketplace not directly managed by a state authority." The second was a small state whose duties included "accelerating the process of capitalist accumulation."[68] Jeffrey McNairn has criticized McKay's emphasis on property, which he said runs the risk of treating liberalism as "little more than a rationalization for bourgeois values or market relations."[69] Although McKay has acknowledged that liberalism and capitalism are distinct phenomena that have not always gone hand in hand, he also explained that "after the 1840s, they also could not be easily separated" in Canada. The liberal conception of private property, he said, provided the "interface between liberalism and capitalism."[70] While Canadian liberalism certainly cannot be reduced to private property and free markets, it would be an incomplete study of it that did not examine the connection.

If it is true that Canadian liberalism came to prioritize property and material progress, as McKay has suggested, what accounts for this correlation? This study suggests that the mid-century development and eventual triumph of neutral liberty over Protestant liberty was a necessary precursor for the property-centred liberal capitalism that took root in modern Canada. Before that triumph, Protestant liberals such as the Brownites were often deeply worried about expressions of liberalism that placed material progress above other concerns. This anti-materialist component of the Brownite movement has unfortunately been lost in some recent interpretations of that era. For example, Ian McKay invoked George Brown as an example of how early liberals often combined evangelicalism with a language of "crass economic advantage."[71] However, for Brown and his supporters it was essential that economic concerns be subjected to the greater moral and spiritual direction of Canadian society, and they regularly challenged their Hincksite rivals on this basis. Although the historian Michael S. Cross framed the division between the rival groups as a matter of agrarianism versus urban industrialism, he rightly understood that the Clear Grits emerged because they were concerned with the materialist direction of liberalism under the Hincksites: "Modern liberalism was on a path to financial and industrial capitalism, a path that had no lane for farm folk."[72]

What appeared to Cross to have an urban–rural basis, however, usually manifested itself as an intercultural competition wherein Christianity was key. For example, in 1848, James Lesslie published an article in the *Examiner* called "Man above Property," which argued that governments were inherently corrupt if they valued wealth accumulation above the "social, moral, and spiritual" health of society: "The measurement of social value by wealth alone, is enough to vitiate and disgrace any political constitution … There you will see justice, as drawn by the hand of Mammon, but not as portrayed by the pencil of revelation."[73]

Basing Canadian liberalism on "the pencil of revelation," however, appeared to be a losing political strategy in the bicultural United Province of Canada. As chapter 3 above highlighted, the early critics of Protestant liberty usually formed coalitions across sectional lines by redirecting voters' attention to secular-materialist concerns such as infrastructure investments and trade policy. The supporters of the Liberal-Conservative premier Francis Hincks, for example, decried the Brownites as advocating "politics which should be confined to the pulpit."[74] In place of Brown's cultural concerns, the Hincksites imagined a government designed almost exclusively to "advance their happiness and prosperity by Railroads, Canals, and other improvements."[75] Indeed, the English travel writer Charles Mackay believed that a materialistic, profit-driven vision for Canada was the only possibility given the persistent tensions between English Protestants and French Catholics: as he said in 1858, "under the existing circumstances, the best federation which they can establish is the federation of railways."[76] This visitor's instinct ended up being more or less correct in the long run, as the secular-material vision for Canadian society increasingly supplanted the Protestant vision in liberal discourse.

The rise of neutral liberty also required the silencing of alternative perspectives that threatened to disrupt the liberal politicians' new secular-materialist vision for intercultural coexistence. A prime example comes from the case of Mr Bain (see chapter 5), who had publicly objected to Protestants voting for the Roman Catholic candidate in his Toronto riding in 1874. Recognizing Bain's comments as a threat to their new paradigm and to their new Catholic-friendly image, Liberal leaders in succession thoroughly rebuked his comments, one speaker calling them "religious fanaticism and extreme bigotry," a second "an error of bygone days," and a third "narrow, bigoted, intolerant."[77] The Catholic candidate himself went a step further by ruthlessly suggesting that Bain himself was a product of the distant past who would be left behind as Canada advanced: "While the country was progressing in the future, the person who had uttered these sentiments would pass away into 'The vile dust from whence he sprung / Unwept, unhonoured, and unsung.'"[78] Whereas an earlier generation had proudly invoked its Protestant heritage as a guide for political action, the new cadre of Liberal leaders ferociously purged such elements from the party.

Thus, it was not the impersonal forces of capitalism alone that killed this Protestant vision for Canadian liberalism, but the conscious decisions of liberal politicians themselves in response to changing demographics. Historian William Westfall identified capitalism itself as instigating the decline in Protestant influence, saying that Protestants "lost their authority because capitalism was destroying the worlds they had once explained and creating many problems that the new culture had to address."[79] However, examining the political side of the story makes clear the role of human agency in this decline.

Seeing the opportunity to form government in the early 1870s, Liberal leaders Alexander Mackenzie, Edward Blake, and Oliver Mowat repackaged their message in order to reach out to Catholic leaders and voters, and deliberately suppressed the Protestant visionaries (e.g., Lucius Huntington) within their ranks. Whether they sincerely believed that the old Protestant–Catholic conflicts had been "settled and swept away" at the time of Confederation,[80] or whether they simply chose that message as a matter of electoral strategy, the liberals of the early national period exerted enormous effort to keep religious divisions out of Canadian politics. In place of emphasizing the Protestant-liberty perspective that had been prevalent in Upper Canadian politics for almost half a century, from the origins of the reform movement to the aftermath of Confederation, the Liberal party had come to embrace an expression of liberalism that put all its faith in economic liberalization, neutral institutions and procedure, and avoidance of church–state controversies whenever possible.

In the course of this strategic reorientation, liberal leaders had secured the dominance of a new liberal myth that would prove remarkably durable. This myth envisioned Canada as a *tabula rasa*, a blank slate, whose neutral institutions (Parliament, legislatures, constitution, courts, civil services, and so on) would ensure the coexistence and material prosperity of its individual inhabitants. If the institutions remained blind to religious differences, the theory went, the inter-religious conflicts of the past would gradually subside. This perspective was articulated by several public figures in the early national period, including Governor General Lord Dufferin, who idealized Canada as a "stainless paradise" where the equal treatment of Protestants and Catholics had negated any reason to import the "ancient feuds" of the old world.[81] It was affirmed by Judge Richards, conducting the trial for the accused killer of Thomas D'Arcy McGee, who lambasted the defendant's claims of anti-Catholic mistreatment: "Every man in this country," he insisted, "is equal in the eye of the law, and ... is no man especially disregarded on account of his religion or country."[82]

And it was exemplified by the young politician Wilfrid Laurier, who said in 1877 that even the conquered French Canadians who lost to the British in 1759 would have looked on in approval if they could see the "the institutions which we have at present; those institutions were granted to us and loyally applied." Whether Protestant or Catholic, of English or French origin, Laurier said, any given Canadian could "feel proud of the institutions which protect him."[83] In the following decades, as leader of the federal Liberals and as prime minister, he would come to embody the new liberal ethos of compromise across cultural lines, a precedent already set by Edward Blake and company in the 1870s.[84] Rather than crediting their society's freedom and prosperity to a particular cultural heritage as earlier Protestant liberals had done, the new generation had deliberately removed culture from the equation and credited instead the apparatuses of government itself.

But in the absence of a cultural foundation, little remained to guide Canadian liberal society other than secular materialism. Some English Canadians began to notice this absence, as indicated by William Foster's call in 1871 for Canadians to find "some cement more binding than geographical contact; some bond more uniting than a shiftless expediency; some lodestar more potent than a mere community of profit."[85] The historian Arthur Lower would later also lament the apparent secularization of Canadian liberalism. Though a passionate liberal himself, he expressed grave concerns about what he perceived to be its failure to assert a broader set of values beyond meaningless consumerism. In a 1937 essay, he worried that his generation "drifts about, not bound together by the older ideas, a set of atoms, sheep without a shepherd, save in so far as the movie, the comic strip, and the athletic hero constitute shepherds and supply what does duty for a code of conduct."[86]

Ian McKay shared Lower's concerns about the atomization and consumerization of the world around him. Indeed, he depicted in stark terms what he saw as the dehumanizing effects of the liberal order: "As deep, non-commercial ties between people become ever weaker," he feared, Canadians have become little more than "tiny, replaceable parts in an unpredictable machine no one can remember making."[87] He proposed moving away from the liberal tradition towards a form of democratic socialism, which would treat people not as "atomized competitive individuals but [as] human beings bonded to each other by ties of common interest and shared values."[88]

What his assessment neglected to answer, however, was that perennial question which haunted Canada's early liberal politicians: what common interests? What shared values? Canadian liberals in the 1870s asked themselves such questions, but had no ready answer. Exorcised of its Protestant soul, and in the absence of any coherent alternative, what path remained for Canadian liberalism except to cultivate, as Foster observed, "a mere community of profit"?

Appendix A

Religious Demographics of Upper Canada / Ontario, 1842–1881

	1842	1848	1851	1861	1871	1881
Roman Catholic	13.4	16.4	17.6*	18.5	16.9†	16.7
Anglican	22.1	22.9	23.4	22.3	20.4	19.0
Prot. Dissenter	(47.8)	(48.8)	(54.5)	(57.4)	(61.5)	(63.6)
Baptist	3.4	3.9	4.8	4.4	5.3	5.5
Methodist	17.0	19.0	22.4	25.1	28.5	30.7
Presbyterian	19.9	20.4	21.4	21.7	22.0	21.8
Other‡	7.5	5.5	5.9	6.2	5.7	5.6
No preference / no creed	16.7	11.9	4.5	1.8	1.2	0.8

* Catholics were concentrated in Toronto, where they made up 25.8 per cent of the population in 1851, up from 16.8 per cent in 1842. See William J. Smyth, *Toronto, the Belfast of Canada: The Orange Order and the Shaping of Municipal Culture* (Toronto: University of Toronto Press, 2015), 43.

† Although the percentage of Catholics in the province was down from their peak the previous decade, their concentration in a handful of ridings (i.e., Glengarry, Ottawa, and Prescott) meant that politicians continued to treat them as a significant voting bloc. Historian Margaret Evans identified eleven ridings where a concentrated Catholic population had a significant influence on election results. See Margaret Evans, *Sir Oliver Mowat* (Toronto: University of Toronto Press, 1992), 119.

‡ The historian John Webster Grant grouped together a variety of Protestant denominations as "other," which he says included Lutherans, Mennonites, and Quakers. For a more accurate estimate of the total number of Protestant Dissenters (as defined in this study), it would be ideal to break down this "other" category to have specific numbers for Congregationalists and Quakers, since the small number of Lutherans and Mennonites would not normally be considered among the Dissenters of the British tradition. See Grant, *A Profusion of Spires*, 224–5.

Source: Adapted from John Webster Grant, *A Profusion of Spires: Religion in Nineteenth-Century Ontario* (Toronto: University of Toronto Press, 1988), 224.

Appendix B

Election Results for United Province of Canada, 1848–1863

	1848	1851	1854	1857	1861	1863
Upper Canada						
Conservative	18	20	15	22	30	22
Liberal (Baldwinite / Hincksite)*	24	18†	12			
Independent Liberal (Brownite)	–	2	29	39	29	41
Lower Canada						
Conservative	9	12	30	36	35	34
Liberal	33	30	35	19	28	24
Result	Baldwin-LaFontaine 57 of 84 seats	Hincks-Morin 48 of 84 seats	MacNab-Morin-Hincks 62 of 130 seats	Macdonald-Cartier 58 of 130 seats	Macdonald-Cartier 65 of 130 seats	Sandfield-Dorion 65 of 130 seats

Note: Since party allegiances were often informal and fluid, these numbers should be considered approximate. In some cases, the totals do not add up to an even forty-two seats per section (or sixty-five per section, starting in 1854) due to the fact that some sat as independents.

* In 1854 the parties realigned: the Clear Grits split from the Hincksites, who joined a coalition with the Conservatives. After 1854, the Hincksites and Conservatives essentially merged into one party sometimes referred to as the Liberal-Conservatives and sometimes as just the Conservatives.

† After the 1851 election, eighteen reformers from Upper Canada agreed to support Hincks's ministry. Yet, as William Ormsby and J.M.S. Careless have written, the caucus was already divided in half between the moderate Hincksites and the Clear Grits. Thus, even though George Brown was numbered among the independent liberals who refused to support Hincks, he was able to exert considerable pressure on Hincks's caucus from the outside. See William Ormsby, "Sir Francis Hincks," 166; J.M.S. Careless, *Union of the Canadas,* 178–9.

Sources: J.M.S. Careless, *The Union of the Canadas: The Growth of Canadian Institutions, 1841–1857* (Toronto: McClelland and Stewart, 1967), 117–18, 178–9, 191–2; William G. Ormsby, "Sir Francis Hincks," in J.M.S. Careless, ed., *The Pre-Confederation Premiers: Ontario Government Leaders, 1841–1867* (Toronto: University of Toronto, 1980), 166, 180–3; "The Political Prospect!" *Globe,* 10 Aug. 1854; "Results of the Election," *Globe,* 16 Jan. 1858; Bruce W. Hodgins, "John Sandfield Macdonald," in J.M.S. Careless, ed., *The Pre-Confederation Premiers: Ontario Government Leaders, 1841–1867* (Toronto: University of Toronto Press, 1980), 264–5, 282; J.M.S. Careless, *Brown of the Globe, Vol. II: Statesman of Confederation* (Toronto: Macmillan, 1963), 47–8, 96–7.

Notes

Introduction

1 "Lord Dufferin on Party Spirit," *Gleaner*, 3 Oct. 1878.

2 William J. Smyth, *Toronto, the Belfast of Canada: The Orange Order and the Shaping of Municipal Culture* (Toronto: University of Toronto Press, 2015), 49.

3 "Lord Dufferin on Party Spirit," *Gleaner*, 3 Oct. 1878.

4 Janet Ajzenstat, *The Canadian Founding: John Locke and Parliament* (Montreal and Kingston: McGill-Queen's University Press, 2007), 84.

5 Ibid., 84, 86.

6 As William Westfall put it, "To a remarkable degree the history of the Protestant Reformation formed an important part of the collective memory of Ontario. Events that happened in the sixteenth and seventeenth centuries were as fresh in people's minds as if they had taken place only a few years before. People observed the rituals of the Reformation with devotion, and the division between Protestant and Catholic remained one of the primary facts of the religious and social life of the province well beyond the nineteenth century." William Westfall, *Two Worlds: The Protestant Culture of Nineteenth-Century Ontario* (Montreal and Kingston: McGill-Queen's University Press, 1989), 12.

7 J.R. Miller, "Anti-Catholic Thought in Victorian Canada," *Canadian Historical Review* 66, no. 4 (1985): 491–2.

8 Ian Radforth, "Collective Rights, Liberal Discourse, and Public Order: The Clash over Catholic Processions in Mid-Victorian Toronto," *Canadian Historical Review* 95, no. 4 (2014): 539–40.

9 "The Roman Catholic Church in Canada," *Globe*, 7 Aug. 1852.

10 John Marshall, *John Locke: Resistance, Religion and Responsibility* (Cambridge: Cambridge University Press, 1994), 53.

11 For example, at a rally expressing opposition to separate Catholic schools at Queen's Park in Toronto, the Protestant crowd reportedly cheered for the "memory of King William III." See "Separate School Question: Mass Meeting Yesterday," *Leader*, 15 April 1863; see also Christopher Moore, *1867: How the Fathers Made a Deal* (Toronto: McClelland & Stewart, 1997), 10–11.

12 The focus on economic opportunity as an alternative to religious questions is especially notable during the leadership of Francis Hincks; see chapter 3.

13 This transition towards the dominance of neutral liberty within the Liberal party is explored in chapter 5.

14 For example, Ian McKay lists the following five characteristics of the classical liberal order in Canada: 1) free-market economy made up of profit-seeking private entities, 2) a small state with limited functions, 3) a political system with limited franchise, 4) a system of law based mostly on individuals, with collective rights for some minorities, and 5) attachment to the British constitution. See Ian McKay, "Canada as a Long Liberal Revolution: On Writing the History of Actually Existing Canadian Liberalisms, 1840s–1940s," in Jean-François Constant and Michel Ducharme, eds., *Liberalism and Hegemony: Debating the Canadian Liberal Revolution* (Toronto: University of Toronto Press, 2009), 356–7.

15 For example, see Carol Wilton, *Popular Politics and Political Culture in Upper Canada, 1800–1850* (Montreal and Kingston: McGill-Queen's University Press, 2000), 228–9; Ajzenstat, *The Canadian Founding*, 100–1; Benjamin T. Jones, *Republicanism and Responsible Government: The Shaping of Democracy in Australia and Canada* (Montreal and Kingston: McGill-Queen's University Press, 2014), x, 14–15; Michel Ducharme, *The Idea of Liberty in Canada during the Age of Atlantic Revolutions, 1776–1838*, trans. Peter Feldstein (Montreal and Kingston: McGill-Queen's University Press, 2014), 11.

16 For a more detailed explanation of this study's contribution to existing historiography, see "The Origins of Liberalism: Rethinking Lockean Thought in Canada, 1828–78," in the Conclusion.

17 In particular, chapters 4 and 5 show how these themes translated from the colonial to the national context.

18 Ian McKay, "The Liberal Order Framework: A Prospectus for a Reconnaissance of Canadian History," *Canadian Historical Review* 81 (2000): 623–4.

19 Jeffrey L. McNairn, "In Hope and Fear: Intellectual History, Liberalism, and the Liberal Order Framework," in Jean-François Constant and Michel Ducharme, eds., *Liberalism and Hegemony: Debating the Canadian Liberal Revolution* (Toronto: University of Toronto Press, 2009), 70–1.

20 Ibid., 85–6.

21 Curtis Fahey, *In His Name: The Anglican Experience in Upper Canada, 1791–1854* (Ottawa: Carleton University Press, 1991), 188.

22 For example, see Paul Romney, "On the Eve of Rebellion: Nationality, Religion and Class in the Toronto Election of 1836," in David Keane and Colin Read, eds., *Old Ontario: Essays in Honour of J.M.S. Careless* (Toronto: Dundurn Press, 1990), 200–1; see also George Emery, *Elections in Oxford County, 1837–1875: A Case Study of Democracy in Canada West and Early Ontario* (Toronto: University of Toronto Press, 2012), xvii–xviii.

23 Quoted in Alfred Henchman Crowfoot, *Benjamin Cronyn: First Bishop of Huron* (London, ON: Incorporated Synod of Diocese of Huron, 1957), 66–7; Henry Roper, "The Anglican Episcopate in Canada: An Historical Perspective," *Anglican and Episcopal History* 57, no. 3 (1988): 265.

24 John Webster Grant, *A Profusion of Spires: Religion in Nineteenth-Century Ontario* (Toronto: University of Toronto Press, 1988), 85–90.

25 This changing political environment of the 1850s, including the relationship between Anglicans and the liberal-reform movement, is analysed in chapter 3.

26 Richard W. Vaudry, *Anglicans and the Atlantic World: High Churchmen, Evangelicals, and the Quebec Connection* (Montreal and Kingston: McGill-Queen's University Press, 2003), 8–9.

27 Michael R. Watts, *The Dissenters, Vol. 1: From the Reformation to the French Revolution* (Oxford: Clarendon Press, 1978), 1–2.

28 Robynne Rogers Healey, *From Quaker to Upper Canadian: Faith and Community among Yonge Street Friends, 1801–1850* (Montreal and Kingston: McGill-Queen's University Press, 2006), 12.

29 On the divisions among Methodists, see chapters 1 and 2; on those among Presbyterians, chapter 2.

30 John Seed, "History and Narrative Identity: Religious Dissent and the Politics of Memory in Eighteenth-Century England," *Journal of British Studies* 44 (Jan. 2005): 48.

31 David Bebbington and David Ceri Jones, "Introduction: Evangelicalism, Dissent and Their Historians," in David Bebbington and David Ceri

Jones, eds., *Evangelicalism and Dissent in Modern England and Wales* (London: Routledge, 2021), 3–4.

32 Hilary M. Carey, *God's Empire: Religion and Colonialism in the British World, c. 1801–1908* (Cambridge: Cambridge University Press, 2010), 177–8.

33 Ibid., 177.

34 See Appendix A: Religious Demographics of Upper Canada / Ontario, 1842–1881.

35 For example, see Romney, "On the Eve of Rebellion," 200–1.

36 Emery, *Elections in Oxford County*, xvii–xviii.

37 Grant, *A Profusion of Spires*, 85–90.

38 In addition to referring to ibid., Curtis Fahey, *In His Name*, and William Westfall, *Two Worlds*, this study has benefitted from a number of informative works on Canadian church–state relations, including Marguerite Van Die, "Religion and Law in British North America," in Stephen Stein, ed., *The Cambridge History of Religions in America, Vol. 2* (Cambridge: Cambridge University Press, 2012); Michael Gauvreau, "The Dividends of Empire: Church Establishments and Contested British Identities in the Canadas and the Maritimes, 1780–1850," in Nancy Christie, ed., *Transatlantic Subjects: Ideas, Institutions, and Social Experience in Post-Revolutionary British North America* (Montreal and Kingston: McGill-Queen's University Press, 2008), 199–250; Michael Gauvreau, "Reluctant Voluntaries: Peter and George Brown: The Scottish Disruption and the Politics of Church and State in Canada," *Journal of Religious History* 25, no. 2 (June 2001): 134–57; Goldwin French, *Parsons and Politics: The Role of the Wesleyan Methodists in Upper Canada and the Maritimes from 1780 to 1855* (Toronto: Ryerson Press, 1962).

39 For example, see Janet Noel, *Canada Dry: Temperance Crusades before Confederation* (Toronto: University of Toronto Press, 1995); Allen P. Stouffer, *The Light of Nature and the Law of God: Antislavery in Ontario, 1833–1877* (Montreal and Kingston: McGill-Queen's University Press, 1992).

40 For more background on American Dissenting churches' vigorous embrace of eighteenth-century evangelicalism, see Patricia U. Bonomi, *Under the Cope of Heaven: Religion, Society, and Politics in Colonial America* (New York: Oxford University Press, 1986); and Jon Butler, *Awash in a Sea of Faith: Christianizing the American People* (Cambridge, MA: Harvard University Press, 1990). For evangelicalism in the Canadian colonies during and after the American Revolution, see G.A. Rawlyk, *The Canada Fire: Radical Evangelicalism in British North America, 1775–1812* (Montreal and Kingston: McGill-Queen's University Press, 1994).

41 David W. Bebbington, *Evangelicalism in Modern Britain: A History from the 1730s to the 1980s* (New York: Routledge, 1989), 3.

42 Grant, *A Profusion of Spires*, 90.

43 "Latest European News: Religious Equality Refused by the Commons," *Globe*, 19 May 1863.

44 J.M.S. Careless, "Mid-Victorian Liberalism in Central Canadian Newspapers, 1850–67," *Canadian Historical Review* 31, no. 3 (Sept. 1950): 235.

45 Todd Webb, *Transatlantic Methodists: British Wesleyans and the Formation of an Evangelical Culture in Nineteenth-Century Ontario and Quebec* (Montreal and Kingston: McGill-Queen's University Press, 2013), 8–9.

46 Ibid., 8.

47 Denis McKim, "Anxious Anglicans, Complicated Catholics, and Disruptive Dissenters: Christianity and the Search for Social Order in the Age of Revolution," in Elizabeth Mancke, Jerry Bannister, Denis B. McKim, and Scott W. See, eds., *Violence, Order, and Unrest: A History of British North America, 1749–1876* (Toronto: University of Toronto Press, 2019), 55, 69–70.

48 David Hempton, *Methodism: Empire of the Spirit* (New Haven, CT: Yale University Press, 2005), 5–6.

49 For more on the nineteenth-century liberal-reform movement in Britain, see Robert Kelley, *The Transatlantic Persuasion: The Liberal-Democratic Mind in the Age of Gladstone* (New York: Knopf, 1969); Michael R. Watts, *The Dissenters, Vol. 2: The Expansion of Evangelical Nonconformity, 1791–1859* (Oxford: Clarendon Press, 1995); and Eugenio F. Biagini, *Liberty, Retrenchment, and Reform: Popular Liberalism in the Age of Gladstone, 1860–1880* (Cambridge: Cambridge University Press, 1992).

50 Arthur R.M. Lower, *Colony to Nation: A History of Canada* (Toronto: Longmans, 1946), 164; William Kilbourn, *The Firebrand: William Lyon Mackenzie and the Rebellion in Upper Canada* (Toronto: Clarke & Irwin, 1956), 37–8. For the historiography of this subject, see the Conclusion.

51 Westfall, *Two Worlds*, 197.

52 For example, Michel Ducharme's *The Idea of Liberty in Canada* suggested that the colonists' religious rhetoric was limited to a few isolated issues, and it "did not relate to liberty or state legitimacy so much as to the relationship between church and state, between temporal power and spiritual power" (10–11).

53 Mark A. Noll, "What Happened to Christian Canada?" *Church History* 75, no. 2 (June 2006): 272–3.

54 Kevin P. Anderson, *Not Quite Us: Anti-Catholic Thought in English Canada since 1900* (Montreal and Kingston: McGill-Queen's University Press, 2019), 240.
55 Brad S. Gregory, *The Unintended Reformation: How a Religious Revolution Secularized Society* (Cambridge, MA: Harvard University Press, 2012), 2, 21, 383.
56 Larry Siedentop, *Inventing the Individual: The Origins of Western Liberalism* (Cambridge, MA: Belknap Press of Harvard University Press, 2014), 332.
57 Ibid., 333–4.
58 James T. Kloppenberg, *Toward Democracy: The Struggle for Self-Rule in European and American Thought* (New York: Oxford University Press, 2016), 6, 144–5, 152–7.
59 "Persecution," *Colonial Advocate*, 20 Dec. 1827.
60 For example, Ajzenstat, *The Canadian Founding*, xiii; see also Russell Blackford, *Freedom of Religion and the Secular State* (Chichester: Wiley-Blackwell, 2012), 53.
61 Kloppenberg, *Toward Democracy*, 156–7.
62 Marshall, *John Locke*, 357–8.
63 John Locke, "A Letter Concerning Tolerance [1689]," in Ian Shapiro, ed., *Two Treatises of Government and A Letter Concerning Tolerance* (New Haven, CT: Yale University Press, 2003), 245–6.
64 Ajzenstat, *The Canadian Founding*, 103.
65 "Protestantism Endangered," *Banner*, 15 Sept. 1843.
66 Linda Colley, *Britons: Forging the Nation, 1707–1837*, 6th ed. (New Haven, CT: Yale University Press, 2009), 29–30, 54.
67 J.P. Ellens, *Religious Routes to Gladstonian Liberalism: The Church Rate Conflict in England and Wales, 1832–1868* (University Park: Pennsylvania State University Press, 1994), 264.
68 Ibid., 269.
69 Michael Gauvreau, "Protestantism Transformed: Personal Piety and the Evangelical Social Vision," in George A. Rawlyk, ed., *The Canadian Protestant Experience, 1760–1990* (Burlington, ON: Welch, 1990), 57.
70 Kelley, *Transatlantic Persuasion*, 376.
71 Goldwin Smith, *The Political Destiny of Canada* (Toronto: Willing & Williamson, 1878), 11, 13.
72 Rev. Stuart Acheson, *Quebec's Blow: Separate School Act, 1863* (Toronto: Canadian Bureau of Patriotic Literature, n.d.), 12. Library and Archives Canada (LAC), Ottawa, ON.

73 John Rolph, *Speeches of Dr. John Rolph, and Christop'r A. Hagerman, Esq., His Majesty's Solicitor General, on the Bill for Appropriating the Proceeds of the Clergy Reserves to the Purposes of General Education* (Toronto: M. Reynolds, 1837), 12.

74 Quoted in J.M.S. Careless, *Brown of the Globe, Vol. 1: The Voice of Upper Canada, 1818–1859* (Toronto: Macmillan, 1959), 150.

75 Edward Miall, *Defects of our System of Government: delivered by Mr. Edward Miall before the Literary and Historical Society of Ottawa, on 3rd February 1877* (Ottawa: C.W. Mitchell, 1892), 6.

76 McKay, "The Liberal Order Framework," 635–6.

77 Ibid., 640.

78 *Gleaner* (Huntingdon, QC), 11 Nov. 1875.

79 Ibid.

80 Carmen Nielson Varty, "The City and the Ladies: Politics, Religion, and Female Benevolence in Mid-Nineteenth-Century Hamilton, Canada West," *Journal of Canadian Studies* 38, no. 2 (spring 2004): 151–71.

81 David A. Wilson, *Thomas D'Arcy McGee, Vol. II: The Extreme Moderate, 1857–1868* (Montreal and Kingston: McGill-Queen's University Press, 2011), 303.

82 Robert Hill, *Voice of the Vanishing Minority: Robert Sellar and the Huntingdon Gleaner, 1863–1919* (Montreal and Kingston: McGill-Queen's University Press, 1998), 77–80.

83 Fahey, *In His Name*, 174–5.

84 Mark McGowan, *Michael Power: The Struggle to Build the Catholic Church on the Canadian Frontier* (Montreal and Kingston: McGill-Queen's University Press, 2005), 268.

85 Bruce Curtis, *Building the Educational State: Canada West, 1836–1871* (London, ON: Althouse Press, 1988), 150.

86 J.M.S. Careless, *The Union of the Canadas* (Toronto: McClelland and Stewart, 1967), 182–3.

87 Ibid., 182–3.

88 Miller, "Anti-Catholic Thought," 479–80.

89 Charles Lindsey, *Rome in Canada: The Ultramontane Struggle for Supremacy over the Civil Authority* (Toronto: Lovell Brothers, 1877), 6.

90 In addition to quoting foreign Catholic leaders, Lindsey documented the anti-liberal writings of several *Programmistes* in Canada, which he summarized as an "army of writers[,] journalists, pamphleteers, authors of comedies, anti-Gallican treatises and sermons, who acknowledged Bishop

Bourget as commander-in-chief." Lindsey, *Rome in Canada*, 157. For Lindsey's extensive documentation of Catholic anti-liberalism, see that volume's chapters 8, 9, and 10.

91 George Brown, "Letter to the Roman Catholic Committee [1871]," in Alexander Mackenzie, ed., *The Life and Speeches of Hon. George Brown* (Toronto: Globe, 1882), 126.

92 Ibid., 125.

93 "Constitution Granted to the North West Territories," n.d., Richard W. Scott Papers, LAC.

94 Janet Epp Buckingham, *Fighting over God: A Legal and Political History of Religious Freedom in Canada* (Montreal and Kingston: McGill-Queen's University Press, 2014), 38–43.

95 For example, city of Ottawa MLA Richard W. Scott (who later served in Mackenzie's federal cabinet) was one such Catholic liaison for Sir John A. Macdonald. During the 1863 election, Scott conveyed the impression that he could command the Catholic vote throughout the colony. In one letter to Macdonald, Scott states, "I have written a number of letters on behalf of Jones to M.S.R. of Leeds, which I think will secure for him the Catholic Vote … I generally send off a batch every day to different parts of Upper Canada … Our chances throughout U.C. look well. Is Sidney Smith to run or Dunford? I have just written a friend to keep every Catholic Vote from Dunford." Letter from R.W. Scott to John A. Macdonald, 30 May 1863, Richard W. Scott Papers.

96 Alexander Galt, *Church and State* (Montreal: Dawson Brothers, 1876), 27.

97 Letter from Alexander Mackenzie to George Brown, 22 Jan. 1876, Alexander Mackenzie Papers, LAC.

98 "Mr. Meredith's Speech at London, December 16th, 1889," in Separate Schools Scrapbook, Oliver Mowat Family Papers, Archives of Ontario (AO).

99 William H. McNeill, "Mythistory, or Truth, Myth, History, and Historians," in *Mythistory and Other Essays* (Chicago: University of Chicago Press, 1986), 15–16.

100 "Toronto, Nov. 5 – To-day being Guy Fawkes' Day it was celebrated here with more than usual éclat in the evening by the younger portion of the community; bonfires and tar barrels were burning in every direction, and several drum and fife bands were parading the streets." *Gleaner*, 11 Nov. 1875.

101 W.F. Clarke, "The History of Nonconformity in England in 1662," in *Canadian Bicentenary Papers* (Toronto: W.C. Chewett & Co., 1862), 6.

102 Ibid., 6.

103 Originally published in the *Montreal Herald* in February 1876. Quoted in Alexander Galt, *Civil Liberty in Lower Canada* (Montreal: D. Bentley, 1876), 11.

104 For example, see "Riot at Montreal," *Banner*, 5 Sept. 1845.

105 *Gleaner*, 16 Dec. 1875.

106 "Lord Dufferin on Party Spirit," *Gleaner*, 3 Oct. 1878.

107 Wilfrid Laurier, "The New Party Leader [2 Aug. 1887]," in Arthur Milnes, ed., *Canada Always: The Defining Speeches of Sir Wilfrid Laurier* (Toronto: McClelland & Stewart, 2016), 124 (emphasis added).

108 Grant, *A Profusion of Spires*, 89.

109 Some of the early research for this chapter appeared in James Forbes, "'God has opened the eyes of the People': Religious Rhetoric in the Upper Canada Rebellion of 1837," *Journal for the Study of Radicalism* 12, no. 1 (spring 2018): 1–25.

110 "The Roman Catholic Bishops on Politics," *Globe*, 23 Aug. 1859.

111 For example, in 1889 Ontario's Liberal Minister of Education G.W. Ross responded to critics of his government's increase in state support for the separate Catholic school system by arguing that education policy ought to be "progressive." See G.W. Ross, "Report of a Speech delivered by the Minister of Education at the Reform Demonstration, Toronto, June 29th, 1889," Mowat Family Papers, Separate Schools Scrapbook, AO.

Chapter One

1 "To the Electors of the County of York," *Colonial Advocate*, 3 Jan. 1827.

2 Carol Wilton, *Popular Politics and Political Culture in Upper Canada, 1800–1850* (Montreal and Kingston: McGill-Queen's University Press, 2000), 44 5.

3 *Constitution*, 29 Nov. 1837.

4 Ian McKay, "Canada as a Long Liberal Revolution: On Writing the History of Actually Existing Canadian Liberalisms, 1840s–1940s," in Jean-François Constant and Michel Ducharme, eds., *Liberalism and Hegemony: Debating the Canadian Liberal Revolution* (Toronto: University of Toronto Press, 2009), 353.

5 Curtis Fahey, *In His Name: The Anglican Experience in Upper Canada, 1791–1854* (Ottawa: Carleton University Press, 1991), xvi, 2–3.

6 George Emery, *Elections in Oxford County, 1837–1875: A Case Study of Democracy in Canada West and Early Ontario* (Toronto: University of Toronto Press, 2012), xvii–xviii (emphasis added).

7 For example, see Paul Romney, "On the Eve of Rebellion: Nationality, Religion and Class in the Toronto Election of 1836," in David Keane and Colin Read, eds., *Old Ontario: Essays in Honour of J.M.S. Careless* (Toronto: Dundurn Press, 1990), 200–1.

8 *Constitution*, 29 Nov. 1837.

9 For example, see Michel Ducharme, *The Idea of Liberty in Canada during the Age of Atlantic Revolutions, 1776–1838*, trans. Peter Feldstein (Montreal and Kingston: McGill-Queen's University Press, 2014), 11; Benjamin T. Jones, *Republicanism and Responsible Government: The Shaping of Democracy in Australia and Canada* (Montreal and Kingston: McGill-Queen's University Press, 2014), x, 14–15.

10 Albert Schrauwers, *'Union Is Strength': W.L. Mackenzie, the Children of Peace, and the Emergence of Joint Stock Democracy in Upper Canada* (Toronto: University of Toronto Press, 2009), chap. 6; Robynne Rogers Healey, *From Quaker to Upper Canadian: Faith and Community among Yonge Street Friends, 1801–1850* (Montreal and Kingston: McGill-Queen's University Press, 2006), 4, 13–14.

11 Colin M. Coates, "Liberty in Time and Space: A Commentary on Ducharme," *Canadian Historical Review* 94, no. 1 (March 2013): 85.

12 Gerald Craig, *Upper Canada: The Formative Years, 1784–1841*, 2nd ed. (Don Mills, ON: Oxford University Press, 2013), 249.

13 Colin Read and Ronald Stagg, *The Rebellion of 1837 in Upper Canada: A Collection of Documents* (Ottawa, ON: Carleton University Press, 1985), lvii.

14 Maxime Dagenais and Julien Mauduit, ed., *Revolutions across Borders: Jacksonian America and the Canadian Rebellion* (Montreal and Kingston: McGill-Queen's University Press, 2019), 13–14.

15 J.I. Little, *Borderland Religion: The Emergence of an English-Canadian Identity, 1792–1852* (Toronto: University of Toronto Press, 2004); see also J.I. Little, *Loyalties in Conflict: A Canadian Borderland in War and Rebellion, 1812–1840* (Toronto: University of Toronto Press, 2008).

16 Nancy Christie, "'In these Times of Democratic Rage and Delusion': Popular Religion and the Challenge to the Established Order, 1760–1815," in George A. Rawlyk, ed., *The Canadian Protestant Experience, 1760 to 1990* (Montreal and Kingston: McGill-Queen's University Press, 1990), 9–47.

17 Alan Greer, "1837–38: Rebellion Reconsidered," *Canadian Historical Review* 76, no. 1 (1995): 13.

18 Jones, *Republicanism and Responsible Government*, 74.

19 Ducharme, *The Idea of Liberty*, 6–7.

20 For example, see "Will the Canadians Declare Their Independence and Shoulder Their Muskets?" *Constitution*, 5 July 1837.

21 Alan Greer, *The Patriots and the People: The Rebellion of 1837 in Rural Lower Canada* (Toronto: University of Toronto Press, 1993), x–xi, chap. 3.

22 Ibid., 239.

23 Ducharme, *The Idea of Liberty*, 9, 161.

24 E. Jane Errington, *The Lion, The Eagle, and Upper Canada: A Developing Colonial Ideology* (Montreal and Kingston: McGill-Queen's University Press, 1987), 93.

25 John Webster Grant, *A Profusion of Spires: Religion in Nineteenth-Century Ontario* (Toronto: University of Toronto Press, 1988), 89.

26 Quoted in Fahey, *In His Name*, 67.

27 J.K. Johnson, *Becoming Prominent: Regional Leadership in Upper Canada, 1791–1841* (Montreal and Kingston: McGill-Queen's University Press, 1989), 151, 237.

28 "Parliamentary Reports: Doctor Strachan's Misrepresentations, and The Episcopalian University Charter," *Colonial Advocate*, 27 March 1828.

29 "Report on the Petition of Christians of all denominations against Doctor Strachan's University Charter, Church Monopoly, &c, &c. &c," *Colonial Advocate*, 3 April 1828.

30 Fahey, *In His Name*, 67–8.

31 "Report on the Petition of Christians."

32 "A Very Clever Letter Upon Strachanism or Jesuitism," *Colonial Advocate*, 8 Nov. 1827.

33 Paul Romney, "Re-inventing Upper Canada: American Immigrants, Upper Canadian History, English Law, and the Alien Question," in Roger Hall, William Westfall, and Laurel Sefton MacDowell, eds., *Patterns of the Past: Interpreting Ontario's History, A Collection of Historical Articles Published on the Occasion of the Centenary of the Ontario Historical Society* (Toronto: Dundurn Press, 1988), 78–9.

34 David Mills, *The Idea of Loyalty in Upper Canada, 1784–1850* (Montreal and Kingston: McGill-Queen's University Press, 1988), 34–5.

35 Paul Romney, *Getting It Wrong: How Canadians Forgot Their Past and Imperilled Confederation* (Toronto: University of Toronto Press, 1999), 35–6.

36 Errington, *The Lion*, 181.

37 "Report on the Petition of Christians of Different Denominations in Upper Canada (Continued)," *Colonial Advocate*, 24 April 1828.

38 Errington, *The Lion*, 52.
39 Grant, *A Profusion of Spires*, 89.
40 Mills, *The Idea of Loyalty*, 55–6.
41 Errington, *The Lion*, 247fn62.
42 "The Vision," *Colonial Advocate*, 3 Jan. 1828.
43 Egerton Ryerson, "To the Hon. and Rev. Dr. Strachan, &c. &c, No. 3 [dated 7 May 1828]," *Colonial Advocate*, 26 June 1828.
44 Wilton, *Popular Politics*, 228.
45 "Fredericksburgh, 5th Jan. 1828," *Colonial Advocate*, 24 Jan. 1828.
46 "Report on the Petition of Christians of Different Denominations in Upper Canada (Continued)," *Colonial Advocate*, 8 May 1828.
47 Egerton Ryerson, "To the Hon. and Rev. Dr. Strachan, &c. &c., No. 4," *Colonial Advocate*, 10 July 1828.
48 Fahey, *In His Name*, 99–100.
49 "The Seeker," *Colonial Advocate*, 28 Feb. 1828.
50 "To the Editor of the Canadian Freeman," reprinted in the *Colonial Advocate*, 10 July 1828.
51 "The Vision," *Colonial Advocate*, 3 Jan. 1828. The biblical phrase "Wo to ye! Scribes and Pharisees" is a reference to Matthew 23 (King James Version [KJV]).
52 "Persecution," *Colonial Advocate*, 20 Dec. 1827.
53 William Lyon Mackenzie wrote that he was opposed to "ecclesiastical supremacy," but not to the Anglican church itself: "The editor of the Colonial Advocate, though not a member of the protestant episcopal church, commonly called the establishment, feels, and ever did feel, friendly to it. That church, both in England, Scotland, Ireland, & the United States, has produced many eminently pious men, and doubtless numbers within her pales, a vast body of faithful servants of their divine master … We repeat, that, tho' opposed to ecclesiastical supremacy, we are not at enmity with those who *conscientiously* uphold the doctrine, worship and discipline, of the religion professed and taught by a Hervey and a Newton." See "Religious Freedom," *Colonial Advocate*, 8 May 1828.
54 "Parliamentary Reports" (27 March 1828).
55 Fahey, *In His Name*, 240–1.
56 Egerton Ryerson, "To the Hon. And Rev. Dr. Strachan, &c. &c. No. 5 [dated 14 May 1828]," *Colonial Advocate*, 22 July 1828; for the parable of the wise man and the foolish man, see Matthew 7:24–7 (KJV).
57 William Lyon Mackenzie, "Speech, of Mr. Mackenzie, at the Fifth Meeting of the Constitutional Society of Upper Canada, on a motion to elect

Mr. Francis Collins, (Editor of the Canadian Freeman) a member of the Society," *Colonial Advocate*, 13 March 1828.

58 "York, Thursday, July 31st, 1828," *Colonial Advocate*, 31 July 1828; "County of York Election," *Colonial Advocate*, 31 July 1828.

59 Peter H. Russell, *Canada's Odyssey: A Country Based on Incomplete Conquests* (Toronto: University of Toronto Press, 2017), 100–1.

60 David Willson, *Sacred Impressions of the Mind, in Praise and Prayer, devoted to God in worship by the Children of Peace in Sharon* (Newmarket, ON: S.n., 1853), 257.

61 Ibid., 259, 263.

62 Romney, *Getting It Wrong*, 30–2.

63 Ibid., 33.

64 Ibid., 33.

65 Bryan Palmer, "Popular Radicalism and the Theatrics of Rebellion: The Hybrid Discourse of Dissent in Upper Canada in the 1830s," in Nancy Christie, ed., *Transatlantic Subjects: Ideas, Institutions, and Social Experiences in Post-Revolutionary British North America* (Montreal and Kingston: McGill-Queen's University Press, 2008), 416–20.

66 "Colleges in Upper Canada," *Colonial Advocate*, 3 Dec. 1829.

67 Ibid.

68 See John 10:11–15 (KJV).

69 *Christian Guardian*, 7 Nov. 1832.

70 William Lesslie Diary, March 1832, Lesslie Family Fonds, box 1, Dundas Museum and Archives, Dundas, ON.

71 For example, see Matthew 12:1–25 (KJV).

72 Matthew 23:27 (KJV). See also entire chapter.

73 Willson, *Impressions of the Mind*, 263–4.

74 Exodus 12:19–20, 13:3 (KJV).

75 Matthew 16:6–12 (KJV).

76 "Three Days Debate on the Question of Whether the Proceeds of the Clergy Reserves Should be applied to the Education of the Youth of the Province, or appropriated for the support of the Clergy of one or more Churches," *Constitution*, 21 Dec. 1836.

77 1 Corinthians 5:6–8; Galatians 5:3–9 (KJV).

78 John Rolph, *Speeches of Dr. John Rolph, and Christop'r A. Hagerman, Esq., His Majesty's Solicitor General, on the Bill for Appropriating the Proceeds of the Clergy Reserves to the Purposes of General Education* (Toronto: M. Reynolds, 1837), 11.

79 "Electors of Upper Canada – see that ye sleep not in the hour of danger!" *Colonial Advocate*, 7 Oct. 1830.

80 "Dissolution of the Legislature," *Colonial Advocate*, 16 Sept. 1830.
81 "County of York Election," *Colonial Advocate*, 28 Oct. 1830.
82 Wilton, *Popular Politics*, 57.
83 Ibid., 51.
84 "Meeting of Friends of Religious Liberty," *Colonial Advocate*, 16 Dec. 1830.
85 Wilton, *Popular Politics*, 53.
86 "The Doctrines and Spirit of Church and State Union in Canada," *Christian Guardian*, 15 Oct. 1831.
87 "Colleges in Upper Canada," *Colonial Advocate*, 3 Dec. 1829.
88 "Report of the Sabbath School Union Society," *Colonial Advocate*, 29 Jan. 1829.
89 "Religious Liberty," *Colonial Advocate*, 16 Dec. 1830.
90 Wilton, *Popular Politics*, 96–7.
91 Ibid., 86.
92 "To the People of Upper Canada," *Colonial Advocate*, 12 Jan. 1832.
93 Ibid.
94 Wilton, *Popular Politics*, 9.
95 "The Progress of Misgovernment," *Colonial Advocate*, 28 March 1832.
96 Wilton, *Popular Politics*, 106.
97 Ibid., 105–6.
98 Reprinted in the *Colonial Advocate.* "The organization of the officials, as the great Catholic Body, to beat down the Protestants of York, explained by Mr. George Gurnett, one of the Secretaries to the Union," *Colonial Advocate*, 28 March 1832.
99 "The Progress of Misgovernment."
100 Neil Semple, *The Lord's Dominion: The History of Canadian Methodism* (Montreal and Kingston: McGill-Queen's University Press, 1996), 75.
101 Grant, *A Profusion of Spires*, 89.
102 Goldwin S. French, *Parsons and Politics: The Role of Wesleyan Methodists in Upper Canada and the Maritimes from 1780 to 1855* (Toronto: Ryerson University Press, 1962), 138–9.
103 "Remarks by the Editor of the Guardian," *Christian Guardian*, 29 Aug. 1832.
104 "To the Patrons, Subscribers and Readers of the Guardian," *Christian Guardian*, 29 Aug. 1832.
105 "The Late Bishop Richardson," *Globe*, 11 March 1875.
106 "Religious Grants," *Christian Guardian*, 3 July 1833.

107 "Not False Accusers," *Christian Guardian*, 10 July 1833.
108 Todd Webb, *Transatlantic Methodist: British Wesleyanism and the Formation of an Evangelical Culture in Nineteenth-Century Ontario and Quebec* (Montreal and Kingston: McGill-Queen's University Press, 2013), 79.
109 French, *Parsons and Politics*, 140, 150.
110 "Answer of the British to the Canadian Conference," *Christian Guardian*, 2 Oct. 1833.
111 [Egerton Ryerson], "Impressions made by my late visit to England," *Christian Guardian*, 30 Oct. 1833.
112 "Our Principles and Opinions," *Christian Guardian*, 27 Nov. 1833.
113 For more on voluntarism in the Methodist church, the reaction to Ryerson's comments about British politics, and the controversy surrounding the union with the British Wesleyan Methodists, see James Forbes, "Contesting the Protestant Consensus: Voluntarists, Methodists, and the Persistence of Evangelical Dissent in Upper Canada, 1829–1854," *Ontario History* 108, no. 2 (autumn 2016): 189–214.
114 Wilton, *Popular Politics*, 53.
115 [Egerton Ryerson], "Impressions made by my late visit to England."
116 Egerton Ryerson, *The Story of My Life: Being Reminiscences of Sixty Years' Public Service in Canada*, ed. J. George Hodgins (Toronto: William Briggs, 1883), 119, 121.
117 French, *Parsons and Politics*, 137.
118 Romney, "On the Eve of Rebellion," 200.
119 Ibid., 213.
120 French, *Parsons and Politics*, 152.
121 Semple, *The Lord's Dominion*, 91.
122 "Ryerson's Attack on Hume," *Colonial Advocate*, 7 Nov. 1833.
123 Gerald Craig, *Upper Canada*, 223–4.
124 W.L. Mackenzie, *The Seventh Report from the Select Committee of The House of Assembly of Upper Canada on Grievances* (Toronto: M. Reynolds, 1835), xvi.
125 Craig, *Upper Canada*, 181.
126 Willson, *Impressions of the Mind*, 263–4.
127 Peter Burroughs, *The Canadian Crisis and British Colonial Policy, 1828–1841* (Toronto: Macmillan, 1972), 76.
128 Alan Wilson, *The Clergy Reserves of Upper Canada: A Canadian Mortmain* (Toronto: University of Toronto Press, 1968), 123–4.

129 "Three Days Debate on the Question of Whether the Proceeds of the Clergy Reserves Should be applied to the Education of the Youth of the Province, or appropriated for the support of the Clergy of one or more Churches [Part 2]," *Constitution*, 28 Dec. 1836.
130 Originally in a letter from William Ryerson to Egerton Ryerson, 14 June 1836. Quoted in Gordon Barkwell, "The Clergy Reserves in Upper Canada: A Study in the Separation of Church and State, 1791–1854," PhD dissertation, University of Chicago, 1953, 186.
131 "The Rectories," *Constitution*, 22 March 1837.
132 Palmer, "Popular Radicalism," 407.
133 "Rural Verse," *Constitution*, 19 Oct. 1836.
134 "Birth and Reign of Kings," *Constitution*, 26 Oct. 1836.
135 "Religious Liberty," *Colonial Advocate*, 16 Dec. 1830.
136 "Colleges in Upper Canada," *Colonial Advocate*, 3 Dec. 1829.
137 "Three Days Debate" (21 Dec. 1836).
138 Read and Stagg, eds., *The Rebellion of 1837*, xxvi.
139 "Sir F.B. Head's Reply to an Address of Toronto Electors [20 May 1836]," in Colin Read and Ronald J. Stagg, eds., *The Rebellion of 1837 in Upper Canada: A Collection of Documents* (Ottawa: Carleton University Press, 1985), 8–9.
140 Romney, *Getting It Wrong*, 61.
141 Quoted in Ryerson, *Story of My Life*, 171.
142 Ibid., 171.
143 Ibid., 167–8.
144 Read and Stagg, eds., *The Rebellion of 1837*, xxviii.
145 Ryerson, *Story of My Life*, 168.
146 Read and Stagg, eds., *The Rebellion of 1837*, xxx.
147 The British prime minister's official residence was and is 10 Downing Street, London. "Will the Canadians declare Their Independence and Shoulder Their Muskets?" *Constitution*, 5 July 1837.
148 "The Political Unions," *Constitution*, 13 Sept. 1837.
149 *Constitution*, 29 Nov. 1837.
150 "W.L. Mackenzie's Appeal to Arms," in Colin Read and Ronald J. Stagg, eds., *The Rebellion of 1837 in Upper Canada: A Collection of Documents* (Ottawa: Carleton University Press, 1985), 110–13.
151 Read and Stagg, eds., *The Rebellion of 1837*, lvii.
152 Chris Raible, "'Uncertain as to Future Fate': Reflections on the Boxes and Their Makers," in Chris Raible, John C. Carter, and Darryl Withrow, eds.,

From Hands Now Striving to be Free: Boxes Crafted by 1837 Rebellion Prisoners, an Analysis and Inventory of 94 Boxes (Toronto: York Pioneer and Historical Society, 2009), 53.

153 "YP42 – Maker: Jesse Cleaver," in Chris Raible, John C. Carter, and Darryl Withrow, eds., *From Hands Now Striving to be Free: Boxes Crafted by 1837 Rebellion Prisoners, an Analysis and Inventory of 94 Boxes* (Toronto: York Pioneer and Historical Society, 2009), 20; see also Healey, *From Quaker to Upper Canadian*, 148.

154 For a brief historiographical summary of the 1837 rebellion, see Palmer, "Popular Radicalism," 430–2fn4–9.

155 Jones, *Republicanism and Responsible Government*, 41.

156 Ibid., 67–8.

157 Ibid., 16.

158 Ibid., 7–8, 16.

159 Ibid., 146.

160 Westfall, *Two Worlds*, 23–4.

161 For example, Egerton Ryerson argued that church establishments would persecute Dissenters in Upper Canada "if they had the power." Thus the goal was to limit that power by insisting on a strict separation of church and state. "The Doctrines and Spirit of Church and State Union in Canada," *Christian Guardian*, 15 Oct. 1831.

162 Jones, *Republicanism and Responsible Government*, 15–16.

163 Ducharme, *The Idea of Liberty*, 7–8.

164 Ibid., 10–11.

165 *Constitution*, 29 Nov. 1837.

166 Ducharme, *The Idea of Liberty*, 75.

167 For more background on Mackenzie's interest in the Bible, see Stuart Barnard, "Religious Print Culture and the British and Foreign Bible Society in Canada, 1820–1904," PhD dissertation, University of Calgary, 2016, 51–64.

168 "Common Sense," *Constitution*, 19 July 1837.

169 "To the Convention of Farmers, Mechanics, Labourers, and other Inhabitants of Toronto, met at the Royal Oak Hotel, to consider of and take measures for effectually maintaining in this colony, a free constitution and democratic form of government," *Constitution*, 15 Nov. 1837.

170 "Birth and Reign of Kings," *Constitution*, 26 Oct. 1836.

171 Egerton Ryerson, "To the Hon. and Rev. Dr. Strachan, &c. &c., No. 4," *Colonial Advocate*, 10 July 1828.

172 "Three Days Debate" (21 Dec. 1836).

Chapter Two

1 Albert Schrauwers, *Awaiting the Millennium: The Children of Peace and the Village of Hope, 1812–1889* (Toronto: University of Toronto Press, 1993), 180.
2 Egerton Ryerson, *Story of My Life: Being Reminiscences of Sixty Years' Public Service* (Toronto: W. Briggs, 1884), 252–3.
3 The Earl of Durham, "Report on the Affairs of British North America, from the Earl of Durham [11 Feb. 1839]," in *Lord Durham's Report on the Affairs of British North America, Vol. 2: Text of the Report*, ed. C.P. Lucas (Oxford: Clarendon Press, 1912), 149.
4 David Mills, *The Idea of Loyalty in Upper Canada, 1784–1850* (Montreal and Kingston: McGill-Queen's University Press, 1988), chap. 7.
5 Michael S. Cross, *A Biography of Robert Baldwin: The Morning-Star of Memory* (Don Mills, ON: Oxford University Press, 2012), 38–9.
6 J.M.S. Careless, *Brown of the Globe, Vol. I: The Voice of Upper Canada* (Toronto: MacMillan, 1959), 28–30.
7 John Ralston Saul, *Louis-Hippolyte LaFontaine and Robert Baldwin* (Toronto: Penguin, 2010), 5–6, 201; Cross, *Robert Baldwin*, 5.
8 "Sectarian Political Preferences – Persecution," *Examiner*, 3 May 1848.
9 For the divisions in the reform party in 1849, see Careless, *Brown of the Globe, Vol. I*, 104–11.
10 Cross, *Robert Baldwin*, 56.
11 Isaac Buchanan, *First Series of Five Letters, Against the Baldwin Faction, by an Advocate of Responsible Government, and of The New College Bill* (Toronto: British Colonist, 1844), 31.
12 Ian McKay, "The Liberal Order Framework: A Prospectus for a Reconnaissance of Canadian History," *Canadian Historical Review* 81 (2000): 632; Michel Ducharme, *The Idea of Liberty in Canada during the Age of Atlantic Revolutions, 1776–1838*, trans. Peter Feldstein (Montreal and Kingston: McGill-Queen's University Press, 2014), 86, 186.
13 Some historians have described the 1840s as the beginning of a Protestant consensus in Ontario, and indeed some major Protestant leaders such as Egerton Ryerson and John Strachan found themselves more willing to cooperate to pursue common aims. For example, see William Westfall, *Two Worlds: The Protestant Culture of Nineteenth-Century Ontario* (Montreal and Kingston: McGill-Queen's University Press, 1989), 49; Mark A. Noll, "Canadian Evangelicalism: A View from the United States," in G.A. Rawlyk, ed., *Aspects of the Canadian Evangelical Experience* (Montreal

and Kingston: McGill-Queen's University Press, 1997), 4. Despite their conciliatory attitude, however, there is much evidence to suggest the old divisions ran deeper than a few leaders could address. For a deeper analysis, see James Forbes, "Contesting the Protestant Consensus: Methodists, Voluntarists, and the Persistence of Evangelical Dissent in Upper Canada, 1829–1854," *Ontario History* 108, no. 2 (autumn 2016): 189–214.

14 J.M.S. Careless, *The Union of the Canadas: The Growth of Canadian Institutions, 1841–1857* (Toronto: McClelland and Stewart, 1967), 3.

15 Cross, *Robert Baldwin*, 75.

16 "Friday, December 20," *Examiner*, 8 Jan. 1840.

17 See chapter 1 for more on Mackenzie's concern about Anglican influence.

18 Todd Webb, "Faiths of '37: Methodism and Anti-Catholicism in Rebellion-Era Canada," Canadian Society for Church History President's Address (2009), 111.

19 Richard W. Vaudry, *Anglicans and the Atlantic World: High Churchmen, Evangelicals, and the Quebec Connection* (Montreal and Kingston: McGill-Queen's University Press, 2003), 155–6.

20 For example, Peter Brown argued that "Popery and High-Church-of-Englandism" were "essentially the same in substance." See "Alarming Demonstration of the Jesuits," *Banner*, 26 Dec. 1845.

21 "Riot at Montreal," *Banner*, 5 Sept. 1845.

22 William J. Smyth, *Toronto, the Belfast of Canada: The Orange Order and the Shaping of Municipal Culture* (Toronto: University of Toronto Press, 2015), 43.

23 Mark G. McGowan, *Michael Power: The Struggle to Build the Catholic Church on the Canadian Frontier* (Montreal and Kingston: McGill-Queen's University Press, 2005), 201; appendix 3.

24 Ibid., 184–7.

25 Ibid., 268.

26 Brian P. Clarke, *Piety and Nationalism: Lay Voluntary Associations and the Creation of an Irish-Catholic Community in Toronto, 1850–1895* (Montreal and Kingston: McGill-Queen's University Press, 1993), 34–40, 55–6.

27 Yvan Lamonde, *The Social History of Ideas in Quebec, 1760–1896*, trans. Phyllis Aronoff and Howard Scott (Montreal and Kingston: McGill-Queen's University Press, 2013), 248.

28 "Thursday, December 19," *Examiner*, 1 Jan. 1840.

29 Diary of John Lesslie, 2 March 1842, Lesslie Family Fonds, Dundas Museum and Archives, Dundas, ON.

30 "Protestantism Endangered," *Banner*, 15 Sept. 1843.

31 Beginning in 1839, William J. Smyth notes five inter-religious riots in the 1840s in Toronto alone, a trend that became less frequent but persisted into the 1880s. See Smyth, *Toronto*, 48.
32 Cross, *Robert Baldwin*, 38–9.
33 Mills, *The Idea of Loyalty*, 8–9.
34 Cross, *Robert Baldwin*, 57–8.
35 Carol Wilton, *Popular Politics and Political Culture in Upper Canada, 1800–1850* (Montreal and Kingston: McGill-Queen's University Press, 2000), 194–5, 219–20.
36 "Meeting of the Reformers of Toronto," *Examiner*, 1 Jan. 1840; "Township of Niagara Meeting," *Examiner*, 15 Jan. 1840; "East Gwillimbury Twp. Meeting," *Examiner*, 15 Jan. 1840.
37 "Home District Township Meetings," *Examiner*, 8 Jan. 1840.
38 "Whitchurch Township Meeting," *Examiner*, 15 Jan. 1840.
39 "Protests Against the Union," *Examiner*, 1 Jan. 1840.
40 "U.C. Provincial Parliament," *Examiner*, 1 Jan. 1840.
41 "Friday, December 20," *Examiner*, 8 Jan. 1840. This phrase comes from the Genesis story of the twins Esau and Jacob. When Esau returned home exhausted from labouring in a field, he begged his brother for a bowl of porridge, or "pottage." Before Jacob fed his brother, he demanded that Esau promise him his inheritance, or "birthright." Only when Esau relinquished his birthright did Jacob give him the food he required. See Genesis 25:23–34 (KJV).
42 Jacques Monet, *The Last Cannon Shot: A Study of French-Canadian Nationalism, 1837–1850* (Toronto: University of Toronto Press, 1969), 89–90.
43 Cross, *Robert Baldwin*, 142.
44 Ibid., 144–5.
45 McGowan, *Michael Powers*, 268; Cross, *Robert Baldwin*, 147.
46 Cross, *Robert Baldwin*, 205.
47 As Monet wrote, "By agreeing to work within the Union as a united political group, they [French Canadians] had taken the first step towards circumventing Durham's sentence of death against their culture." Monet, *The Last Cannon Shot*, 120; see also Cross, *Robert Baldwin*, 70.
48 "Alarming Demonstration of the Jesuits," *Banner*, 26 Dec. 1845.
49 Ibid.
50 For a brief overview of his public life, see "Hon. Isaac Buchanan," *Globe*, 1 Oct. 1883; see also Cross, *Robert Baldwin*, 205.
51 Buchanan, *First Series of Five Letters*, 9–10.

52 Ibid., 17.
53 Ibid., 17–19.
54 Douglas McCalla, "Buchanan, Isaac," *Dictionary of Canadian Biography*, vol. 11, University of Toronto / Université Laval, 2003. http://biographi.ca/en/bio/buchanan_isaac_11E.html <26 Oct. 2021>.
55 Buchanan, *First Series of Five Letters*, 26.
56 Ibid., 12.
57 Cross, *Robert Baldwin*, 106–7.
58 McGowan, *Michael Power*, 268.
59 Buchanan, *First Series of Five Letters*, 9.
60 Letter from W.L. Mackenzie to Isaac Buchanan, 21 Dec. 1845, Mackenzie–Lindsey Family Fonds, Archives of Ontario (AO), Toronto, ON.
61 Buchanan, *First Series of Five Letters*, 13.
62 David Willson, "The Merits of Isaac Buchanan," *Examiner*, 17 Jan. 1844.
63 "To the editor of the Examiner," *Examiner*, 17 Jan. 1844.
64 Buchanan, *First Series of Five Letters*, 31.
65 For the Irish migration to Toronto in 1847, see Mark McGowan, *Death or Canada: The Irish Famine Migration to Toronto, 1847* (Toronto: Novalis, 2009); Hereward Senior, *The Fenians in Canada* (Toronto: MacMillan, 1978), 10–11; Smyth, *Toronto*, 44–7.
66 For example, see "Great Meeting in Behalf of the Irish," *Banner*, 26 Feb. 1847.
67 Ibid.
68 "Remedy for the Distress in Ireland and Scotland," *Banner*, 26 Feb. 1847.
69 "Government Plan of Relief for Ireland," *Banner*, 12 March 1847.
70 "Irish Emigration Scheme," *Banner*, 7 May 1847.
71 Letter from James Lesslie to W.L. Mackenzie, 4 March 1847, Mackenzie–Lindsey Family Fonds.
72 "Emigration – Disease: Prudential Arrangements," *Examiner*, 25 Aug. 1847.
73 Letter from James Lesslie to W.L. Mackenzie, 4 March 1847, Mackenzie–Lindsey Family Fonds.
74 "Emigration – Disease: Prudential Arrangements."
75 "Clergy Reserves," *Banner*, 24 Dec. 1847.
76 "Social, Educational, and Religious State of the Manufacturing Districts in England," *Christian Guardian*, 9 Aug. 1843; "Letters from President Durbin on the Position of the Wesleyans in England: Letter II, Sheffield Conference, England, 1843: Effect of the Wesleyan People and Preachers –

Much Increased by Sir J. Graham's Bill – Analysis of the Bill," *Christian Guardian*, 20 Sept. 1843.

77 For background on Maynooth, see G.I.T. Machin, *Politics and the Churches in Great Britain, 1832–1868* (Oxford: Clarendon Press, 1977), 169–72.

78 Allen P. Stauffer, *The Light of Nature and the Law of God: Antislavery in Ontario, 1833–1877* (Montreal and Kingston: McGill-Queen's University Press, 1992), 24; David J. Cox, "The Wolves Let Loose at Wolverhampton: A Study of the South Staffordshire Election 'Riots,' May 1835," *Law, Crime and History* (2011): 14.

79 Congregational Meetings (1834–1891), 27, Zion Congregational Church Collection, United Church of Canada Archives, Toronto, ON.

80 Regarding one of Bidwell's earlier letters about Head, Rev. Roaf wrote, "It appears to me to be more courteous to Sir Francis than your former bearing towards him, more courteous than the reports, resolutions and speeches of the House of Assembly, and to imply a respect for the present Government which I have thought you did not feel, and was not deserved … I should have liked to perceive more of that self reliance and hope and indomitable firmness which are evidences of innocence." John Roaf, Letter to Marshall Spring Bidwell, Temperance Hotel, Albany, NY, 19 Dec. 1837, James R. Roaf Fonds, AO.

81 According to historian Joseph Hardwick, colonial officials often designated special Days of Thanksgiving to celebrate a particularly abundant harvest or the termination of a crisis (as in the rebellions of 1837), a tradition that may be traced back to Britain at least as early as the Tudor era. These occasions were "intended to broaden horizons and nurture a sense of shared experience and collective responsibility among colonists." See Joseph Hardwick, "Fasts, Thanksgivings, and Senses of Community in Nineteenth-Century Canada and the British Empire," *Canadian Historical Review* 98, no. 4 (Dec. 2017): 677–8.

82 F.B. Head, "Proclamation," in *Religious Liberty* (Toronto: Palladium, 1838), 3.

83 John Roaf, "To the Editor of the Palladium [1 Feb. 1838]," in *Religious Liberty* (Toronto: Palladium, 1838), 4.

84 "Letter from the Rev. John Roaf: The Premier's Letter on the Clergy Reserves to the Hon. Francis Hincks," *Globe*, 3 Jan 1854.

85 For more on transatlantic liberalism and evangelicalism, see Robert Kelley, *The Transatlantic Persuasion: The Liberal-Democratic Mind in the Age of Gladstone* (New York: Knopf, 1969); Richard Carwardine, *Transatlantic*

Revivalism: Popular Evangelicalism in Britain and America, 1790–1865 (Westport, CT: Greenwood Press, 1978); and Nancy Christie, ed., *Transatlantic Subjects: Ideas, Institutions, and Social Experience in Post-Revolutionary British North America* (Montreal and Kingston: McGill-Queen's University Press, 2008).

86 William Buckingham, *Hon. Alexander Mackenzie: His Life and Times* (Toronto: Rose Publishing, 1892), 100.

87 "Religious Establishments," *Banner*, 22 Aug. 1845.

88 Ibid.

89 The transatlantic evangelical community in the 1840s resembled the mid-eighteenth-century Great Awakening as described by historian Susan O'Brien. As she saw it, that earlier era's proliferation of newsprint and ocean travel enabled a form of evangelicalism that transcended local communities and contexts. See Susan O'Brien, "A Transatlantic Community of Saints: The Great Awakening and the First Evangelical Network, 1735–1755," *American Historical Review* 91, no. 4 (Oct. 1986): 811–32.

90 Richard W. Vaudry, *The Free Church in Victorian Canada, 1844–1861* (Waterloo, ON: Wilfrid Laurier University Press, 1989), xiii, xiv.

91 Ibid., 64–5.

92 Michael Gauvreau, "Reluctant Voluntaries: Peter and George Brown; the Scottish Disruption and the Politics of Church and State in Canada," *Journal of Religious History* 25, no. 2 (June 2001): 135.

93 For the Methodist union of 1833, see chapter 1.

94 Originally from the Wesleyan Methodist Church, *Minutes of the Annual Conference*, 1837. Quoted in Neil Semple, *The Lord's Dominion: The History of Canadian Methodism* (Montreal and Kingston: McGill-Queen's University Press, 1996), 93.

95 Semple, *The Lord's Dominion*, 93–5.

96 Ibid., 97–8.

97 Todd Webb, *Transatlantic Methodists: British Wesleyans and the Formation of an Evangelical Culture in Nineteenth-Century Ontario and Quebec* (Montreal and Kingston: McGill-Queen's University Press, 2013), 93–4.

98 Ibid., 95.

99 John Steady, *The True Briton of the Nineteenth Century: Canadian Patriots and English Chartists, a Correspondence between Mr. Steady, an English farmer, and his brother in Canada* (London: Walter, 1840), 22.

100 Ibid., 8.

101 Ibid., 25.

102 Webb, *Transatlantic Methodists*, 74; Eileen Yeo, "Christianity in Chartist Struggle, 1838–1842," *Past and Present*, no. 91 (May 1981): 115.
103 E.P. Thompson, *The Making of the English Working Class* (New York: Pantheon, 1963), 44; Nathan O. Hatch, *The Democratization of American Christianity* (New Haven, CT: Yale University Press, 1989), 91.
104 Steady, *True Briton*, 8.
105 John Roaf, "To the Editors of the 'Patriot,' 'Christian Guardian,' and 'Commercial Herald' [18 Feb. 1838]," in John Roaf, *Religious Liberty: Being a Letter to the Editor of the "Palladium," upon the Thanksgiving Proclamation* (Toronto: Palladium Office, 1838), 6.
106 John K. Walton, *Chartism* (London: Routledge, 1999), 6–7.
107 Steady, *True Briton*, 9–10.
108 Quoted in Malcolm Chase, *Chartism: A New History* (Manchester: Manchester University Press, 2007), 25.
109 Careless, *Union of the Canadas*, 168–9.
110 Chase, *Chartism*, 193.
111 Ibid., 193–4.
112 Ibid., 196–200.
113 Alex Tyrrell, "Personality in Politics: The National Complete Suffrage Union and Pressure Group Politics in Early Victorian Britain," *Journal of Religious History* 12, no. 4 (1983): 390–1.
114 "Persecution," *Colonial Advocate*, 20 Dec. 1827.
115 Yeo, "Christianity in Chartist Struggle," 126.
116 Chase, *Chartism*, 50–1.
117 Michael Sanders, "'God is our guide! our cause is just!': The National Chartist Hymn Book and Victorian Hymnody," *Victorian Studies* 54, no. 4 (summer 2012): 686.
118 Yeo, "Christianity in Chartist Struggle," 133.
119 Ibid., 123.
120 Nancy Christie and Michael Gauvreau, *Christian Churches and Their Peoples, 1840–1965: A Social History of Religion in Canada* (Toronto: University of Toronto Press, 2010), 24.
121 Sanders, "God is our guide," 685–6.
122 Ibid., 693.
123 Ibid., 689–91.
124 Patrick Joyce, *Visions of the People: Industrial England and the Question of Class, 1848–1914* (New York: Cambridge University Press, 1991), 33–4.
125 Quoted in Yeo, "Christianity in Chartist Struggle," 121.

126 Ibid.

127 Stephens's call for Chartists to follow the bridegroom is a direct reference to the parable of the ten virgins in the Gospel of Matthew, wherein the young women prepare to enter a wedding feast. Half of them lighted their lamps with oil and were thus permitted to enter, whereas the other half neglected to prepare and were shut out. The parable ends with a warning for listeners to prepare for the coming of Christ: "Watch therefore, for ye know neither the day nor the hour wherein the Son of man cometh." See Matthew 25:1–13 (KJV).

128 "To the Free & Independent Electors of the County of Oxford," *Examiner*, 1 Jan. 1840.

129 For more on Dissenters' persecution narratives, see Jonathan Seed, "History and Narrative Identity: Religious Dissent and the Politics of Memory in Eighteenth-Century England," *Journal of British Studies* 44 (Jan. 2005): 61.

130 On millennialism in Upper Canada, see William Westfall, *Two Worlds*, chap. 6.

131 Michael Gauvreau, *The Evangelical Century: College and Creed in English Canada from the Great Revival to the Great Depression* (Montreal and Kingston: McGill-Queen's University Press, 1991), 112–13.

132 For example, see Ryerson, *Story of My Life*, 252–3; Earl of Durham, "Report on the Affairs of British North America," 149.

133 Curtis Fahey, *In His Name: The Anglican Experience in Upper Canada, 1791–1854* (Ottawa: Carleton University Press, 1991), 174–5.

134 John Rolph, *Speeches of Dr. John Rolph, and Christop'r A. Hagerman, Esq., His Majesty's Solicitor General, on the Bill for Appropriating the Proceeds of the Clergy Reserves to the Purposes of General Education* (Toronto: M. Reynolds, 1837), 11.

135 "Clergy Reserves," *Examiner*, 1 Jan. 1840.

136 "The Course of the Editor of 'The Church,'" *Christian Guardian*, 22 July 1840.

137 "Sectarianism – No. II," *Christian Guardian*, 13 Jan. 1841.

138 "Religious Establishments," *Banner*, 22 Aug. 1845.

139 "The Course of the Editor of 'The Church.'"

140 Richard E. Bennett, "Plucking Not Planting: Mormonism in Eastern Canada, 1830–1850," in Brigham Y. Card et al., eds., *The Mormon Presence in Canada* (Edmonton: University of Alberta Press, 1990), 27–8.

141 J.I. Little, "Millennial Invasion: Millerism in the Eastern Townships of Lower Canada," in Richard Connors and Andrew Collin Gow, eds.,

Anglo-American Millennialism, from Milton to the Millerites (Boston: Brill, 2004), 183–4; J.I. Little, *Borderland Religion: The Emergence of an English-Canadian Identity, 1792–1852* (Toronto: University of Toronto Press, 2004), chaps. 6 and 10; see also Westfall, *Two Worlds*, 167.

142 Westfall, *Two Worlds*, 165–6.

143 John Roaf, *Lectures on the Millennium* (Toronto, 1844), 5–6, 9–10.

144 Ibid., 99–100; see also Westfall, *Two Worlds*, 182–3.

145 Westfall, *Two Worlds*, 183–4; Vaudry, *Anglicans in the Atlantic World*, 141–2.

146 Westfall, *Two Worlds*, 184–6.

147 Gauvreau, *The Evangelical Century*, 121–3.

148 Roaf, *Lectures on the Millennium*, 79–80.

149 Ibid., 81–2.

150 Ibid., 94–5.

151 Ibid., 84.

152 Ibid., 85.

153 Vaudry, *Anglicans in the Atlantic World*, 155–6.

154 Roaf, *Lectures on the Millennium*, 94–5.

155 Ibid., 85.

156 "Religious Establishments," *Banner*, 22 Aug. 1845.

157 "Sectarian Political Preferences – Persecution," *Examiner*, 3 May 1848.

158 "County of York Election," *Examiner*, 22 Dec. 1847.

159 "The Toronto Election: James Beatty," *Banner*, 24 Dec. 1847.

160 "The Past Year," *Banner*, 8 Jan. 1847.

161 "The Provincial Elections," *Banner*, 24 Dec. 1847.

162 "The Past Year," *Banner*, 8 Jan. 1847.

163 Letter from James Lesslie to W.L. Mackenzie, 9 Aug. 1848, Mackenzie–Lindsey Family Fonds.

164 Letter from J.H. Price to Rev. J. Winterbotham, 25 Dec. 1849, James Hervey Price Fonds, AO.

Chapter Three

1 "Opening of Parliament – The Royal Speech," *Examiner*, 24 Jan. 1849.

2 "The Reserves and Rectory Question – Mr. Lesslie's Explanations in the Upper House," *North American*, 21 May 1850.

3 "Legislative Council," *North American*, 21 May 1850.

4 Michael S. Cross, *A Biography of Robert Baldwin: The Morning-Star of Memory* (Don Mills, ON: Oxford University Press, 2012), 346.

5 The divisions in the reform movement were complicated and changed a few times during this period. At first, George Brown assailed the Clear Grits when they emerged in 1849, on the basis of their affinity for American elective institutions and self-professed radicalism. He even ran as a Baldwinite in the 1851 Haldimand by-election. However, when Francis Hincks offered support for Catholic separate schools later in 1851, Brown withdrew the *Globe*'s support for the Baldwin ministry and gradually began to side with the Grits. William McDougall, the editor of Clear Grit newspaper the *North American*, saw Brown's withdrawal as an opportunity to advocate reform unity and increase his paper's influence. He offered it as the new organ of the Hincks ministry in exchange for Grit representation in the cabinet in 1851. Brown lambasted the move as a compromise of principle, and reformers who still opposed the Hincks ministry could now begin to see Brown as a better representative. See J.M.S. Careless, *Brown of the Globe, Vol. I: The Voice of Upper Canada* (Toronto: Macmillan, 1959), 111–12, 139–41.

6 J.M.S. Careless, "Mid-Victorian Liberalism in Central Canadian Newspapers, 1850–67," *Canadian Historical Review* 31, no. 3 (Sept. 1950): 224.

7 "To Thinking Reformers," *North American*, 2 Aug. 1853.

8 For example, see "The Fanatics," *North American*, 8 July 1853.

9 "The Reserves and Rectories," *Globe*, 9 Sept. 1852.

10 Isaac Buchanan, *First Series of Five Letters, Against the Baldwin Faction, by an Advocate of Responsible Government, and of The New College Bill* (Toronto: British Colonist, 1844), 17.

11 "Mr. Merritt and the Clergy Reserves," *North American*, 21 May 1850.

12 "The Convention: Opinions of the Press," *Globe*, 23 Nov. 1859.

13 G.I.T. Machin, *Politics and the Churches in Great Britain, 1832 to 1868* (Oxford: Clarendon Press, 1977), 216–18.

14 "Papal Aggression: The Measure of John Russell," *Examiner*, 12 March 1851.

15 Rev. William McClure, *The Character and Fatal Tendency of Puseyism, Defined and Exposed, being a course of lectures delivered in the Temperance Street Chapel, Toronto* (Toronto: T.T. Howard, 1850), 12, 25.

16 Letter from William McDougall to Charles Clarke, 2 Feb. 1853, Charles Clarke Fonds, Archives of Ontario (AO), Toronto, ON.

17 Bruce Curtis, *Building the Educational State* (London: Althouse Press, 1988), 150.

18 "Separate Schools," *Globe*, 26 Dec. 1855.

19 Donald M. MacRaild, "Transnationalising 'Anti-Popery': Militant Protestant Preachers in the Nineteenth-Century Anglo-World," *Journal of Religious History* 39, no. 2 (June 2015): 238; William J. Smyth, *Toronto, the Belfast of Canada: The Orange Order and the Shaping of Municipal Culture* (Toronto: University of Toronto Press, 2015), 47–8.
20 "Thursday, December 19," *Examiner*, 1 Jan. 1840.
21 "Romanism," *Examiner*, 26 Feb. 1851.
22 "The Roman Catholic Bishops on Politics," *Globe*, 23 Aug. 1859.
23 Paul Romney, *Getting It Wrong: How Canadians Forgot Their Past and Imperiled Confederation* (Toronto: University of Toronto Press, 1999), 29–30.
24 Letter from James Lesslie to W.L. Mackenzie, 20 March 1850, Mackenzie–Lindsey Family Fonds, AO.
25 "Mr. Baldwin," *North American*, 2 Aug. 1850.
26 Curtis, *Building the Educational State*, 123–31; Cross, *Robert Baldwin*, 287–8.
27 Cross, *Robert Baldwin*, 306.
28 "Repudiation of State Interference with Religion by the Congregationalists," *Examiner*, 12 July 1848.
29 "Opening of Parliament – The Royal Speech," *Examiner*, 24 Jan. 1849.
30 "Great Meeting on the Clergy Reserve Question," *Globe*, 11 May 1850.
31 For example, see "Anti-Clergy Reserve Association," *Globe*, 10 July 1851; "The Premier's Letter on the Clergy Reserves!" *Globe*, 3 Jan. 1854; "The Commutation Trick," *Globe*, 22 March 1855.
32 Letter from James Lesslie to W.L. Mackenzie, 20 March 1850, Mackenzie–Lindsey Fonds.
33 "Parliamentary Rhymes: Old Black Coat," *North American*, 18 June 1850.
34 "Mr. Baldwin," *North American*, 2 Aug. 1850
35 "Reserves and Rectories," *North American*, 7 June 1850.
36 "Debate on Clergy Reserves Continued," *North American*, 25 June 1850.
37 "Clergy Reserve – The Cloven Foot at Last – The Organ's Lies," *North American*, 25 June 1850.
38 "Mr. Merritt and the Clergy Reserves," *North American*, 21 May 1850.
39 Romney, *Getting It Wrong*, 12, 18.
40 Ibid., 28.
41 Letter from James Lesslie to W.L. Mackenzie, 20 March 1850, Mackenzie–Lindsey Fonds.
42 "Reserves and Rectories," *North American*, 7 June 1850.
43 "Mr. Baldwin," *North American*, 2 Aug. 1850.
44 "The Juggling Ministry," *North American*, 2 July 1850.

45 McClure, *The Character and Fatal Tendency of Puseyism*, 25.
46 "Debate on Clergy Reserves Continued," *North American*, 25 June 1850.
47 Letter from James Lesslie to W.L. Mackenzie, 20 March 1850, Mackenzie–Lindsey Fonds.
48 Linda Colley, *Britons: Forging the Nation, 1707–1837*, 4th ed. (New Haven, CT: Yale University Press, 2009), 29–30, 54.
49 "The Juggling Ministry," *North American*, 2 July 1850.
50 "Debate on Clergy Reserves Continued," *North American*, 25 June 1850.
51 Lilian F. Gates, *After the Rebellion: The Later Years of William Lyon Mackenzie* (Toronto: Dundurn Press, 1988), 174.
52 Ibid., 175–6, 180.
53 J.M.S. Careless, "Robert Baldwin," in J.M.S. Careless, ed., *The Pre-Confederation Premiers: Ontario Government Leaders, 1841–1867* (Toronto: University of Toronto Press, 1980), 140–1; see also Gates, *After the Rebellion*, 182–4.
54 "Mr. Baldwin in 1846, 1847, and in 1851," *Examiner*, 25 June 1851.
55 "Dr. Rolph," *Examiner*, 22 Oct. 1851.
56 Careless, "Robert Baldwin," 141–2.
57 Cross, *Robert Baldwin*, 346–7.
58 John Ralston Saul, *Louis-Hippolyte LaFontaine and Robert Baldwin* (Toronto: Penguin, 2010), 217–18.
59 Ibid., 223.
60 Cross, *Robert Baldwin*, 90–1, 294.
61 "Mr. Merritt and the Clergy Reserves," *North American*, 21 May 1850.
62 George Emery, *Elections in Oxford County, 1837–1875: A Case Study of Democracy in Canada West and Early Ontario* (Toronto: University of Toronto Press, 2012), 79–80.
63 George Brown, "Anti-Clergy Reserve Meeting [26 July 1851]," in Alexander Mackenzie, ed., *The Life and Speeches of Hon. George Brown* (Toronto: Globe, 1882), 241–2.
64 Ibid., 242.
65 Ibid., 243–4.
66 "Dinner to Mr. George Brown at Port Sarnia," *Globe*, 27 Dec. 1851.
67 William G. Ormsby, "Sir Francis Hincks," in J.M.S. Careless, ed., *The Pre-Confederation Premiers: Ontario Government Leaders, 1841–1867* (Toronto: University of Toronto, 1980), 166.
68 "The Prospect," *Globe*, 15 Jan. 1852.
69 "Result of the Elections," *Lambton Shield*, 9 Jan. 1852.

70 "First Riding of York," *Globe*, 20 Dec. 1851.
71 Emery, *Elections in Oxford County*, 76–80.
72 For example, as we saw above, reformer James Hervey Price lost his seat in South York to a conservative because the reform vote was split between multiple reform candidates. "First Riding of York," *Globe*, 20 Dec. 1851.
73 Letter from William McDougall to Charles Clarke, 26 July 1851, Charles Clarke Fonds.
74 Careless, *Brown of the Globe, Vol. I*, 139–41.
75 "Haldimand Election," *Examiner*, 23 April 1851.
76 "Counties of Kent and Lambton," *Globe*, 30 Sept. 1851.
77 "The Electoral Contest," *North American*, 14 Nov. 1851.
78 "The Separate School Question," *North American*, 7 Nov. 1851.
79 "Separate Schools – Protestant Intolerance," *North American*, 20 April 1852.
80 Jeffrey L. McNairn, "In Hope and Fear: Intellectual History, Liberalism, and the Liberal Order Framework," in Michel Ducharme and Jean-François Constant, eds., *Liberalism and Hegemony: Debating the Canadian Liberal Revolution* (Toronto: University of Toronto Press, 2009), 77, 86.
81 Dan Horner, "'Shame on you as men!': Contesting Authority in the Aftermath of Montreal's Gavazzi Riot," *Social History* 44, no. 87 (May 2011): 30–1.
82 The article further states, "We trust that the [Protestants of Quebec] will learn a lesson from the event; that it will teach them to put forth all their moral strength in order that they may overawe the Romish bands, and liberty may be obtained to speak, write, and print freely at all times." "Father Gavazzi in Quebec," *Globe*, 9 June 1853.
83 "Father Gavazzi's Lecture," *Globe*, 28 June 1853.
84 Ibid.
85 "The Late Riots – Public Feeling in Upper Canada," *Globe*, 25 June 1853.
86 "The Fanatics," *North American*, 8 July 1853.
87 "The Gavazzi Riots," *North American*, 2 Aug. 1853.
88 Michel Ducharme, *The Idea of Liberty in Canada during the Age of Atlantic Revolutions, 1776–1838*, trans. Peter Feldstein (Montreal and Kingston: McGill-Queen's University Press, 2014), 5–7.
89 Jeffrey L. McNairn, *The Capacity to Judge: Public Opinion and Deliberative Democracy in Upper Canada, 1791–1854* (Toronto: University of Toronto Press, 2000), 14–15.
90 "The Roman Catholic Church in Canada," *Globe*, 7 Aug. 1852.

91 Brown, "Anti–Clergy Reserve Meeting," 242.
92 "Conditions of Political Partnership," *Examiner*, 8 Oct. 1851.
93 Although many of the laws restricting alcohol and Sabbath-day activities were not implemented until much later in the nineteenth century, they were widely proposed and advocated by Protestants in the years before Confederation. John Webster Grant, *A Profusion of Spires: Religion in Nineteenth-Century Ontario* (Toronto: University of Toronto Press, 1988), 97–8, 189–90; see also Jan Noel, *Canada Dry: Temperance Crusades before Confederation* (Toronto: University of Toronto Press, 1995), 84–6.
94 Bruce Curtis, *Building the Educational State*, 275–6.
95 "Father Gavazzi's Lecture," *Globe*, 28 June 1853.
96 "Politics and Christianity, No. II: Leaven," *Examiner*, 9 Aug. 1848.
97 "The Waterloo Dinner," *North American*, 22 July 1853.
98 "Religion in Schools," *North American*, 16 April 1852.
99 Ormsby, "Sir Francis Hincks," 179–80, 190–1.
100 "Ministers in the West," *North American*, 2 Aug. 1853.
101 "The Waterloo Dinner," *North American*, 22 July 1853.
102 Ian McKay, "Canada as a Long Liberal Revolution: On Writing the History of Actually Existing Canadian Liberalisms, 1840s–1940s," in Jean-François Constant and Michel Ducharme, eds., *Liberalism and Hegemony: Debating the Canadian Liberal Revolution* (Toronto: University of Toronto Press, 2009), 413–14.
103 "The Position of the Conservatives," *Globe*, 20 July 1854.
104 Ormsby, "Sir Francis Hincks," 183–5.
105 "Parliamentary Rhymes: The Opening of the Session," *North American*, 7 June 1850.
106 "The Late Riots – Public Feeling in Upper Canada," *Globe*, 25 June 1853.
107 "Protestant Union," *Globe*, 6 Sept. 1853.
108 "The Waterloo Dinner," *North American*, 22 July 1853.
109 Letter from William McDougall to Charles Clarke, 2 Feb. 1853, Charles Clarke Fonds.
110 "A Defective Nomenclature," *Daily Leader*, 16 Aug. 1854.
111 Ormsby, "Francis Hincks," 182–3.
112 Careless, *Brown of the Globe, Vol. I*, 193.
113 Emery, *Elections in Oxford County*, 85.
114 Careless, *Brown of the Globe, Vol. I*, 188, 190–1.
115 Ormsby, "Francis Hincks," 182–3.
116 "Provincial Parliament," *Daily Leader*, 19 Oct. 1854.

117 "The Ministerial Defeat – The Dissolution of the House," *Examiner*, 28 June 1854.
118 "The Dissolution – The Government – The Elections," *Examiner*, 5 July 1854.
119 "The Political Prospect!" *Globe*, 10 Aug. 1854.
120 "The Prospect of the Liberals," *Examiner*, 9 Aug. 1854.
121 Careless, *Brown of the Globe, Vol. I*, 188, 190–1.
122 Ormsby, "Francis Hincks," 182–3.
123 "The Coalition Ministry," *Examiner*, 20 Sept. 1854.
124 "The Scheme of Churchmen and Roman Catholics," *Examiner*, 15 Nov. 1854.
125 "Old Tache's [*sic*] Tool," in James Lesslie Scrapbook, Lesslie Family Fonds, Dundas Museum and Archives, Dundas, ON.
126 "Mr. Cauchon," *Examiner*, 14 March 1855.
127 "Clergy Reserve Bill," *North American*, 25 March 1853.
128 Ormsby, "Francis Hincks," 177.
129 For more on the Dissenters' dissatisfaction with the MacNab government's secularization bill, see James Forbes, "Contesting the Protestant Consensus: Voluntarists, Methodists, and the Persistence of Evangelical Dissent in Upper Canada," *Ontario History* 108, no. 2 (autumn 2016): 210–12.
130 Careless, *Brown of the Globe, Vol. I*, 203.
131 "Separate Schools," *Globe*, 14 Dec. 1855.
132 "Separate Schools: Bishop Charbonnel in the Field," *Globe*, 11 Dec. 1855.
133 David A. Wilson, *Thomas D'Arcy McGee, Vol. I: Passion, Reason, and Politics, 1825–1857* (Montreal and Kingston: McGill-Queen's University Press, 2008), 344–6.
134 "Great Protestant Demonstration! Three Thousand Irishmen in St. Lawrence Hall," *Globe*, 11 Feb. 1856.
135 Ibid.
136 Whereas the clergy reserves had directly pitted Anglicans against non-Anglican Protestants, after 1854 Upper Canadian liberals generally depicted subsequent church–state issues as conflicts between Protestants and Catholics. For example, see the discussion of the 1863 bill in chapter 4.

For more about the political orientation of the Anglican clergy before and after 1854, see Curtis Fahey, *In His Name: The Anglican Experience in Upper Canada, 1791–1854* (Ottawa: Carleton University Press, 1991), 188–90.
137 "Union of Romanists and Churchmen," *Examiner*, 5 July 1854.

138 George Emery, *Elections in Oxford County, 1837–1875: A Case Study of Democracy in Canada West and Early Ontario* (Toronto: University of Toronto Press, 2012), 126–7.

139 William Westfall, *Two Worlds: The Protestant Culture of Nineteenth-Century Ontario* (Montreal and Kingston: McGill-Queen's University Press, 1989), 49.

140 For more about attitudes towards Anglicanism in the early reform movement under William Lyon Mackenzie's leadership, see the discussion of anti-clericalism in chapter 1.

141 "Representation by Population! Justice to Upper Canada!" *Globe*, 4 Dec. 1857.

142 "Mr. Brown's Meeting in Saint Lawrence Hall!" *Globe*, 12 Dec. 1857.

143 "A General Election," *Globe*, 23 Nov. 1857.

144 "Compulsory Piety," *Daily Leader*, 28 Oct. 1854.

145 "General Election," *Globe*, 15 Dec. 1857.

146 "St. Andrew's Ward: Meeting in the Temperance Hall," *Globe*, 11 Dec. 1857.

147 Cecil J. Houston and William J. Smyth, *The Sash Canada Wore: A Historical Geography of the Orange Order in Canada* (Toronto: University of Toronto Press, 1980), 148.

148 Bruce W. Hodgins, "John Sandfield Macdonald," in J.M.S. Careless, ed., *The Pre-Confederation Premiers: Ontario Government Leaders, 1841–1867* (Toronto: University of Toronto Press, 1980), 247, 261–2.

149 Careless, *Brown of the Globe, Vol. I*, 202–3.

150 "Results of the Election," *Globe*, 16 Jan. 1858.

151 Ged Martin, "John A. Macdonald: Provincial Premier," *British Journal of Canadian Studies* 20, no. 1 (May 2007): 106–7, 111.

152 Ibid., 112–13; see also Richard Gwyn, *The Life and Times of John A. Macdonald, Vol. I: 1815–1867* (Toronto: Random House, 2007), chap. 11.

153 George Brown, "Policy of the Brown–Dorion Administration [1858]," in Alexander Mackenzie, ed., *The Life and Speeches of the Hon. George Brown* (Toronto: Globe, 1882), 268, 284–5.

154 "The Roman Catholic Bishops on Politics," *Globe*, 23 Aug. 1859.

155 "The Convention: Opinions of the Press," *Globe*, 23 Nov. 1859.

156 "The Convention," *Globe*, 22 Oct. 1859.

157 Romney, *Getting It Wrong*, 29–30.

158 A.I. Silver, *The French-Canadian Idea of Confederation, 1864–1900* (Toronto: University of Toronto Press, 1982), 34–5.

159 Romney, *Getting It Wrong*, 279–80.

160 Ibid., 27.
161 Ibid., 76–7.
162 "The Roman Catholic Church in Canada," *Globe*, 7 Aug. 1852.
163 Charles Mackay, *Life and Liberty in America* (New York: Harper & Brothers, 1859), 398.
164 "Protestant Union," *Globe*, 6 Sept. 1853.

Chapter Four

1 A.I. Silver, *The French-Canadian Idea of Confederation, 1864–1900* (Toronto: University of Toronto Press, 1982), 15–16.
2 Paul Romney, *Getting It Wrong: How Canadians Forgot Their Past and Imperilled Confederation* (Toronto: University of Toronto Press, 1999), 94–5.
3 P.B. Waite, *The Life and Times of Confederation, 1864–1867: Politics, Newspapers, and the Union of British North America* (Toronto: University of Toronto Press, 1962), 120, 128–9, 132–3.
4 Ibid., 120.
5 Donald Creighton, *The Road to Confederation: The Emergence of Canada, 1863–1867* (Toronto: Macmillan, 1964), 40–2.
6 Ibid., 45–7.
7 J.M.S. Careless, *Brown of the Globe, Vol. II: Statesman of Confederation, 1860–1880* (Toronto: Macmillan, 1963), 168.
8 Romney, *Getting It Wrong*, 94–5.
9 Ibid., 91–2.
10 Christopher Moore, *1867: How the Fathers Made a Deal* (Toronto: McClelland & Stewart, 1997), 119–22.
11 Christopher Moore, *Three Weeks in Quebec City: The Meeting That Made Canada* (Toronto: Allen Lane, 2015), 164–5.
12 Daniel Heidt, "Introduction: Reconsidering Confederation," in Daniel Heidt, ed., *Reconsidering Confederation: Canada's Founding Debates, 1864–1999* (Calgary: University of Calgary Press, 2018), 13–14.
13 We may usefully compare the Quebec and the Ontario chapters in the recent *Reconsidering Confederation.* On Quebec's cultural interests in the Confederation debates, historians Marcel Martel et al. wrote, "While discussing the powers to be allocated to the federal government and the provinces, French-Canadian representatives insisted that education be controlled by the future provincial governments because denominational

divides across the country ran deep, and local circumstances required accommodation." Marcel Martel, Colin M. Coates, Martin Paquet, and Maxime Gohier, "Quebec and Confederation: Gains and Compromise," in Daniel Heidt, ed., *Reconsidering Confederation: Canada's Founding Debates, 1864–1999* (Calgary: University of Calgary Press, 2018), 80. By contrast, a chapter on Ontario did not mention religion among issues over which residents expected provincial control. Daniel Heidt, "Ontario: The Centre of Confederation?" in ibid., 62.

14 For example, Eugenie Brouillet et al. recently described George Brown as representing "the commercial and industrial interests of Toronto and of reformers from the Canadian West." In such configurations, questions of religion and culture are often mentioned only in reference to Quebec. See Eugenie Brouillet et al., "Introduction: 1864, a Pivotal Year in the Advent of Canadian Confederation," in Eugenie Brouillet, Alain-G. Gagnon, and Guy Laforest, eds., *The Quebec Conference of 1864: Understanding the Emergence of the Canadian Federation* (Montreal and Kingston: McGill-Queen's University Press, 2018), 5.

15 "The Roman Catholic Bishops on Politics," *Globe*, 23 Aug. 1859.

16 George Brown, "Confederation Resolutions" [8 Feb. 1865], in Alexander Mackenzie, ed., *Life and Speeches of the Hon. George Brown* (Toronto: Globe, 1882), 302.

17 "The Fenian Raid," *Canadian Independent*, Aug. 1866.

18 For example, for a recent study that emphasizes the financial ends of Confederation, see Elsbeth Heaman, *Tax, Order, and Good Government: A New Political History of Canada, 1867–1917* (Montreal and Kingston: McGill-Queen's University Press, 2017); see also Andrew Smith, "Toryism, Classical Liberalism, and Capitalism: The Politics of Taxation and the Struggle for Canadian Confederation," *Canadian Historical Review* 89, no. 1 (March 2008): 1–25.

19 Janet Ajzenstat, *The Canadian Founding: John Locke and Parliament* (Montreal and Kingston: McGill-Queen's University Press, 2007), 100–4.

20 Janet Ajzenstat, Paul Romney, Ian Gentles, and William D. Gairdner, eds., *Canada's Founding Debates*, 2nd ed. (Toronto: University of Toronto Press, 2003), 285–90.

21 Thomas Thorner, ed., *A Few Acres of Snow: Documents in Pre-Confederation Canadian History*, 2nd ed. (Peterborough, ON: Broadview Press, 2003), 420–2, 432–5. For a more complete transcript of the speech, see Brown, "Confederation Resolutions," 299–347.

22 For example, see "The World's Union Prayer Meeting," *Canadian Independent*, Feb. 1860.

23 James Lesslie recorded in his diary, "This day the Atlantic Telegraph Fleet arrived safely on the coast of Newfoundland having under the good Providence of God, successfully laid the cable connecting Europe with the American Continent." 27 July 1866, James Lesslie Diaries, Lesslie Family Fonds, Dundas Museum and Archives, Dundas, ON.

24 "Retiring Chairman's Address," *Canadian Independent*, July 1865.

25 "Fenianism and the Witness," *Irish Canadian*, 12 April 1865.

26 "Political Catechism for England and Ireland," *Canadian Independent*, April 1866.

27 George Spaight, *Trial of Patrick James Whelan for the murder of the Hon. Thomas d'Arcy McGee* (Ottawa: Ottawa Times, 1868), 87.

28 "Mr. McGee's Letters," *Globe*, 11 July 1859.

29 David A. Wilson, *Thomas D'Arcy McGee, Vol. II: The Extreme Moderate, 1857–1868* (Montreal and Kingston: McGill-Queen's University Press, 2011), 173.

30 "Mr. McGee's Letters," *Globe*, 11 July 1859.

31 John Webster Grant, *A Profusion of Spires: Religion in Nineteenth-Century Ontario* (Toronto: University of Toronto Press, 1988), 224.

32 Henry T. Newton Chesshyre, *Canada in 1864: A Settler's Handbook* (London: S. Low, Son, and Marston, 1864), 125.

33 "The Twelfth of July in Ottawa," *Irish Canadian*, 19 July 1865.

34 Chesshyre, *Canada in 1864*, 132–3.

35 "We need to be revived, we can be revived, and we will be revived," *Canadian Independent*, Feb. 1860.

36 Phoebe Palmer, *The Life and Letters of Mrs. Phoebe Palmer*, ed. Richard Wheatley (New York: W.C. Palmer, Jr., 1876), chap. 9.

37 "The World's Union Prayer Meeting," *Canadian Independent*, Feb. 1860.

38 See entry on 22 January 1860, James Lesslie Diaries.

39 Letter from James Hervey Price to James Lesslie, 29 Oct. 1860, James Hervey Price Fonds, Archives of Ontario (AO), Toronto, ON.

40 David M. Thompson, "The Liberation Society, 1844–1868," in Patricia Hollis, ed., *Pressure from Without in Early Victorian England* (London: Edward Arnold, 1974), 210; see also Timothy Larsen, *Friends of Religious Equality: Nonconformist Politics in Mid-Victorian England* (Rochester, NY: Boydell & Brewer, 1999).

41 Thompson, "The Liberation Society," 218.

42 "Mails by the 'Scotia' from our own Correspondent," *Globe*, 7 Dec. 1863.
43 N.H. Keeble, "Introduction," in N.H. Keeble, ed., *'Settling the Peace of the Church': 1662 Revisited* (Oxford: Oxford University Press, 2014), 27.
44 Timothy Larsen, "Victorian Nonconformity and the Memory of the Ejected Ministers: The Impact of the Bicentennial Commemorations of 1862," in R.N. Swanson, ed., *The Church Retrospective: Papers Read at the 1995 Summer Meeting and the 1996 Winter Meeting of the Ecclesiastical History Society* (Woodbridge, England: Boydell Press, 1997), 461–2.
45 Ibid., 463; T. Binney, *Farewell Sunday and Saint Bartholomew's Day: Two Sermons Preached at the King's Weigh-House Chapel, Fish Street Hill, On Sunday, the 17th, and Sunday, the 24th of August, 1862* (London: Jackson, Walford and Hodder, 1862), 4, 7.
46 W.F. Clarke, "The History of Nonconformity in England in 1662," in *Canadian Bicentenary Papers* (Toronto: W.C. Chewett & Co., 1862), 31.
47 F.H. Marling, "Reasons for Nonconformity in Canada in 1862," in *Canadian Bicentenary Papers* (Toronto: W.C. Chewett & Co., 1862), 68.
48 "The Drinking Usages and Temperance Act of 1864," *Canadian Independent*, Dec. 1864.
49 "Roman Catholic Separate Schools," *Canadian Independent*, April 1863.
50 For example, see George Emery, *Elections in Oxford County, 1837–1875: A Case Study of Democracy in Canada West and Early Ontario* (Toronto: University of Toronto Press, 2012), 126–7.
51 "French Canadian Aspirations: A Remarkable Letter," *Globe*, 28 Jan. 1860.
52 "Mr. McGee's Letters," *Globe*, 11 July 1859.
53 "The Emigration Question," *Globe*, 4 Dec. 1861.
54 "Emigration," *Globe*, 15 Feb. 1869.
55 "The Emigration Question," *Globe*, 4 Dec. 1861.
56 "Canadian Emigration Agents," *Globe*, 22 Jan. 1862.
57 "An Emigration Company," *Globe*, 22 July 1863.
58 "Emigration Agencies," *Globe*, 19 March 1869.
59 "Mr. McGee's Letters," *Globe*, 11 July 1859.
60 "City Election: Grand Rally of Mr. Brown's Friends!" *Globe*, 5 July 1861.
61 "Norfolk Election," *Globe*, 16 July 1861.
62 Bruce W. Hodgins, "John Sandfield Macdonald," in J.M.S. Careless, ed., *The Pre-Confederation Premiers: Ontario Government Leaders, 1841–1867* (Toronto: University of Toronto Press, 1980), 264–5.
63 Emery, *Elections in Oxford County*, 126–7.
64 "Political Priests," *Globe*, 22 July 1861.

65 "Results of the Contest!" *Globe*, 13 July 1861.
66 "The Great Issue," *Globe*, 15 Nov. 1861.
67 Hodgins, "John Sandfield Macdonald," 264–6.
68 Ibid., 275–8; Careless, *Brown of the Globe, Vol. II*, 90–2.
69 John S. Moir, *Church and State in Canada West: Three Studies in the Relation of Denominationalism and Nationalism, 1841–1867* (Toronto: University of Toronto Press, 1959), 171.
70 Letter from E.J. [Edward John Horan] Bp. of Kingston to Richard W. Scott, 13 April 1860, Richard W. Scott Fonds, Library and Archives Canada (LAC), Ottawa, ON.
71 Letter from E.J. Bp. of Kingston to Richard W. Scott, 4 April 1862, Richard W. Scott Fonds.
72 Careless, *Brown of the Globe, Vol. II*, 89.
73 Moir, *Church and State*, 171–2.
74 "The Separate School Question: The St. Lawrence Hall Last Night, The Meeting Broken Up!!" *Leader*, 8 April 1863.
75 "Separate School Question: Mass Meeting Yesterday," *Leader*, 15 April 1863.
76 "Roman Catholic Separate Schools," *Canadian Independent*, April 1863.
77 "The Reform Demonstration at Brantford," *Globe*, 11 August 1863.
78 Thomas D'Arcy McGee, *A Plea for Separate Schools, 1863: A Great Statesman's Masterly Presentation* (S.I.: S.n., 1863), 5–6.
79 Ibid., 1.
80 "The School Bill in the Legislative Council," *Leader*, 18 April 1863.
81 "Representation by Population," *Globe*, 1 June 1863.
82 "The Issue," *Globe*, 22 June 1863.
83 Letter from R.W. Scott to John A. Macdonald, 30 May 1863, Richard W. Scott Fonds.
84 Letter from R.W. Scott to John A. Macdonald, n.d. [1863], Richard W. Scott Fonds. Alonzo Wright represented Quebec's County of Ottawa in the legislature of the united province and then in Parliament until 1891.
85 "Political Priests," *Globe*, 14 July 1863.
86 Hodgins, "John Sandfield Macdonald," 282.
87 Careless, *Brown of the Globe, Vol. II*, 96–100.
88 "The Reform Demonstration at Brantford," *Globe*, 11 Aug. 1863.
89 "God Save the Queen," *Canadian Independent*, May 1864.
90 Paul Romney, *Getting It Wrong*, 24–5.
91 "Union!" *Globe*, 26 Aug. 1864.
92 Heaman, *Tax, Order, and Good Government*, 15–16.
93 Ibid., 27–8.

94 "The 'Constant Irishman,'" *Globe*, 4 Sept. 1863.
95 "The Great Issue," *Globe*, 6 Oct. 1863.
96 Heaman, *Tax, Order, and Good Government*, 46.
97 Ajzenstat, *The Canadian Founding*, 84.
98 Ian McKay, *Rebels, Reds, Radicals: Rethinking Canada's Left History* (Toronto: Between the Lines, 2005), 54–5.
99 William Westfall, *Two Worlds: The Protestant Culture of Nineteenth-Century Ontario* (Montreal and Kingston: McGill-Queen's University Press, 1989), 4.
100 Silver, *The French-Canadian Idea of Confederation*, 45.
101 "The 'Constant Irishman,'" *Globe*, 4 Sept. 1863.
102 "French Domination," *Globe*, 14 Aug. 1863.
103 Hodgins, "John Sandfield Macdonald," 290–1.
104 "Going Backwards," *Globe*, 1 April 1864.
105 "Corruption Re-established," *Globe*, 4 April 1864.
106 "The Reform Demonstration at Brantford," *Globe*, 11 Aug. 1863.
107 "Latest from Quebec: Very Full Caucus of the Upper Canada Liberals," *Globe*, 22 June 1864.
108 "The Roman Catholic Bishops on Politics," *Globe*, 23 Aug. 1859.
109 "The Ministerial Crisis," *Globe*, 18 June 1864.
110 "Latest from Quebec: Very Full Caucus of the Upper Canada Liberals," *Globe*, 22 June 1864.
111 "Parliament Last Night: The Crisis Terminated!" *Globe*, 23 June 1864.
112 For example, see Creighton, *Road to Confederation*, 41–3; Careless, *Brown of the Globe, Vol. II*, 118–20.
113 Richard Gwyn, *John A., The Man Who Made Us: The Life and Times of John A. Macdonald, Volume One, 1815–1867* (Toronto: Random House, 2007), 291.
114 Carmen Nielson, "A Much-Fathered Nation: Feminist Biography and Confederation Politics," *Canadian Historical Review* 98, no. 2 (June 2017): 365–6.
115 Ibid., 367.
116 Paul Romney, "George Brown and Oliver Mowat on the Quebec Resolutions and Confederation: Reality and Myth," in Eugenie Brouillet, Alain-G. Gagnon, and Guy Laforest, eds., *The Quebec Conference of 1864: Understanding the Emergence of the Canadian Federation* (Montreal and Kingston: McGill-Queen's University Press, 2018), 161–3.
117 Creighton, *Road to Confederation*, 45–7.
118 Romney, "George Brown and Oliver Mowat," 156, 171–2.
119 "Parliament Last Night: The Crisis Terminated!" *Globe*, 23 June 1864.

120 "The Ministry – Its Task," *Globe*, 1 July 1864.
121 "Have We a Coalition Ministry?" *Globe*, 5 July 1864.
122 "The Great Confederation," *Globe*, 4 Oct. 1864.
123 Silver, *The French-Canadian Idea of Confederation*, 41–2.
124 *Canada's Founding Debates*, 298.
125 Doug Owram, *Promise of Eden: The Canadian Expansionist Movement and the Idea of the West, 1856–1900* (Toronto: University of Toronto Press, 1980), 5–6.
126 "The Foundation of Many Generations," *Canadian Independent*, March 1867.
127 "Centenary of Methodism in America," *Globe*, 24 Oct. 1866.
128 "Annual Soiree of Cooke's Church," *Globe*, 11 Dec. 1866.
129 Joseph Hardwick, "Fasts, Thanksgivings, and Senses of Community in Nineteenth-Century Canada and the British Empire," *Canadian Historical Review* 98, no. 4 (Dec. 2017): 693–4.
130 "Thanksgiving Day, Its Observance in Toronto," *Globe*, 19 Oct. 1865.
131 Matthew 21:43 (KJV). For full context, see Matthew 21:18–46.
132 Matthew 21:45 (KJV).
133 "The Withered Fig Tree," *Canadian Independent*, Oct. 1863.
134 "Intemperance in High Places," *Globe*, 3 Sept. 1866.
135 "Intemperance in High Places [Part II]," *Globe*, 10 Sept. 1866.
136 "The Foundation of Many Generations," *Canadian Independent*, March 1867.
137 Unknown origin. Quoted in "Literary Notices," *Canadian Independent*, May 1863.
138 For example, Janet Ajzenstat wrote that "the formula devised by the Fathers of Confederation … depends on maintaining at the national level the dimension of political life in which particularity does not count." See Ajzenstat, *The Canadian Founding*, 108.
139 For a list of provincial powers under the British North America Act (1867), see sections 92, 93, and 95. "British North America Act, 1867," Department of Justice, Government of Canada, https://www.justice.gc.ca/eng/rp-pr/csj-sjc/constitution/lawreg-loireg/p1t11.html <29 Oct. 2021>.
140 Brown, "Confederation Resolutions," 317.
141 Ibid., 302.
142 Ajzenstat, *The Canadian Founding*, 81.
143 Ibid., 20.
144 For example, ibid., 108–9.

145 Ian McKay, "Canada as a Long Liberal Revolution: On Writing the History of Actually Existing Canadian Liberalisms, 1840s–1940s," in Jean-François Constant and Michel Ducharme, eds., *Liberalism and Hegemony: Debating the Canadian Liberal Revolution* (Toronto: University of Toronto Press, 2009), 352–3.

146 Moore, *1867*, 10–11.

147 *Canada's Founding Debates*, 348.

148 George Brown, "Confederation Resolutions," 301.

149 Moir, *Church and State in Canada West*, 178–9.

150 Creighton, *Road to Confederation*, 399–400.

151 Moir, *Church and State in Canada West*, 178–9.

152 "The McGee Manifesto," *Globe*, 21 May 1867.

153 "We're Irish Everywhere," *Irish Canadian*, 20 June 1866.

154 "Saint Patrick's Day in Toronto," *Irish Canadian*, 22 March 1865.

155 "Communications: South Lanark Election," *Globe*, 20 Feb. 1869.

156 "The Twelfth of July: Orange Procession at St. Catharines," *Globe*, 13 July 1869.

157 "Annual Address to the Students of the Congregational College of British North America [11 Oct. 1865]," *Canadian Independent*, Jan. 1866.

158 William J. Smyth, *Toronto, the Belfast of Canada: The Orange Order and the Shaping of Municipal Culture* (Toronto: University of Toronto Press, 2015), 48.

159 Wilson, *Thomas D'Arcy McGee, Vol. II*, 229–30.

160 Ibid., 230.

161 "Saint Patrick's Day in Toronto," *Irish Canadian*, 22 March 1865.

162 James Lesslie, 17 March 1866 and 2 April 1866, James Lesslie Diaries.

163 For more on this invasion and the battle that followed, see Peter Vronsky, *Ridgeway: The American Fenian Invasion and the 1866 Battle That Made Canada* (Toronto: Allen Lane, 2011).

164 James Lesslie, 1, 2, and 5 June 1866, James Lesslie Diaries.

165 Wilson, *Thomas D'Arcy McGee, Vol. II*, 304–5.

166 Ibid., 281.

167 Wilson, *Thomas D'Arcy McGee, Vol. I*, 44–5.

168 Wilson, *Thomas D'Arcy McGee, Vol. II*, 233–7.

169 Ibid., 313, 322.

170 David A. Wilson, *Irish Nationalism in Canada* (Montreal and Kingston: McGill-Queen's University Press, 2009), 55–6.

171 "Execution of Whelan," *Globe*, 12 Feb. 1869.

172 Spaight, *Trial of Patrick James Whelan*, 87–8.
173 Ibid., 62.
174 Wilson, *Thomas D'Arcy McGee, Vol. II*, 281.
175 Spaight, *Trial of Patrick James Whelan*, 88.
176 "Communications: South Lanark Election," *Globe*, 20 Feb. 1869.
177 "The Foundation of Many Generations," *Canadian Independent*, March 1867.

Chapter Five

1 George Brown, "Letter to the Roman Catholic Committee," in Alexander Mackenzie, ed., *Life and Speeches of the Hon. George Brown* (Toronto: Globe, 1882), 126.
2 *Gleaner*, 11 Nov. 1875.
3 Ian McKay, "The Liberal Order Framework: A Prospectus for a Reconnaissance of Canadian History," *Canadian Historical Review* 81 (2000): 635–6.
4 Evans identified eleven provincial ridings in Ontario that had a large percentage of Catholics in the 1870s: "The Roman Catholics made up about one-sixth of Ontario's population, enough to swing elections in the ridings of Prescott, Russell, Ottawa, Glengarry, North Essex, South Renfrew, and Stormount which were heavily Catholic, and perhaps in others such as West Peterborough, South Bruce, South Essex, and West Hastings which had a substantial Catholic minority." See A. Margaret Evans, *Sir Oliver Mowat* (Toronto: University of Toronto Press, 1992), 119.
5 Ramsay Cook, *The Regenerators: Social Criticism in Late Victorian English Canada* (Toronto: University of Toronto Press, 1985); David B. Marshall, *Secularizing the Faith: Canadian Protestant Clergy and the Crisis of Belief, 1850–1940* (Toronto: University of Toronto Press, 1992).
6 Marshall, *Secularizing the Faith*, 24.
7 Ibid., 21–2, 66–7.
8 Marguerite Van Die, *An Evangelical Mind: Nathanael Burwash and the Methodist Tradition in Canada, 1839–1918* (Montreal and Kingston: McGill-Queen's University Press, 1989); Phyllis D. Airhart, *Serving the Present Age: Revivalism, Progressivism, and the Methodist Tradition in Canada* (Montreal and Kingston: McGill-Queen's University Press, 1992); Nancy Christie and Michael Gauvreau, *A Full-Orbed Christianity: The Protestant Churches and Social Welfare in Canada, 1900–1940* (Montreal and Kingston: McGill-Queen's University Press, 1996).

9 Phyllis D Airhart, "Ordering a New Nation and Reordering Protestantism, 1867–1914," in George A. Rawlyk, ed., *The Canadian Protestant Experience, 1760–1990* (Burlington, ON: Welch Publishing, 1990), 117, 125.

10 "Speech of Mr. Huntington at Grenville," *Globe*, 31 Dec. 1875.

11 Robert Hill, *Voice of the Vanishing Minority: Robert Sellar and the* Huntingdon Gleaner, *1863–1919* (Montreal and Kingston: McGill-Queen's University Press, 1998), 77–80.

12 Letter from Alexander Mackenzie to George Brown, 22 Jan. 1876, Alexander Mackenzie Papers, Library and Archives Canada (LAC), Ottawa, ON; see also Dale C. Thomson, *Alexander Mackenzie: Clear Grit* (Toronto: Macmillan, 1960), 259.

13 Alexander Galt, *Civil Liberty in Lower Canada* (Montreal: D. Bentley, 1876), 15–16; Charles Lindsey, *Rome in Canada: The Ultramontane Struggle for Supremacy over the Civil Authority* (Toronto: Lovell Brothers, 1877), 9.

14 Thomson, *Alexander Mackenzie*, 255–9.

15 Peter B. Waite, *Arduous Destiny: Canada, 1874–1896* (Toronto: McClelland and Stewart, 1971), 44–5; see also chapter 3, "Blake, Religion, and Laurier, 1873–1877."

16 Waite, *Arduous Destiny*, 51–2.

17 Ben Forster, "Mackenzie, Alexander," in *Dictionary of Canadian Biography*, vol. 12, University of Toronto / Université Laval, 2003–, http://www.biographi.ca/en/bio/mackenzie_alexander_12E.html <30 Oct. 2021>.

18 Keith D. Smith, *Liberalism, Surveillance, and Resistance: Indigenous Communities in Western Canada, 1877–1927* (Athabasca, AB: Athabasca University Press, 2009), 8–9; Ian McKay, "Canada as a Long Liberal Revolution: On Writing the History of Actually Existing Canadian Liberalisms, 1840s–1940s," in Jean-François Constant and Michel Ducharme, eds., *Liberalism and Hegemony: Debating the Canadian Liberal Revolution* (Toronto: University of Toronto Press, 2009), 380–1, 414.

19 For example, see Michel Ducharme, *The Idea of Liberty in Canada during the Age of Atlantic Revolutions, 1776–1838*, trans. Peter Feldstein (Montreal and Kingston: McGill-Queen's University Press, 2014), 11; Benjamin T. Jones, *Republicanism and Responsible Government: The Shaping of Democracy in Australia and Canada* (Montreal and Kingston: McGill-Queen's University Press, 2014), x, 14–15.

20 Brown, "Letter to the Roman Catholic Committee."

21 J.M. Bumsted, *Louis Riel v. Canada: The Making of a Rebel* (Winnipeg: Great Plains Publications, 2001), 125, 135–6.

22 "The North-West Question," *Globe*, 31 March 1870.

23 "The Latest Arrivals from Red River," *Globe*, 12 April 1870.
24 Carl Berger, *The Sense of Power: Studies in the Ideas of Canadian Imperialism* (Toronto: University of Toronto Press, 1970), 59–60.
25 Doug Owram, *Promise of Eden: The Canadian Expansionist Movement and the Idea of the West, 1856–1900* (Toronto: University of Toronto Press, 1980), 91–2.
26 Bumsted, *Louis Riel v. Canada*, 133–4.
27 Owram, *Promise of Eden*, 99.
28 "The Red River Rebellion, Public Meeting: The Policy of the Government Denounced," *Globe*, 23 July 1870.
29 A.I. Silver, *The French-Canadian Idea of Confederation, 1864–1900* (Toronto: University of Toronto Press, 1982), 79.
30 Thomson, *Alexander Mackenzie*, 114–15.
31 "The Red River Rebellion, Public Meeting."
32 Waite, *Arduous Destiny*, 42–3.
33 J.M.S. Careless, *Brown of the Globe, Vol. II: Statesman of Confederation, 1860–1880* (Toronto: Macmillan, 1963), 281.
34 George Brown, "Letter to the Roman Catholic Committee," 125.
35 "The Red River Rebellion, Public Meeting."
36 Brown, "Letter to the Roman Catholic Committee," 126.
37 "Election Intelligence," *Globe*, 1 March 1871.
38 "Mr. Blake to his Constituents," *Globe*, 2 March 1871.
39 "Grand Mass Meeting, Mr. Mackenzie's Speech," *Globe*, 4 March 1871.
40 "The Reform Meeting in Hamilton: Mr. Blake's Oration," *Globe*, 17 March 1871.
41 "The Murder of Scott, and the Orangemen," *Globe*, 1 March 1871.
42 "Orangemen and the Election," *Globe*, 13 March 1871. The reference to selling out for a "mess of pottage" comes from the biblical story of Esau and Jacob found in Genesis 25.
43 "Reformers of Middlesex, Demonstration at Strathoy," *Globe*, 6 June 1871.
44 "North Wellington Reformers, Dinner to Mr. McKim," *Globe*, 22 June 1871.
45 Brown, "Letter to the Roman Catholic Committee," 126.
46 Bruce W. Hodgins, "John Sandfield Macdonald," in J.M.S. Careless, ed., *The Pre-Confederation Premiers: Ontario Government Leaders, 1841–1867* (Toronto: University of Toronto Press, 1980), 302.
47 Ibid., 275–8; see also chapter 4 for more on the Scott Act of 1863.
48 Letter from R.W. Scott to John A. Macdonald, Toronto, 20 Dec. 1871, R.W. Scott Fonds, LAC.

49 Telegraph from R.W. Scott to Hon. James Skead or W.G. Perley, 20 Dec. 1871, R.W. Scott Fonds.
50 Telegraph from John A. Macdonald to R.W. Scott, 21 Dec. 1871, R.W. Scott Fonds.
51 Letter from John Carling to John A. Macdonald, 30 Nov. 1871, R.W. Scott Fonds.
52 Brian P. Clarke, "Scott, Sir Richard William," *Dictionary of Canadian Biography*, vol. 14, University of Toronto/Université Laval, 2003–, biographi.ca/en/bio/scott_richard_william_14E.html <30 Oct. 2021>.
53 Letter from Mr. Jarnot to Alexander Mackenzie, 11 Dec. 1871, Alexander Mackenzie Fonds.
54 "Carleton and Simcoe Elections," *Globe*, 4 Jan. 1872.
55 Letter from Mr. McCauley to Alexander Mackenzie, 13 Dec. 1871, Alexander Mackenzie Fonds.
56 John Webster Grant, *A Profusion of Spires: Religion in Nineteenth-Century Ontario* (Toronto: University of Toronto Press, 1988), 224.
57 Margaret Evans identifies eleven provincial ridings in Ontario in the 1870s where Catholic votes significantly affected election results. See Evans, *Sir Oliver Mowat*, 119.
58 David B. Marshall, "Religion in Canada, 1867–1945," in Stephen J. Stein, ed., *Cambridge History of Religions in America* (Cambridge: Cambridge University Press, 2012), 677.
59 "East Division of Toronto: Mass Meeting of Reformers, Nomination of Mr. John O'Donohoe," *Globe*, 10 July 1872.
60 "Catholic Reformers and the Reform Party: Letter from the Hon. George Brown," *Globe*, 8 Aug. 1872.
61 "Shameful!" *Globe*, 27 July 1872.
62 J. Murray Beck, *Pendulum of Power: Canada's Federal Elections* (Scarborough, ON: Prentice-Hall, 1968), 15–16.
63 Ibid., 16.
64 Careless, *Brown of the Globe, Vol. II*, 299–300.
65 George Brown, "Toronto, August 22, 1872," in Alexander Mackenzie, ed., *Life and Speeches of the Hon. George Brown* (Toronto: Globe, 1882), 235.
66 Pierre Berton, *The National Dream: The Great Railway, 1871–1881* (Toronto: McClelland and Stewart, 1970), 90–3.
67 Thomson, *Alexander Mackenzie*, 150–1, 166–70.
68 "The City Elections: East Toronto," *Globe*, 23 Jan. 1874.
69 "East Toronto Election: Splendid Demonstration," *Globe*, 22 Jan. 1874.

70 Waite, *Arduous Destiny*, 20.
71 2 Feb. and 1 April 1872, James Lesslie Diaries, Lesslie Family Fonds, Dundas Museum and Archives, Dundas, ON.
72 22 Nov. 1872, James Lesslie Diaries.
73 6 April 1872, James Lesslie Diaries.
74 "Conditions of Political Partnership," *Examiner*, 8 Oct. 1851.
75 1 Jan. 1872, James Lesslie Diaries.
76 Evans, *Sir Oliver Mowat*, 120–3.
77 Letter from John [Walsh] Bp. of London to R.W. Scott, 9 March 1873, Richard W. Scott Fonds, LAC.
78 Waite, *Arduous Destiny*, 43–4.
79 Wilfrid Laurier, "Plea against Louis Riel's expulsion from the Commons [15 April 1874]," in Arthur Milnes, ed., *Canada Always: The Defining Speeches of Sir Wilfrid Laurier* (Toronto: McClelland & Stewart, 2016), 38.
80 Ibid., 35.
81 Ibid., 45–6.
82 Ibid., 50.
83 "The North-West Question," *Globe*, 31 March 1870.
84 Letter from Luther Holton to Alexander Mackenzie, 26 Jan. 1875, Alexander Mackenzie Fonds, LAC.
85 Waite, *Arduous Destiny*, 44–5.
86 "The North-West Question, Government Policy: Notice Motion by Hon. A. Mackenzie," *Globe*, 9 Feb. 1875.
87 "Dominion Parliament," *Globe*, 13 Feb. 1875.
88 "Constitution Granted to the North West Territories," n.d., Richard W. Scott Fonds.
89 Thomson, *Alexander Mackenzie*, 230–1.
90 Ian Radforth, "Collective Rights, Liberal Discourse, and Public Order: The Clash over Catholic Processions in Mid-Victorian Toronto," *Canadian Historical Review* 95, no. 4 (Dec. 2014): 516, 524–8.
91 Ibid., 535–8.
92 "Something for Young Men," *Gleaner*, 12 Feb. 1874.
93 *Gleaner*, 11 Nov. 1875.
94 *Gleaner*, 16 Dec. 1875.
95 "Speech of Mr. Huntington at Grenville," *Globe*, 31 Dec. 1875.
96 Letter from Alexander Mackenzie to George Brown, 17 Jan. 1876, Alexander Mackenzie Fonds.

97 Letter from Alexandre-Antonin Taché to Joseph Cauchon, 6 Jan. 1876 (translation from the original French), Alexander Mackenzie Fonds.
98 Letter from Alexandre-Antonin Taché to Joseph Cauchon, 10 Jan. 1876 (translation from the original French), Alexander Mackenzie Fonds.
99 Letter from Joseph Cauchon to Alexandre-Antonin Taché, 8 Jan. 1876 (translation from the original French), Alexander Mackenzie Fonds.
100 Letter from Alexandre-Antonin Taché to Joseph Cauchon, 12 Jan. 1876 (translation from the original French), Alexander Mackenzie Fonds.
101 Letter from Luther Holton to Alexander Mackenzie, 23 Jan. 1876, Alexander Mackenzie Fonds.
102 Letter from Luther Holton to Alexander Mackenzie, 28 Jan. 1876, Alexander Mackenzie Fonds.
103 Letter from Alexander Mackenzie to George Brown, 22 Jan. 1876, Alexander Mackenzie Fonds.
104 "A New Departure," *Nation*, 14 Jan. 1876.
105 *Gleaner*, 17 Feb. 1876.
106 "Dominion Parliament," *Gleaner*, 17 Feb. 1876.
107 Timothy Verhoeven, "Transatlantic Connections: American Anti-Catholicism and the First Vatican Council (1869–70)," *Catholic Historical Review* 100, no. 4 (autumn 2014): 718.
108 Alexander Galt, *Civil Liberty in Lower Canada* (Montreal: D. Bentley, 1876), 15–16.
109 Robert Hill, *Voice of the Vanishing Minority*, 92–3.
110 Peter Waite argues that narratives of economic depression 1874–96 were exaggerated for partisan purposes and that gross national product (GNP) actually continued to grow at an average of 4 per cent per year. Still, there is evidence that these years saw a cyclical decline in GNP growth compared with previous eras and that some industries such as those reliant on staple exports were disproportionately affected. Waite, *Arduous Destiny*, 74–7.
111 W.A. Foster, "Canada First; or, Our New Nationality" [1871], in *Canada First: A Memorial of the Late William A. Foster, Q.C.* (Toronto: Hunter Rose, 1890), 13–47.
112 Berger, *The Sense of Power*, 61–2, 66.
113 Thomson, *Alexander Mackenzie*, 200–2.
114 Ibid., 213–16.
115 Joseph Schull, *Edward Blake, Vol. I: The Man of the Other Way* (Toronto: Macmillan, 1975), 147.

116 Foster, "Canada First," 39.
117 Ibid., 41.
118 Smith summarized the purpose of the movement as he saw it, however vague: "All however united in striving to cultivate Canadian patriotism, to raise Canada above the rank of a mere dependency, and to give her the first place in Canadian hearts." Goldwin Smith, "Introduction," in *Canada First: A Memorial of the Late W.A. Foster* (Toronto: Hunter Rose, 1890), 3.
119 Berger, *The Sense of Power*, 62–6.
120 Foster, "Canada First," 31–2.
121 Ibid., 43.
122 Ibid., 43.
123 W.A. Foster, "Address to the Canadian National Association, Delivered at Toronto, February, 1875," in *Canada First: A Memorial of the Late W.A. Foster* (Toronto: Hunter Rose, 1890), 69.
124 "Mr. O'Donohoe and East Toronto," *Globe*, 19 Dec. 1874.
125 Foster, "Address to the Canadian National Association," 69–70.
126 "Canada First: Address of the Canadian National Association to the People of Canada," in *Canada First: A Memorial of the late William A. Foster, Q.C.* (Toronto: Hunter Rose, 1890), 52.
127 For further discussion of Thomas D'Arcy McGee, see chapter 4 of this study.
128 Foster, "Canada First," 42–3. The phrase "living water" appears in several biblical passages, such as John 4:10–11 and Jeremiah 17:13 (KJV).
129 Foster, "Address to the Canadian National Association," 65.
130 Wilson, *Thomas D'Arcy McGee, Vol. II*, 392.
131 "The Outlook at Ottawa," *Nation*, 2 April 1874.
132 Thomson, *Alexander Mackenzie*, 240–3.
133 For example, see Hon. A. Mackenzie, *Reform Government in the Dominion, The Pic-Nic Speeches delivered in the Province of Ontario during the Summer of 1877* (Toronto: Globe, 1878), 7–9.
134 "Articles on the Premier's Visit, from the Scottish Press," in *Speeches of the Hon. Alexander Mackenzie during his Recent Visit to Scotland, with His Principal Speeches in Canada* (Toronto: James Campbell & Son, 1876), 116.
135 Alexander Mackenzie, "Presentation of the Freedom of the City of Perth [1875]," in *Speeches of the Hon. Alexander Mackenzie during his Recent Visit to Scotland, with His Principal Speeches in Canada* (Toronto: James Campbell & Son, 1876), 62–3.
136 Alexander Mackenzie, "Address from the Workingmen of Dundee [1875]," in *Speeches of the Hon. Alexander Mackenzie during his Recent Visit to*

Scotland, with His Principal Speeches in Canada (Toronto: James Campbell & Son, 1876), 53.

137 Letter from Egerton Ryerson to Goldwin Smith, 8 Feb. 1875, Goldwin Smith Fonds, LAC.

138 Bruce Curtis, *Building the Educational State: Canada West, 1836–1871* (London, ON: Althouse Press, 1988), 275–6.

139 William Buckingham, *The Hon. Alexander Mackenzie: His Life and Times* (Toronto: Rose Publishing, 1892), 122.

140 Alexander Mackenzie, "Presentation of the Freedom of the Borough of Irvine," in *Speeches of the Hon. Alexander Mackenzie during his Recent Visit to Scotland, with His Principal Speeches in Canada* (Toronto: James Campbell & Son, 1876), 113.

141 William Westfall, *Two Worlds: The Protestant Culture of Nineteenth-Century Ontario* (Montreal and Kingston: McGill-Queen's University Press, 1989), 49. As we saw in chapter 3, in the 1850s Upper Canadian Protestants began to speak as though they shared common political interests in order to combat the perceived common enemy of Catholic political influence. Still, significant differences existed among Protestants, particularly between the evangelical Dissenting sects and the Anglicans. See James Forbes, "Contesting the Protestant Consensus: Voluntarists, Methodists, and the Persistence of Evangelical Dissent, 1829–1854," *Ontario History* 108, no. 2 (autumn 2016): 189–214.

142 H. Blair Neatby, *Laurier and a Liberal Quebec: A Study in Political Management* (Toronto: McClelland and Stewart, 1973), 4.

143 Hill, *Voice of the Vanishing Minority*, 77.

144 Verhoeven, "Transatlantic Connections," 699–700.

145 Yvan Lamonde, *The Social History of Ideas in Quebec, 1760–1896*, trans. Phyllis Aronoff and Howard Scott (Montreal and Kingston: McGill-Queen's University Press, 2013), 316–17.

146 J.R. Miller, *Equal Rights: The Jesuits' Estates Act Controversy* (Montreal: McGill-Queen's University Press, 1979), 28–9.

147 "The Doubtful Visitor: A Short Drama Lately Performed in Toronto," *Grip*, 10 June 1876.

148 Lindsey, *Rome in Canada*, 6.

149 Ibid., 15, 22–3, 210–11.

150 Ibid., 6.

151 Ibid., 220.

152 Ibid., 6–7.

153 Lamonde, *The Social History of Ideas in Quebec*, 311–12.

154 Neatby, *Laurier and a Liberal Quebec*, 5–6.

155 Wilfrid Laurier, "On Political Liberalism [1877]," in Arthur Milnes, ed., *Canada Always: The Defining Speeches of Sir Wilfrid Laurier* (Toronto: McClelland & Stewart, 2016), 56.

156 Ibid., 60–1.

157 Ibid., 58–9.

158 Ibid., 64.

159 Ibid., 56–7, 60–1.

160 Lamonde, *The Social History of Ideas in Quebec*, xxv–xxvi.

161 Laurier, "Plea against Louis Riel's Expulsion," 35, 45–6.

162 Laurier, "On Political Liberalism," 74.

163 Ibid., 61.

164 Neatby, *Laurier and a Liberal Quebec*, 4.

165 Hon. A. Mackenzie, *Reform Government in the Dominion, The Pic-Nic Speeches delivered in the Province of Ontario during the Summer of 1877* (Toronto: Globe, 1878), 3.

166 For example, Mackenzie emphasized that in fulfilling Macdonald's 1871 promise to British Columbia to build the transcontinental railway, the government must do so "without resorting to additional taxation for the purpose." He also extensively compared his government's expenditures with its immediate predecessor's and emphasized that his had worked "to place the contract system on a sounder and better footing than ever it was before" to avoid "insinuations of corruption." Mackenzie, *Reform Government in the Dominion*, 3, 7, 9.

167 Ibid., 3.

168 Alexander Mackenzie, *Workingmen's Demonstration at Toronto, Thursday, May 30th, 1878* (Cornwall, ON: Freeholder, 1878), 15.

169 Ibid., 1–2.

170 Ibid., 3.

171 Ibid., 10.

172 For more on the secularization of King's College, see chapters 1 and 2.

173 Mackenzie, *Workingmen's Demonstration*, 14.

174 Mackenzie, *Reform Government*, 3.

175 Alexander Mackenzie, "Presentation of Address at Rimouski [1875]," in *Speeches of the Hon. Alexander Mackenzie during his Recent Visit to Scotland, with His Principal Speeches in Canada* (Toronto: James Campbell & Son, 1876), 192–3.

176 "The Contest in Niagara," *Globe*, 9 Sept. 1878.

177 "The Glengarry Demonstration: Hon. Mr. Mackenzie's Speech," *Globe*, 4 Sept. 1878.
178 "Centre Toronto: Rousing Meeting of Reformers Last Night," *Globe*, 5 Sept. 1878.
179 "The Election: Rev. Macdonnell's Advice to Voters," *Globe*, 16 Sept. 1878.
180 "The Result," *Globe*, 18 Sept. 1878.
181 Waite, *Arduous Destiny*, 20, 91.
182 Beck, *Pendulum of Power*, 31–2.
183 *Gleaner*, 24 Oct. 1878.
184 "The Catholic Vote," *Globe*, 1 Oct. 1878.
185 "The Result," *Globe*, 18 Sept. 1878.
186 "West Toronto, Rally of West End Reformers," *Globe*, 1 Nov. 1875.
187 Schull, *Edward Blake, Vol. I*, 209–10.
188 Edward Blake, "The Teeswater Demonstration [24 Sept. 1877]," in *Reform Government in the Dominion: The Pic-Nic Speeches* (Toronto: Globe, 1878), 141.
189 Quoted in Schull, *Edward Blake, Vol. I*, 202.
190 Carless, *Brown of the Globe, Vol. II*, 366–7, 371.
191 Laurier, "On Political Liberalism," 74.
192 Ibid., 61.
193 Alexander Mackenzie, *Political Points and Pencillings, Being Selections from Various Addresses Delivered by Hon. Alex. Mackenzie* (Toronto: Grip, 1878), 3.

Conclusion

1 Margaret Evans, *Sir Oliver Mowat* (Toronto: University of Toronto Press, 1992), 119; William J. Smyth, *Toronto, the Belfast of Canada: The Orange Order and the Shaping of Municipal Culture* (Toronto: University of Toronto Press, 2015), 43.
2 McKay argues that the version of liberalism that came to dominate Canadian society in the nineteenth century prioritized "property" in the Lockean prescription for the individual's right to life, liberty, and property. Ian McKay, "The Liberal Order Framework: A Prospectus for a Reconnaissance of Canadian History," *Canadian Historical Review*, vol. 81 (2000): 624.
3 John Ralston Saul, *Louis-Hippolyte LaFontaine and Robert Baldwin* (Toronto: Penguin, 2010), 5–6.
4 Ibid., 218.

5 Ibid., 223.
6 See the section on "Religion and the Fall of Robert Baldwin" in chapter 3.
7 Saul, *Louis-Hippolyte LaFontaine and Robert Baldwin*, 220.
8 Michael S. Cross, *A Biography of Robert Baldwin: The Morning-Star of Memory* (New York: Oxford University Press, 2012), 56.
9 Ibid., 89–90.
10 Russell Blackford, *Freedom of Religion and the Secular State* (Chichester: Wiley-Blackwell, 2012), 53.
11 Janet Ajzenstat, *The Canadian Founding: John Locke and Parliament* (Montreal and Kingston: McGill-Queen's University Press, 2007), xvi, 81, 108–9.
12 Jeffrey L. McNairn, "In Hope and Fear: Intellectual History, Liberalism, and the Liberal Order Framework," in Michel Ducharme and Jean-François Constant, eds., *Liberalism and Hegemony: Debating the Canadian Liberal Revolution* (Toronto: University of Toronto Press, 2009), 85–6.
13 Michel Ducharme, *The Idea of Liberty in Canada during the Age of Atlantic Revolutions, 1776–1838*, trans. Peter Feldstein (Montreal and Kingston: McGill-Queen's University Press, 2014), 5–7.
14 Ibid., 181–4.
15 Jakob De Roover and S.N. Balagangadhara, "John Locke, Christian Liberty, and the Predicament of Liberal Toleration," *Political Theory* 36, no. 5 (Aug. 2008): 524.
16 James T. Kloppenberg, *Toward Democracy: The Struggle for Self-Rule in European and American Thought* (New York: Oxford University Press, 2016), 156–7.
17 J.C.D. Clark, *The Language of Liberty, 1660–1832: Political Discourse and Social Dynamics in the Anglo-American World* (Cambridge: Cambridge University Press, 1994), 45.
18 "To the Electors of the County of York," *Colonial Advocate*, 3 Jan. 1827.
19 "W.L. Mackenzie's Appeal to Arms," in Colin Read and Ronald J. Stagg, eds., *The Rebellion of 1837 in Upper Canada: A Collection of Documents* (Ottawa: Carleton University Press, 1985), 110–13.
20 Isaac Buchanan, *First Series of Five Letters, Against the Baldwin Faction, by an Advocate of Responsible Government, and of The New College Bill* (Toronto: British Colonist, 1844), 12, 17–19.
21 "Irish Emigration Scheme," *Banner*, 7 May 1847.
22 "Romanism," *Examiner*, 26 Feb. 1851.
23 "The Convention: Opinions of the Press," *Globe*, 23 Nov. 1859.
24 "The Roman Catholic Bishops on Politics," *Globe*, 23 Aug. 1859.

25 "Parliament Last Night: The Crisis Terminated!" *Globe*, 23 June 1864.
26 "The Foundation of Many Generations," *Canadian Independent*, March 1867.
27 "The Great Confederation," *Globe*, 4 Oct. 1864; see also A.I. Silver, *The French-Canadian Idea of Confederation, 1864–1900* (Toronto: University of Toronto Press, 1982), 41–2.
28 "The Foundation of Many Generations."
29 Carol Wilton, *Popular Politics and Political Culture in Upper Canada, 1800–1850* (Montreal and Kingston: McGill-Queen's University Press, 2000), 228–9.
30 "The Juggling Ministry," *North American*, 2 July 1850.
31 George Emery, *Elections in Oxford County, 1837–1875: A Case Study of Democracy in Canada West and Early Ontario* (Toronto: University of Toronto Press 2012), xvii–xviii, 126–7.
32 Jeffrey L. McNairn, *The Capacity to Judge: Public Opinion and Deliberative Democracy in Upper Canada, 1791–1854* (Toronto: University of Toronto Press, 2000), 14–15.
33 McNairn, *Capacity to Judge*, 15.
34 Ducharme, *The Idea of Liberty*, 10–11.
35 Ajzenstat, *The Canadian Founding*, 100–1.
36 *Constitution*, 29 Nov. 1837.
37 "Sectarian Political Preferences – Persecution," *Examiner*, 3 May 1848.
38 William Westfall, *Two Worlds: The Protestant Culture of Nineteenth-Century Ontario* (Montreal and Kingston: McGill-Queen's University Press, 1989), 197.
39 Nancy Christie, "'In These Times of Democratic Rage and Delusion': Popular Religion and the Challenge to the Established Order, 1760–1815," in G.A. Rawlyk, ed., *The Canadian Protestant Experience, 1760–1990* (Montreal and Kingston: McGill-Queen's University Press, 1990), 11, 43.
40 G.A. Rawlyk, *The Canada Fire: Radical Evangelicalism in British North America, 1775–1812* (Montreal and Kingston: McGill-Queen's University Press, 1994), xv.
41 David Bebbington, "Canadian Evangelicalism: A View from Britain," in George A. Rawlyk, ed., *Aspects of the Canadian Evangelical Experience* (Montreal and Kingston: McGill-Queen's University Press, 1997), 44, 50–2.
42 William Kilbourn, *The Firebrand: William Lyon Mackenzie and the Rebellion in Upper Canada* (Toronto: Clarke & Irwin, 1956), 37–8.
43 Arthur R.M. Lower, *Colony to Nation: A History of Canada* (Toronto: Longmans, 1946), 164.

44 Robert Kelley, *Transatlantic Persuasion: The Liberal-Democratic Mind in the Age of Gladstone* (New York: Knopf, 1969), xx, 49.
45 Linda Colley, *Britons: Forging the Nation, 1707–1837*, 6th ed. (New Haven, CT: Yale University Press, 2009), 29–30, 54.
46 Clark, *Language of Liberty*, 45.
47 Kloppenberg, *Toward Democracy*, 6, 16.
48 J.P. Ellens, *Religious Routes to Gladstonian Liberalism: The Church Rate Conflict in England and Wales, 1832–1868* (University Park: Pennsylvania State University Press, 1994), viii, 1–2.
49 Ajzenstat, *The Canadian Founding*, xiii.
50 Ibid., 81–2.
51 Ibid., 103–4.
52 John Marshall, *John Locke: Resistance, Religion and Responsibility* (Cambridge: Cambridge University Press, 1994), 53.
53 J.C. Walmsley and Felix Waldman, "John Locke and the Toleration of Catholics: A New Manuscript," *Historical Journal* 62, no. 4 (2019): 1102–3, 1115.
54 Marshall, *John Locke*, 110–11.
55 Ibid., 357–8.
56 De Roover and Balagangadhara, "John Locke," 524.
57 John Locke, "A Letter Concerning Tolerance [1689]," in Ian Shapiro, ed., *Two Treatises of Government and A Letter Concerning Tolerance* (New Haven, CT: Yale University Press, 2003), 245.
58 Scott Sowerby, *Making Toleration: The Repealers and the Glorious Revolution* (Cambridge, MA: Harvard University Press, 2013), 257.
59 Locke, "Letter Concerning Toleration," 244–5; see also Sowerby, *Making Toleration*, 256–7.
60 Regarding Atheists, Locke says, "Those are not at all to be tolerated who deny the being of God. Promises, covenants, and oaths, which are the bonds of human society, can have no hold upon an atheist." On "Mahometans," Locke writes, "It is ridiculous for any one to profess himself to be a Mahometan only in religion, but in every thing else a faithful subject to a Christian magistrate." See Locke, "Letter Concerning Toleration," 245–6.
61 "Persecution," *Colonial Advocate*, 20 Dec. 1827.
62 Albert Schrauwers, *'Union is Strength': W.L. Mackenzie, the Children of Peace, and the Emergence of Joint Stock Democracy in Upper Canada* (Toronto: University of Toronto Press, 2009), 138–9.

63 David Willson, *Impressions of the Mind, to which are added Some Remarks on Church and State Discipline, and the Acting Principles of Life* (Toronto, 1835), 257, 259.

64 "The Doctrines and Spirit of Church and State Union in Canada," *Christian Guardian*, 15 Oct. 1831.

65 McKay, "Liberal Order Framework," 617–18.

66 Ibid., 635–6.

67 Ibid., 624.

68 Ian McKay, "Canada as a Long Liberal Revolution: On Writing the History of Actually Existing Canadian Liberalisms, 1840s–1940s," in Jean-François Constant and Michel Ducharme, eds., *Liberalism and Hegemony: Debating the Canadian Liberal Revolution* (Toronto: University of Toronto Press, 2009), 356–7.

69 McNairn, "In Hope and Fear," 70–1, 75.

70 McKay, "Canada as a Long Liberal Revolution," 385.

71 Ibid., 414.

72 Cross, *Baldwin*, 294.

73 "Politics of Christianity, No. X: Man above Property," *Examiner*, 11 Oct. 1848. The term "mammon" comes from biblical passages such as one in the Gospel of Luke, in which Jesus says, "If therefore ye have not been faithful in the unrighteous mammon, who will commit to your trust the true riches? … No servant can serve two masters: for either he will hate the one, and love the other; or else he will hold to the one, and despise the other. Ye cannot serve God and mammon." See Luke 16:11–13 (KJV)

74 "To Thinking Reformers," *North American*, 2 Aug. 1853.

75 "Ministers in the West," *North American*, 2 Aug. 1853.

76 Charles Mackay, *Life and Liberty in America* (New York: Harper & Brothers, 1859), 398.

77 "The City Elections," *Globe*, 23 Jan. 1874.

78 "The City Elections: East Toronto," *Globe*, 23 Jan. 1874.

79 Westfall, *Two Worlds*, 10.

80 Brown, "Letter to the Roman Catholic Committee," 126.

81 "Lord Dufferin on Party Spirit," *Gleaner*, 3 Oct. 1878.

82 George Spaight, *Trial of Patrick James Whelan for the murder of the Hon. Thomas d'Arcy McGee* (Ottawa: Ottawa Times, 1868), 88.

83 Wilfrid Laurier, "On Political Liberalism [1877]," in Arthur Milnes, ed., *Canada Always: The Defining Speeches of Sir Wilfrid Laurier* (Toronto: McClelland & Stewart, 2016), 80–2.

84 H. Blair Neatby, *Laurier and a Liberal Quebec: A Study in Political Management* (Toronto: McClelland and Stewart, 1973), 207–8.

85 W.A. Foster, "Canada First; or, Our New Nationality [1871]," in *Canada First: A Memorial of the Late William A. Foster, Q.C.* (Toronto: Hunter Rose, 1890), 39.

86 Arthur Lower, "Our Shoddy Ideals [1937]," in Welf H. Heick, ed., *History and Myth: Arthur Lower and the Making of Canadian Nationalism* (Vancouver: UBC Press, 1975), 145.

87 Ian McKay, *Rebels, Reds, Radicals: Rethinking Canada's Left History* (Toronto: Between the Lines, 2005), 70.

88 Ibid., 27–8.

Index